WHERE TO GET MONEY FOR EVERYTHING

Also by Paula Nelson

The Joy of Money

WHERE TO GET MONEY FOR EVERYTHING

A Strategic Guide
to Today's Money Sources

• Paula Nelson •

William Morrow and Company, Inc.
New York • 1982

Grateful acknowledgment is made for permission to reprint the
Home Improvements Chart on pages 150–153. Source: Don
Logay/Newsweek Remodeling Supplement, April 1982.

Library of Congress Cataloging in Publication Data
Nelson, Paula.
    Where to get money for everything.
    Includes index.
    1. Loans, Personal—Handbooks, manuals, etc.
2. Credit—Handbooks, manuals, etc.   I. Title.
HG3755.N365   1982   332.7′43′0202   82-12614
ISBN 0-688-00536-5

Printed in the United States of America

First Edition

1 2 3 4 5 6 7 8 9 10

BOOK DESIGN BY LINEY LI

To David

and

to Heidi

My sincerest appreciation and gratitude to two talented and committed editors, Amy Louise Shapiro and Richard Trubo, for their professionalism and humanity.

Special thanks to Marilee Zdenek, Bill Kerstetter, Susan Mauntel, Doris Siegel, and Judy Hollis for their kindness and support throughout this project; to Hillel Black and to Bill Adler for their essential initial enthusiasm; to Patricia Lindh, Don Marts, Dennis McKenzie, Norton Kiritz, and Don Logay for giving so freely of their time and expertise in reviewing the manuscript.

Contents

Let us all be happy and live within our means,
even if we have to borrow the money to do it with.

—ARTEMUS WARD
Natural History

A MONEY SOLUTION FOR THE TIMES

Where to Get Money for Everything is a direct response to a need made clear to me by people from all over this country, from all walks of life. The book was inspired by an experience I shared with millions of other Americans.

The concept took shape during an appearance on the Phil Donahue show. We were getting set for air time; the audience was seated, our microphones were neatly pinned to our jackets, and the television crew was busy checking last-minute details.

I asked Phil if I could address a question to the audience while we were waiting for the show to begin.

"Just for fun, how many of you are millionaires?" I asked.

One hand went up.

"How many of you could use a $5,000 loan?"

Nearly every hand in the studio shot up.

Then the show started, and for the next twenty minutes the talk ranged from mortgage-rate trends to Theory Z. It struck me as an array of topics weighty enough to impress a classroom full of Economics I students.

During the first break for commercials, my thoughts kept returning to the audience's reaction to my initial questions. It was evident that what motivated their interest in the general problems of the economy was a desire for specific solutions. They needed to know how and where to get money—to send their kids to college, to pay their bills, to buy a house, or perhaps even to start a small business of their own. In the next segment of the show I decided to raise that overriding issue directly.

"I know it's interesting to talk about sophisticated economic subjects," I began, "but let's get down to earth. We all know it takes money to make money, to get ahead. I'd welcome any questions about that."

The questions flew, and so did the balance of the hour.

When I got back to my hotel, I listed every question I'd heard on a yellow pad, as well as the thoughts they provoked in my own mind. The heading I wrote at the top of the page was *Where to Get Money for Everything.*

Over the next few weeks, with that list in mind, I listened intently to queries from lecture audiences, television and newspaper interviewers, and friends. They formed a distinct pattern.

From college students to executives of Fortune 500 companies—and just about everyone in between—people wanted to know how to get the cash they needed. They were all concerned about the credit crunch, the bewildering changes in interest rates, the new options for creative financing. Obtaining money had clearly become *everyone's* problem, whether the color of their collar was white, blue, or pink.

For the average person, borrowing money might once have involved only a relatively simple decision, but these days it requires the expertise of a financial pro. Borrowing is now an essential part of most of our lives, and most of us are not professionals at that game. But learning about how to get money can be exciting and interesting, and mastering the art of borrowing and obtaining money in several other ways can be very rewarding.

Let's look realistically at borrowing.

It's the only way the majority of Americans can now maintain their all-time high standard of living. Houses, cars, education, furniture, and an entire shopping list of other "can't-do-without" big-ticket items would be beyond the reach of most of us if we didn't have readily accessible credit and easy credit terms. For many of us, there is no longer a choice between buying these items for cash and buying them on credit; unless we buy them with credit, we can't buy them at all.

You *can* cut the cost of living when you borrow, even though the cost of credit is high and almost certain to go higher. For example, you can take advantage of sales when your own supply of cash is low. You can outsmart inflation by buying the things you need now, rather than later when prices will have soared. And you can pay back the dollars you borrow today with tomorrow's cheaper ones.

You can make money on the money you borrow, provided that you borrow at x percent and get a return of x-plus percent. For example, it is common to borrow against an insurance policy at a low interest rate and then put the cash in higher-returning money-market funds or Treasury bills. You don't have to be a financial wizard to do these things; all you need is assertiveness, ingenuity, and a handy source of good information.

Borrowing *can* help you get your piece of the pie, your share of the American dream. It's clearly no time to be a borrowing novice, but don't let that hold you back. This book will provide you with the information—and, I hope, the inspiration—to make you a pro.

MY PERSONAL MONEY
EDUCATION—AND YOURS

Few of us are born with financial savvy; we accumulate our knowledge over the years, mostly through trial and error. At some point it becomes clear to nearly everyone that there is more to the financial world than a paycheck—that there is, in fact, a money system.

Over the past fifteen years I have learned about that system by being involved in it. Following an all-too-brief stint in college, I entered the business world at the age of eighteen. After one year in the secretarial ranks, I made a firm commitment to move into management— not only to make more money, but also to get as close as possible to the nerve centers of business.

The first step toward that goal was my promotion to a position as contracts administrator of the small aerospace firm where I was working. Within a year I was offered a unique and challenging opportunity: to team up with two of the company's managers and launch a new audio-equipment manufacturing venture to be called Infonics, Inc. Of course, I accepted.

At the age of twenty, I found myself on the firing line in a fledgling company with the opportunity to help make it profitable and successful. In two short years, Infonics sales topped the million-dollar mark, enabling the company to publicly trade its stock over the counter. (I might note that the price of the stock jumped from $5 to $26 a share at that time.)

Along with the challenge and excitement of launching the company came an added bonus: learning the art of borrowing to finance its foundation and its growth. Over the next few years I found out about establishing corporate lines of credit, raising venture capital, and, eventually, generating several million dollars through three public stock issues. Being in daily contact with bankers, lawyers, Wall Street underwriters, and venture-capital experts gave me a firsthand opportunity to learn and apply some invaluable financial "secrets." It was the finest financial education that money *couldn't* buy—it was learning by doing.

After a major New York Stock Exchange company acquired Infonics in 1973, I shifted my attention from corporate finance to personal finance. I gave seminars throughout the country, to inform as many people as possible about the strategies I had developed in the corporate world and adapted for day-to-day personal use. I realized I could potentially reach even more people by gathering all that I'd taught and learned in those seminars into a book.

The Joy of Money was first published in 1976, and it is now in its eleventh printing. (I'm proud to say that it has been called a classic in its field and was hailed by some as the first "women's money book.") Since then I have devoted my energies to passing along information on both the personal and the corporate facets of the money world, not only in lectures and seminars, but through a column in _McCall's_ magazine, as the financial commentator for the "Today" show, through appearances on "PM Magazine," and in guest appearances on many other television shows.

I've come to realize one very important thing since the publication of _The Joy of Money_. Both men and women have a need, and a desire, to learn about _borrowing_ money as well as _making_ money. This book should teach you, in just a few hours of straightforward, easy reading, the essentials about money sources. I've organized the book so that it will be easy for you to find the facts you need to solve any one of a wide range of money-getting problems—from obtaining a signature loan to raising venture capital. _Where to Get Money for Everything_ is a complete sourcebook designed to educate the future borrowing pro—you.

HOW THIS BOOK CAN HELP
YOU GET THE MONEY YOU NEED

- You'll learn the principles and practices of loan-getting success.
- You'll learn how to establish a strong credit rating—even though you may never have had one before.

- You'll learn how to get loans from banks and other money sources—and which source is the best for you.
- You'll learn how to borrow money against your assets—including savings accounts, certificates of deposit, securities, and more.
- You'll learn how to use the equity in your home to borrow—to obtain far larger sums than you could get otherwise.
- You'll learn how to get loans on the best possible terms—and avoid hidden costs.
- You'll learn how to make credit cards one of your most powerful tools for successful personal finance.
- You'll learn about the best ways to get out of unmanageable debt—and the best sources for debt-consolidation loans.
- You'll learn about the most advantageous methods of financing your new car—and whether you're better off leasing or buying.
- You'll learn about the new creative financing techniques for buying or selling your home—to beat high down payments and mortgage interest rates.
- You'll learn how to get the most for your home-improvement dollars—and about the best sources for remodeling loans.
- You'll learn the up-to-date facts on loans and grants for your children's education—or your own.
- You'll learn the skills of obtaining grants—from both private and government sources.
- You'll learn how to get money to start a business and keep it going—and how to write an expert business plan.
- You'll learn the techniques of successful negotiation—from thorough preparation to effective presentation to achieving your money-getting goals.
- You'll learn precisely where to turn for even more de-

tailed information and guidance on the wide variety of subjects included in this book.

In short, you'll learn everything you need to be a money-getting expert. No matter what your needs, you'll know where to go to get the money to fulfill them.

CHAPTER 1

THE ART OF GETTING
BANK LOANS ON YOUR
SIGNATURE ALONE

Do you need $3,000, $4,000, $5,000, or more in a hurry? If you're like most Americans, the first thing you think of is a signature loan, for which your scrawl is your promise to repay. Every kind of bank offers it. All you have to do is fill out a form and sign it, and a check is in your hands or a credit posted to your account in twenty-four to forty-eight hours. It's simple, swift, and sure.

Or is it?

It is if you fit the description of the computer norm, if you're willing to settle for less money than you need, or if you're interested only in a one-shot deal and don't care about building up a credit reservoir for the future.

But if the computer squawks when the bank inputs your data, you won't get what you want by simply filling out an application. You'll have to learn a new art form instead: the art of getting a "yes" on your loan request even though by computer standards you may deserve a "no." That art is based on knowing how a bank's signature-loan system works and how you can make it work for you. In addition, if you need more dollars than the established ceilings, or if you plan to establish an ongoing relationship with a bank so that you will be able to get money when you need it, not just today but in the future, you need to understand the signature-loan system. Successfully obtaining a signature loan can be the essential first step in building a long-term relationship with your bank and the foundation for fulfilling your future borrowing needs.

TEN SIMPLE GUIDELINES
FOR GETTING SIGNATURE LOANS
APPROVED BY YOUR BANK

1. *Get rid of your awe of banks and bankers.*

Loan-getting success is not achieved by mail or by phone, except for making initial contacts. You'll be meeting with your banker, in person, on his or her home court, and if you approach the contest with fear and trembling, you don't have much of a chance. When you walk into a bank, leave your awe outside.

Often when I offer this advice, I hear the not unreasonable protest, "If *they* have the money and *I* need it, it's going to be tough to keep a casual stance."

Let me bolster your self-confidence with an illustration of a positive approach to borrowing. Years ago, when I had my first job working for a small company, the president turned to me at the end of a meeting. "Well," he said, smiling. "Now we know exactly how much money we need for expansion and inventory in the next fiscal year. So I'll call Bill over at the bank . . ."

And ask him for a loan, I mentally leaped ahead of him.

". . . and ask him if he'd like to make some money today."

I didn't think I had heard right. I said, "Pardon me, would you repeat that?"

"Certainly. I'm going to call Bill over at the bank and ask him if he'd like to make some money today."

"If you need money from him, how are you going to get it by offering money to him?" My boss's statement made as much sense to me as a weather forecast of sleet and snow in July.

"That's the approach I always take when I

need a loan," he replied. "It's the only approach to take, because it works. Want to hear me prove it?"

It was an invitation I couldn't refuse. He flipped on the telephone conference hookup so that I could listen, reached Bill (who happened to be the president of the bank), and made small talk for a few moments.

Then my boss made his pitch. "Bill, how would you like to make some money today?"

"We're always looking to make some money," came the hearty reply. "How much do you need?"

"A hundred thousand."

"For how long?"

"One year."

"Going rate?"

"Right."

"Why don't you drop down for lunch Friday? Bring your latest financials and we'll wrap it up."

"See you on Friday."

That ninety-second dialogue taught me an important lesson that irrevocably changed my perception of banks and bankers. I realized that a bank is like a store—a money store—and a banker can be thought of as a merchant who rents out cash for a certain period of time at a certain rate of interest. This understanding broke down my intimidation—a block I'm sure many people face when dealing with banks and talking with bankers.

I've shared this story with hundreds of people who have reported back that its moral gave them the confidence they needed. Just remember: to stay in business, a bank needs to make loans—to you.

2. Deal with the bank you usually bank with.

If you're like most Americans, a bank is the place you go for checking accounts, N.O.W. accounts, traveler's checks, a credit card, for savings accounts, C.D.'s, All Savers certificates, and bank mutual funds; for car financing, home-improvement loans, and money to put your kids through college; for I.R.A. and Keogh plans; for setting up trusts; and even for getting documents notarized. The bank in which you carry out all or most of your other financial transactions is naturally the bank that is most likely to grant your request for a personal loan.

Even if you don't request a personal loan, it's not uncommon for the bank with which you carry on other kinds of transactions to offer you one—perhaps by mail or by telephone. Sometimes—for example, if you're just starting out or need to establish credit—it's advisable to accept the loan even if you have no immediate need for cash. Then pay back the installments *on time.* "One of the first things we look for before approving a second personal loan," one loan officer told me, "is a track record of on-time payments on the first personal loan." Establishing that record is an essential prerequisite to getting the next loan when you need it.

3. Know the details of your credit report and loan point score before you submit your loan application.

Your *loan point score* is a numerical value assigned to the information you supply on the loan application form. Your *credit report ratings* are most commonly a number from 0 to 9, each corresponding to a description of your payment history on other credit accounts. (Bureaus such as TRW use *word* ratings—*excellent, substandard,* and so on—rather than numbers.)

Bank executives have the power to make a loan based solely on their personal judgment. But don't count on it. As a matter of routine, they usually don't finalize their decisions until they have reviewed loan point scores and credit report ratings. If one or the other doesn't meet bank standards, or if both don't, a loan request, under routine circumstances, is virtually certain to be rejected. If you are aware of these factors in advance—by figuring your loan point score and obtaining a copy of your credit report—you can take remedial measures before and during your meeting with the banker and turn a possible or even a certain "no" into a "yes."

To determine your loan point score, ask your bank or lender for a copy of its scoring chart. Each bank or lender uses its own form, each containing different information, but the items in the following composite typically appear. A score of 15 or better on the composite scoring chart indicates that your chances for loan approval are good. (Remember, there is no universal scoring system, but this will give you an indication of the type of information lenders rate, and how you may rank.)

LOAN SCORING CHART

1. Monthly income

Under $1,000	0	———
$1,000–$1,499	1	———
$1,500–$2,000	2	———
$2,000 or more	3	———

2. Monthly obligations

Less than ⅓ of income	3	———
33⅓%–40% of income	2	———
41%–50% of income	1	———
50% or more	0	———

3. Checking account at bank

Yes	1	———
No	0	———

4. Prior loans at this bank branch

Yes	1	_____
No	0	_____

5. Years on present job

10+	4	_____
5–10	3	_____
4–6	2	_____
1–4	1	_____

6. Years at current address

Less than 5 years	1	_____
More than 5 years	2	_____

7. Years at previous address

Less than 5 years	1	_____
More than 5 years	2	_____

8. Telephone number listed on application

Yes	1	_____
No	0	_____

9. Savings account

Yes	1	_____
No	0	_____

10. Purpose of loan—debt consolidation

Yes	−2	_____
No	2	_____

11. Credit references listed

Yes	2	_____
No	0	_____

12. Own home

Yes	3	_____
No	0	_____

If your score is 15 or more, you are in a strong credit position. The credit scoring chart is only one element of the credit-approval process, however. The next is your credit history as reflected on your credit report. If you have scored lower than 15, you will find steps to offset a low point score on page 29.

To find out your credit report rating:

1. Call the chief loan officer, or any other high executive, of your bank and ask for the name, address, and telephone number of the credit bureau to which the bank subscribes. (TRW is the biggest, with 92 million names in its data bank.) Or look up a local credit bureau in the Yellow Pages under "Credit" or "Reporting Services." Almost all the 1,850 or so credit bureaus in the United States have access to the same information, so the chances of finding your report at any credit bureau you contact are excellent. If you have trouble, write or call Associated Credit Bureaus (a trade association), 16211 Park Place 10, P.O. Box 218300, Houston, TX 77218, (713) 492-8155.

2. When you've located the credit bureau that carries your report, request a copy of it by phone or in writing. The credit bureau will send you an authorization form.

3. Fill out the form, attach a check for the fee (usually less than $10), and return the form to the credit bureau. Your report will be mailed promptly. (If you've been turned down for credit within the previous thirty days, the report is free.)

4. Examine the report. It lists information on your credit accounts over the past seven years (ten years if you've gone into bankruptcy within that period of time) as supplied by banks and retail stores. Your report *may* also contain other items relevant to your credit-worthiness, including civil suits, judgments against you, and petitions filed and granted under the bankruptcy

law. You'll very likely find a numerical rating from 0 to 9 (except for 6) adjacent to each credit account listed, or a word rating. Keep in mind, though, that credit reports do not truly rate your credit-worthiness as such. Each creditor makes an independent assessment of your credit history, based on its individual requirements; some are of course more stringent than others. Your credit report is a summary of the information submitted by all those who submit data to the credit bureau (American Express, for example, does not).

WHAT YOUR CREDIT REPORT RATING MEANS

Rating	Meaning
0	Credit approved but not used, or account too new to rate.
1	Pays on due dates, or pays within 30 days of billing.
2	Has history of one payment consistently past due, or pays in more than 30, but less than 60, days.
3	Has history of two payments consistently past due, or pays in more than 60, but less than 90, days.
4	Has history of three payments consistently past due, or pays in more than 90, but less than 120, days.
5	Account is now at least 120 days overdue but not yet rated 9.
7	Making lower payments under voluntary plan, or under Chapter 13 or the Bankruptcy Act.

8   Goods have been repossessed, or goods have been voluntarily returned because of inability to pay.

9   Bankrupt, or account placed for collection, or left town with no forwarding address.

A credit report sometimes contains real surprises when it arrives in the mail. That's what happened to a friend of mine named Sandra Wilson, a computer programmer, after she applied for a loan to the Bank of America in Los Angeles. Her rating showed up as a 9—bankrupt. Her credit report showed that she had defaulted on a loan from the Wells Fargo Bank in San Francisco three years before. She called me in a state of shock.

"You? Bankrupt?" I found it hard to believe. I'd known Sandra for years—long enough to know she was compulsive about paying her bills on time.

"Of course not," she snapped.

"Well, did you ever have a loan with the Wells Fargo Bank in San Francisco?" I asked.

"I haven't been in San Francisco in twenty years!"

It was obvious to me she'd been the victim of the credit bureau's mistake, and I told her so. Credit bureaus—and those who report to them—_do_ make mistakes; TRW, the leading credit reporting firm, admits to about 1.4 million a year.

The burden of proof was on Sandra. Until she could document that she had never gotten a loan from the San Francisco bank, the erroneous information would remain on her report. So Sandra wrote to the president of the bank, requesting a letter stating that she had never gotten a loan there. When she received it, she sent a photocopy to the credit bureau, with a cover letter pointing out the mistake. The credit bureau sent back a note of apology and a new credit report that contained only the accurate numbers.

Sandra had rectified the problem. _You_ can do it just as easily when you spot a mistake on your own credit report.

Under routine circumstances you can forecast a banker's response to your scores. A 17-or-higher loan point score, coupled with a credit report of all 1's, earns a certain "yes" to your loan application. If your credit report shows 2's through 5's, you can expect an iffy "yes," subject to the discretion of the loan officer. If a single 7 or 8 appears, you'd get an almost certain "no"; if there's a 9, a definite "no." A lower-than-17 loan point score decreases your chances for success in each case. But don't be discouraged; what may appear to be a "no" from this calculation is far from the final word.

4. Offset your unacceptable loan point score and credit report ratings by setting the record straight.

Unless you're a deadbeat or a debtaholic, it may not be your fault that you're behind the evaluating system's eight ball. There are always mitigating circumstances that don't show up in the credit reports, and it's often in your banker's interest to be understanding of them. It's _your_ job to tell the banker about them right up front. Feel free to say, "I want you to know that I may not pass your point score test for this loan, but there's a reason...." Explain your reason simply and sincerely, sticking strictly to the facts. Your most powerful tactic is honesty.

Here are some rules for setting the record straight when you talk to a loan officer:

- Be honest. Your character is your most valuable asset.
- Put all the negatives on the table at your first meeting. The banker will find out about them anyway, and it's sudden death to a loan request if he or she feels you deliberately concealed anything.
- Compensate for the negatives with positives, such as "I'm training for a better job," "I'm saving regularly," "I'm due for a raise soon." Document every statement when possible.
- Be sure the credit report your banker receives is free of errors. Don't go in and say, "I know I've got a bad rating, but it's a mistake." Remember, the burden of proof is on you. Get the report corrected _before_ you apply for the loan.
- Verbally explain any extenuating circumstances that caused your poor credit record (loss of job, illness in the family, marital problems, fire, accident, theft, and so on). Your banker may have gone through a similar experience or know someone who has and will probably be sympathetic. Remember, bankers are people, too.
- Prepare a written statement (a hundred words should usually prove adequate) to explain any problems on your credit report and to back up your verbal explanation.
- Prove that you can pay on time every time. The best way is to work out a realistic budget that clearly demonstrates your ability to meet each installment. Present it to your banker in a clear neat format.

5. Deal only with a top bank officer.

If you want to cut the red tape, get the loan you need quickly, and be treated the way you feel you ought to be treated, deal only with the president or the vice-president of your bank.

Although setting up a meeting isn't really necessary for a one-time small loan, it's vital if you will need money for a variety of purposes over the next months or years.

It's no problem at all to set up a meeting with a top bank officer in small or medium-sized communities. Banks in major cities present a somewhat different situation, which I'll come to later.

Several years ago I needed to change banks and bankers. I had been dealing with one of the major banks in California whose service was adequate, but it was oriented more to individual needs than to business needs. With several projects in the works, I was looking for a bank that was accustomed to loaning money for business ventures. I asked my accountant for some suggestions, and he offered to introduce me to a banker he knew well.

The following week we all met for lunch—the executive vice-president of a medium-sized bank, my accountant, and I. Over lunch I told the banker about myself, my current and future projects, and how much money I would need to finance them. (He was familiar with the types of ventures I was proposing.) I asked him various questions about his bank, its policies, and the type of customer to which it catered to assure myself that he could provide all the services I needed.

At the bank that same afternoon, I filled out the form for new accounts, and my first loan application was approved on the spot.

If you pave the way in a professional manner, getting quick loan approval is not unusual. Most bank executives have the ability to approve loans personally within a certain dollar range, typically $25,000 to $300,000, depending on such factors as the size and type of bank and the executive's status. No loan committee; just a bank executive's decision to say "yes."

A week earlier I had in fact set up a similar

meeting with my former banker and the answer had
been "Sorry, no." The trick was to find the right executive at the right bank. My accountant had played the
key role by arranging the crucial meeting. Accountants
are members of your community's "money club"—along
with attorneys, insurance agents, stockbrokers, and
real-estate agents. They make up an informal network of
professionals who deal in finance, and any one of them is
likely to know the bankers you need to know. Don't feel
you're imposing on your accountant or your attorney
when you ask for an introduction. Most of these professional people regard bringing people together as part of
their jobs.

What if you don't have an accountant—probably your most direct link to the banking community? An
"official" introduction to a banker is always good, but
you can be just as effective by telephoning directly: call
your bank and ask for the name of the president or vice-
president of consumer loans. Then don't be shy; call him
or her. Say, "My name is _____, and I'd like to set up a
meeting with you to discuss a loan." Chances are he or
she will be glad to meet with you.

If you're sloughed off with "I'll send you an application form in the mail," say, "I've filled out the form,
but I'm interested in establishing an overall relationship
with your bank." That should pique a banker's interest;
bankers are always eager to have a new customer who
intends to make use of all or most of the bank's services
on a continuing basis.

If you live in a big city, make your contact with
the manager of the local branch of your bank. He or she
might negotiate the loan with you (it happens in smaller
branches) or introduce you to the chief loan officer (a
common procedure in larger branches). In either case
you're dealing with a top officer—and that's what you
want.

6. Get your banker interested in you.

Contrary to popular belief, bankers are human and lead lives much like yours and mine. More important, they are in the "people business." The competition for *your* banking business is keen, and it increases daily now that brokerage and insurance companies are entering the banking world. That means that bankers are eager to make your acquaintance and to make you happy. Understanding that fact is vital and useful. Be friendly and direct when you communicate with your banker. Open up; talk about yourself, what you're doing, your plans, and even your future needs.

Many people miss that first opportunity to present themselves. And it's a mistake. Think for a moment: when people are faced with a stack of ten more or less similar loan applications, who do you think will be the obvious choice: a customer the banker knows, or the other nine who are only data in blanks on an application form? The farther away you get from the cold, impersonal application form, the better are your chances for quick, top-notch banking services.

While doing the research for a television segment on this topic, I interviewed the senior loan officer of a bank who confided that for him, loan decisions were "20 percent science and 80 percent art—the art is knowing people." He told me the story of an earnest young man who had come to him for a personal loan. "The guy said to me, 'I'm tied to my family's money and connections and want to establish a line of credit so I can get started on my own and have a credit track record.' " The banker was impressed with the young man's desire to be independent, and he told me he felt a certain sense of involvement and wanted to help him. "Even though I knew it entailed some risk," the banker said, "I gave him the loan."

After you get your first loan at a new bank, look down the road; you'll probably need another loan in the not-too-distant future. So keep your banker interested in you. Keep him or her posted on what's happening in your life and in your career. If a banker is aware of the progress of your professional and personal affairs, he or she is more likely to be receptive to your loan requests in the coming years.

7. Take advantage of corporate clout.

Corporate accounts are extremely profitable, and bankers turn cartwheels to keep them. If you're a corporate employee on any level, you'll be given special consideration when you apply for a personal loan at the bank that handles your corporation's account.

I found that out when I applied for my first loan. The vice-president of the corporation I worked for introduced me to the bank president. I went in to see him, was treated graciously, and got my loan on the spot. The corporate introduction meant a safe loan from the banker's viewpoint.

Recently a friend of mine whose corporation had transferred him from Los Angeles to New York called me in a mild panic. He needed an interim real-estate loan fast, had no banking contacts in New York, and didn't know what to do. I suggested he call his personnel director, find out what bank his corporation dealt with in New York, and get the name of the bank executive who handled the account. He got the information, made an appointment with the executive, and had a check in his hands in twenty-four hours.

8. Know your loan-getting strengths.

Loan officers typically look for three characteristics in an applicant: Character, Capital, and Capacity.

If you possess these "three *C*'s," your chances of obtaining a loan are excellent.

Character, to a loan officer, means an affirmative answer to the question "Will you pay back the loan?" If you are diligently paying off your mortgage, as well as a car loan and the bills for your children's education, your Character rating is good.

Capital means an affirmative answer to the question "Can you pay back the loan in times of financial crisis?" If you have cash (savings accounts) or assets that could be converted into cash, your banker will probably consider you a good "Capital" risk.

Capacity means a positive answer to "Can you pay every installment on time?" If you have drawn a regular paycheck for many years and have managed your money well over this period, you will more than likely be able to meet your installments when they are due.

Even though you might not have thought about it in these terms, you may possess the three *C*'s— your hidden loan-getting strengths. If you can answer the three preceding questions affirmatively, you should be able to get the loan for which you never thought you could qualify.

9. Businesslike behavior is best.

Many bankers evaluate an applicant's behavior patterns as well as his or her ability to meet tough credit standards (a high loan point score, a positive credit report, and a history of on-time personal loan payments). By following these suggestions, you'll earn a high rating for your business behavior as well:

• Don't approach the situation with a negative attitude. A cheerful and confident stance is best.

- Dress in a manner appropriate for your business and community. Don't let your appearance detract from your purpose.
- Act as you would in any business situation—politely, sincerely, and honestly—and expect the same from the banker.
- Relax. I have seen people freeze when talking to bankers. Take a deep breath and smile.
- Be sure to present a clear, specific purpose for the loan.
- Answer questions straightforwardly. Have the facts clear in your mind. Hesitating, stuttering, or mumbling could be misinterpreted.
- Know what to expect. Bankers are not cheerleaders, so don't lose your temper should the banker's reaction be less than enthusiastic.
- After presenting your case, get a commitment on when you will hear from your banker.

10. Don't settle for less money than you need.

You'll probably get as much money as you need for your first loan if you take one simple action: show the banker a realistic budget proving that you can pay the loan back without strapping yourself. If you feel you've done this and the banker is *still* hesitant to approve your initial loan request, find out exactly where the problems lie; there's a good chance you can overcome them.

Many of the guidelines for obtaining signature loans from banks apply to other kinds of loans as well— from other kinds of financial institutions or from individuals. The most important factor in applying for *any* kind of loan is to persuade the lender that you *can* and *will* pay it back on time.

CHAPTER 2

SOURCES OF PERSONAL LOANS AND HOW TO CHOOSE THE RIGHT ONE FOR YOU

On the way to Los Angeles International Airport one day, a taxi driver offered me his opinion of the "credit crunch." "Lady, from now on, it looks like you'll have to own your own bank to get a loan. . . . The little guy doesn't have a chance."

For the cabbie and for many others, the credit-crunch headlines have obscured a basic fact of economic life today: not only is money available, but it can be obtained from many sources other than banks and at a wide range of interest rates.

It's easy to feel discouraged and to suffer from tunnel vision in a time of daily and often depressing economic changes. But now, more than ever, is the time to know how to take full advantage of your options. Here are the facts. Although commercial banks are the leading source of personal loans, there are eight *additional* sources for signature loans: savings-and-loan associations, savings banks, credit unions, personal-finance companies, employers, family and friends, private loan sources, and credit-card companies. Each of these is a potential loan source for *you*.

In Chapter 1, I outlined the techniques for getting a signature loan from a commercial bank, but there's more to signature loans than that. In this chapter you will learn about the four different *types* of signature loans available from commercial banks. Then I'll introduce you to the various types of banking institutions in the United States, all of which grant signature loans, and offer guidelines to help you choose the one that is most suitable for your needs. I'll also tell you about the five *non*-bank signature-loan sources and spell out their advantages and disadvantages. Equipped with this knowledge, you'll be able to choose the best possible loan source for you.

THE FOUR KINDS OF SIGNATURE LOANS (UNSECURED PERSONAL LOANS)

1. REGULAR SIGNATURE LOANS

You sign a promise to pay—it's really nothing more than an IOU—and the money is yours.

2. READY CREDIT

This functions as a line of credit tied either to your bank account or to your credit card. The line of ready credit available to you ranges from $500 to $2,000 (and in some cases up to $5,000). Special checks are frequently offered for these accounts. As soon as you write a check against the account (and it clears), the account is activated and loan fees begin. You then have the right to pay back the loan on a monthly basis with fees similar to credit-card rates (1½ percent per month).

3. OVERDRAFT CHECKING

This works the same way as ready credit, except that the bank deposits money in your personal checking account rather than into a special account. The maximum amount is usually $2,000.

4. CREDIT-CARD LOANS

With bank credit cards (VISA and MasterCard are the only bank cards) you can draw up to your unused allowable credit limit. In some cases that credit line could be as high as $25,000, but it is usually $2,000.

The application forms for these four types of bank signature loans are quite similar. In fact, banks often issue just one form, where you simply check off the kind of signature loan you desire.

STRATEGIES FOR FILLING OUT A BANK SIGNATURE-LOAN APPLICATION FORM SUCCESSFULLY

When you fill out an application for a signature loan, you can improve your chances for approval. Here are some suggestions that I've found can often make the difference between approval and rejection.

• *Be factual.* It is perfectly appropriate to round out figures to your advantage, but your credit report will probably reveal any serious distortions or exaggerations you inadvertently or intentionally make.

• *If the questions on the form don't permit you to communicate your story fully and fairly, tell it on an attached sheet of paper.* Let's say that you've been at your present job for less than a year, after working for your previous employer for under a year, too. That's a black mark against you, because bankers value stability (which is a sign of character). So on the attached sheet, explain why you left your previous job (moving to a better-paying position is always an acceptable reason) and why you believe your current job will be permanent (good pay, job satisfaction, and opportunity for advancement always meet with bankers' approval).

• *If you have sound investments (C.D.'s, money-market funds, gilt-edged securities, and so on), list them on an attached sheet of paper under the heading "Additional Credit References."*

• *If you're self-employed or work in the arts, attach a statement documenting your capability of repaying the loan.* A letter from an accountant, if you have one, will carry additional weight.

• *Check your responses on the application*

form against your ratings on the Loan Scoring Chart (*page 24*). If you think you can raise your score on any item by means of an explanation, do so on a separate sheet of paper.

BANK SOURCES FOR SIGNATURE LOANS

Now let's assess the advantages and disadvantages of the four kinds of banking and banklike institutions as sources of signature loans.

1. COMMERCIAL BANKS

The nation's oldest type of bank grants more signature loans than any other lending institution. Commercial banks were founded to serve the business community and the wealthy. These days, however, commercial banks serve everybody with a supermarket of customer services.

ADVANTAGES

- The company you work for deals with a commercial bank, and if you patronize the same one, you may have a borrowing edge.
- You can conduct all your banking business in one place—not only a convenience, but a plus in building up your "borrowing track record" with a single institution.
- This kind of bank is accustomed to handling large quantities of signature loans, and so service is efficient and swift (a loan is usually processed in twenty-four hours if your application is problem-free).
- You may take as long as three years to repay, a desirable situation should you want to keep your installment payments small. (You can, of course, pay back the loan in only one or two years, however, and save significantly on interest costs.)

- Rates are reasonable by today's standards (check the financial pages of your newspaper).

DISADVANTAGES

- Credit standards are the highest among financial institutions that grant signature loans.
- Loan requests for less than $1,000 are usually rejected.

2. SAVINGS BANKS

Savings banks came into being early in the last century when farmers, wage earners, small-business owners, and professionals—whom commercial banks turned away—pooled their savings for their mutual benefit. That's why some savings banks are still called "mutual savings banks." There's nothing "mutual" about today's savings banks, however. When you deal with them, you're treated as you would be in any other kind of bank—as a customer.

ADVANTAGES

- Some savings banks offer as complete a line of customer financial services as commercial banks. Thus, you can conduct *all* your banking there and gain a borrowing edge. (Check the specific services offered by the savings bank you have in mind before you open your accounts to be sure it can fulfill not only your present but also your future banking needs.)
- Rates are as reasonable as those of commercial banks.
- The term of the loan can be as long as three years.

DISADVANTAGES

- Small loans (under $3,000) are difficult to obtain.
- Savings banks exist in only sixteen states.*

---

* The sixteen states are Alaska, Connecticut, Delaware, Indiana, Maine, Maryland, Massachusetts, New Hamp-

3. SAVINGS-AND-LOAN INSTITUTIONS

S & L's originated in the early 1800s to satisfy the home-financing needs—and nothing else—of farmers and workers. Today more than 50 percent of the families in the United States own their own homes, but at the beginning of the nineteenth century, homeowning (with the exception of shanties and prairie houses) was a privilege of the rich. So S & L's provided the mortgage money that permitted thousands of low- and middle-income people to purchase their own homes. Mortgages are still the mainstay of the S & L business, and the ceilings on those loans are higher than at other lending institutions. In addition, S & L's now offer a complete line of consumer financial services, much like those of savings banks.

ADVANTAGES

• Like commercial banks and savings banks, S & L's offer many services other than loans and can provide reasonable, competitive interest rates.

DISADVANTAGES

• The disadvantages are the same as for savings banks—except that S & L's operate in all fifty states.

4. CREDIT UNIONS

When I was the financial commentator for the "Today" show, I conducted a study that convinced me that credit unions may be the best source of signature loans for most people. Credit unions (not to be confused with labor unions) are formed by people like you and me. A group of individuals united by a close common

———————————————————————————————————

shire, New Jersey, New York, Oregon, Pennsylvania, Rhode Island, Vermont, Washington, and Wisconsin. Although charters also exist in Minnesota and Ohio, no savings banks have been established in those states.

interest—such as working in the same firm, or being members of the same club, church, or professional association—can obtain a federal charter to operate as a credit union. The union then accepts deposits from its members and makes loans to them, mostly for short durations. Members who save funds with the union earn dividends (interest) on their money, derived from loan repayments. Because they operate under a different set of rules from commercial banks and savings-and-loans, credit unions can offer low interest rates. They are non-profit associations, usually run by the members themselves, and have tax-exempt status.

The chances are good that there is a credit union for which you qualify for membership. To obtain a list of credit-union names, write CUNA (Credit Union National Association), P.O. Box 431, Madison, WI 53701. If you don't qualify for an existing credit union nearby, CUNA will supply you with information about forming your own association with members of a group to which you belong.

ADVANTAGES

- Credit standards are flexible; the object of the credit union is to accommodate its members.
- Rates are the lowest of any lender (from ¼ percent to 2 to 3 percent under those of commercial banks).
- Credit unions specialize in personal loans.
- Service is as quick and efficient as at a commercial bank, but often more personalized.
- You can sometimes take up to twelve years to repay a loan (although three to four years is more common), which can make the amounts of installment payments almost negligible.
- There is usually no limit to the amount you can borrow—but see "Disadvantages."

DISADVANTAGES

- You must be a member of the credit union to apply for a loan.
- Some credit unions set limits on certain kinds of loans; these may be lower than your requirements.

NON-BANK SOURCES FOR SIGNATURE LOANS

Sometimes a bank or banklike institution may not be the right loan source for you. Certain people, perhaps because of a poor credit rating, cannot qualify for loans from a bank or savings-and-loan association. Moreover, not everyone has a credit union to turn to. Often individuals discover that other sources are actually less expensive places from which to borrow.

So, be sure to consider all your options, including the following five non-bank sources for signature loans.

1. YOUR EMPLOYER

Many companies have a standard policy of granting loans to employees. Repayment is made through paycheck deductions.

ADVANTAGES

- Your loan request is almost never rejected.
- You receive the loan within twenty-four hours.
- Interest rates vary from zero to slightly under commercial bank rates.

DISADVANTAGES

- Loan amounts seldom exceed 10 percent of your yearly salary.

- Loans are usually short-term, from six months to a year. The paycheck deduction can leave a big hole in your weekly take-home money.

2. CREDIT-CARD COMPANIES

In collaboration with local banks, American Express offers a Gold Card which permits you to draw on a line of credit of $2,000 or more. (You cannot draw cash on the American Express Green Card.) Diners Club permits you to draw $1,000 over a two-week period, but only outside the United States.

So-called cash advances obtainable with *bank* credit cards are discussed in Chapter 5; let's concentrate on the American Express Gold Card here.

ADVANTAGES

- You can obtain a loan simply by presenting your Gold Card at any American Express office. Cash is also available twenty-four hours a day at automatic cash dispensers.
- Interest rates are the same as for credit-card loans made by commercial banks.
- You can borrow very small sums.

DISADVANTAGES

- None, unless you need more than $2,000.

3. SMALL-LOAN COMPANIES

Also known as "consumer-finance companies" and "personal-loan companies," they were established to provide small loans for the "little guy." (But the "little guy," as it turns out, hasn't made these companies as profitable as they would like to be, so many small-loan companies have shifted to the far more profitable mortgage and second-mortgage markets.)

ADVANTAGES

- Credit standards are low. Almost any employed person can get a loan.
- You can obtain loans for smaller amounts than are available from banks (but not as small as you can get with a credit card).
- You can take up to three years to repay.

DISADVANTAGES

- On the average, the most you can borrow is $2,500. (Ceilings vary from state to state.)
- Rates are high, often twice those of commercial banks.
- A cosigner may be required.

4. _EXECUTIVE LOAN SERVICES_

These agencies provide large loans (sometimes by mail) for high-salaried executives with a history of job stability.

ADVANTAGES

- You can get up to $50,000 overnight.
- You can take up to three years to repay.

DISADVANTAGES

- Rates are 6 to 8 percent higher than those of commercial banks.

5. _YOUR FAMILY AND FRIENDS_

Sometimes your best loan source may be right under your nose. Perhaps your family and friends can profit by lending you money, if they've got the liquid assets. That's the sales pitch to use, and it often works. Who wouldn't prefer the same return a commercial bank would receive for a loan to the 5½ to 15-or-so percent available from deposit accounts and money-market funds?

ADVANTAGES

- If a family member is willing and able, you can get the loan fast, without credit checks or red tape.
- There is no ceiling on the loan.
- You pay the same interest rates as you would at a commercial bank, or less, depending on what you negotiate.
- You can negotiate a mutually convenient duration for the loan.

DISADVANTAGES

- None, provided that you keep the loan on a business-like basis and avoid emotional entanglements. Unfortunately, that's easier said than done! It's frequently touchy just to find out whether a family member or friend has a few thousand dollars to lend. So the entire issue has to be managed with extra care. Think through all the emotional *and* financial ramifications thoroughly when you're considering borrowing from someone close to you.

WHICH SIGNATURE-LOAN SOURCE IS BEST FOR YOU?

Now you must decide which signature-loan source is best for you. I suggest that you do some comparison shopping: investigate all the options I have described, and assess how they fit into your own financial picture.

As you research the various loan sources, you might find it helpful to jot down, in chart form, interest rates, loan ceilings, repayment schedules, and other pertinent information for each source as you make phone calls and visit various bank offices. That way you have a handy means of comparison. Most people can successfully obtain a signature loan if they are willing to do their homework and take the time to become informed borrowers.

CHAPTER 3

HOW TO USE YOUR ASSETS TO GET THE PERSONAL LOAN YOU NEED

A few months ago I got a call from my nephew Scott. After our customary friendly greetings, he said, "Aunt Paula, since you're the family expert on money matters, I'd like to ask you for some advice."

"What's up?" I inquired.

"I have a chance to spend a year in Mexico on a work-study program and need $7,000 to cover my expenses. What's the best way to raise the cash?" He told me that although he had $10,000 in a savings account, he was reluctant to dig into it because he would need it all for college when he got back.

"You don't have to touch that money," I told him. "Call your banker and ask about a savings-backed collateral loan."

Scott is certainly no VIP or wheeler-dealer, but the next day he called me back to report that he had gotten his loan. He suggested to an officer at his bank that he use his savings as collateral and it worked. It always does.

Signature loans, covered in the first two chapters, are simply the most basic kind of loan. They're fine for loans of amounts up to about $2,500, but when the amount you need exceeds 20 percent of your net income, lenders look for something tangible on which to grant a loan. That is where collateral becomes essential for getting the loan you need.

Collateral is anything of value against which you can borrow money. In the event that you don't or can't repay the debt, ownership of the collateral passes to the lender. Collateral, therefore, secures the repayment of the loan. In fact, collateralized loans are commonly called *secured* loans; signature loans are referred to as *unsecured* loans.

In this chapter you will learn about the four kinds of collateral acceptable to banks and other loan sources, and the six non-bank sources for collateralized loans. Each type of collateral is evaluated so that you can make an informed decision about what type to use to get the personal loan you want.

FOUR TYPES OF COLLATERAL

The basic kinds of collateral are savings deposits, real estate, stocks and bonds, and—on rare occasions—investment-quality diamonds, paintings, and other collectibles.

1. SAVINGS DEPOSITS

These include passbook accounts, statement savings accounts, time savings accounts, and C.D.'s (certificates of deposit). The accounts may be held singly or jointly. You can usually borrow an amount up to 100 percent of your savings. (Some banks set a 90 percent limit; check with a bank officer.)

My nephew Scott, as you'll recall, had $10,000 in his savings account. He used $7,000 as collateral, and that amount was frozen the moment he received the loan. Then, starting with his first payment, an amount equal to it (less interest) was freed. He could of course use the remaining $3,000 as he pleased.

Scott preferred to borrow against his savings account, rather than simply withdrawing the $7,000 he needed. I reminded him that the money he kept in the bank account would continue to earn interest while he was out of the country and that his loan would function as a forced repayment plan.

There are other reasons, however, for taking out a savings-backed loan. It can even make sense to take out a loan of this type when you don't necessarily need extra money right away, and I often advise people to do so.

Jennifer McMillan was one such person. At age

twenty-three she had a college degree in journalism, was working as a production assistant at ABC television, and had $3,000 in the bank. She was also making marriage plans for the following year and had mentioned to me that she might want a good-size loan at that time to get started in a new home. Jennifer also told me, however, that "there is no credit report or history on me at all, because nobody has ever reported anything about me, either good or bad."

As I explained in Chapter 1, credit reports are an extremely important factor in determining your eligibility for a signature loan. So I advised Jennifer to take out a savings-backed loan right then, using the $3,000 she had in her savings account as collateral. If she paid it back punctually, she'd have an excellent entry on her credit report and a much-improved chance of receiving that big loan a year later.

This type of planning ahead makes good sense. If you're young, with little or no credit history, but a nest egg in savings, consider taking out a savings-backed loan (the refusal rate is zero) to establish a strong credit rating.

Keep in mind, though, that there are several different types of savings accounts, some of which *cannot* be used as collateral. For example, *All Savers* accounts are special tax-exempt certificates of deposit that were offered to the public for only a fifteen-month period beginning October 1, 1981. The law prohibits borrowing against them.

N.O.W. savings accounts are also ineligible for use as collateral for a loan. Even so, having maintained a steady average balance in your account for at least two years should weigh in your favor when you apply for a signature loan.

Certificates of deposit can be used as collateral

if they are regular C.D.'s and not the special All Savers. If you need cash, it is often a sound idea to borrow against your C.D. rather than withdrawing the funds, because the latter course entails a severe penalty. If you take out a loan, however, your original funds remain intact in the C.D. and continue to earn interest.

When evaluating whether to borrow against your C.D. or withdraw money from the account, have the bank compute the transaction both ways—the cost of taking the funds out early (and paying a penalty) versus borrowing against the funds. This is a common request, and your banker should be happy to make the calculation for you.

2. REAL ESTATE

Homeowners currently constitute 65 percent of the U.S. population, so it's not surprising that real estate is by far the most popular type of collateral. The equity in your home—that is, the current value of your home less the amount you still have to pay on your mortgage—can be one of your most valuable borrowing assets. Because real-estate equity is considered an excellent type of collateral, its use usually guarantees quick loan approval. In general, you can borrow up to 80 to 85 percent of your home equity. Naturally, as your equity builds up over the years, your ability to obtain a larger equity-backed loan will increase as well.

3. STOCKS AND BONDS

Almost all banks accept top-rated bonds and blue-chip stocks as collateral if they are worth at least $15 a share. As a general rule, you can borrow up to 75 percent of the value of qualifying stocks. The specific percentage is based on the stock's rating as determined by Standard and Poor's or Moody's. Also, you should be able to borrow up to 80 percent of the value of qualifying bonds and up to 90 percent of the value of Treasury bills (a kind of bond). There is no ceiling on a loan secured by stocks and/or bonds.

But watch out for the pitfalls of this kind of loan. Banks hold your pledged securities for the duration of the loan, and you can't sell them, even when market conditions dictate that you should. What's more, if the value of your securities drops while the loan is still unpaid, the bank may ask for additional collateral. If you can't come up with it, the bank could call in the loan, asking for immediate repayment in full. In the event that you can't pay in such a situation, the bank could sell securities sufficient to liquidate your debt.

**4. DIAMONDS, GOLD, PAINTINGS, AND OTHER VALUABLE ASSETS**

A bank generally won't accept these as collateral. But if you possess something of value that you think a bank _should_ accept, ask a bank executive. The answer might be "yes," although realistically the chances are slim. A more direct loan source is a dealer who specializes in selling whatever asset you have.

SIX ADDITIONAL SOURCES FOR COLLATERALIZED LOANS

When you're in the market for a loan—whether signature or collateralized—I always recommend that you evaluate _all_ possible money sources, not just the most obvious ones. Banks don't have a monopoly on the collateral-loan marketplace, any more than they do on signature loans. There are six additional sources of money that may fit your needs, several of which offer significantly better rates than banks. These alternative sources are particularly valuable to you if, for instance, your credit rating is poor, or you need more cash than you can get through a bank.

1. LIFE-INSURANCE COMPANIES

Life-insurance companies accept as collateral the cash value—the sum of the paid premiums, plus interest, less certain deductions—of policies they have issued. The cash value grows steadily; a chart incorporated into the policy tells you what the cash value is at any given time. A clause in every cash-value (or "whole-life") insurance policy gives the policyholder the right to borrow up to 95 percent of the cash value on demand. (A whole-life policy is insurance that protects you not just for a certain number of years—a term—but for your whole life.) You cannot, however, borrow against "term" insurance policies, which do not build cash value.

There are so many outstanding advantages to "cash-value" insurance loans that they are certainly worth investigating as a money source. You'll never be refused for this type of loan, because your policy guarantees acceptance. After all, an insurance policy is a binding contract between you and the insurance company. To obtain the loan, all you need to do is make your request in writing to the insurance company. A check is then mailed to you, usually within a week.

The interest rate on insurance loans is low, perhaps the lowest you can get. You can also pay back the loan anytime, in full or in regular (or irregular) installments. In fact, you need never repay the loan. Should you decide not to repay it, the amount of your loan plus interest is deducted from the eventual death benefits.

2. BROKERAGE HOUSES

Earlier you learned that stocks and bonds can be used as collateral for a bank loan. But you can also deal directly with your stockbroker. Some brokers will give cash loans of up to 50 percent of the value of the securities they handle for you. One advantage of dealing with a broker rather than a bank is that the broker grants the loan solely on the basis of collateral. (A banker will check your credit rating as well; if it's poor, no matter how sound the collateral, you may not get the loan.) Another advantage is that you can repay the loan whenever you like. The disadvantages are generally the same as for bank loans secured by stocks and/or bonds. But you'll also pay a higher interest rate than banks charge.

Another borrowing option is available if you have a Cash Management Account (CMA™), pioneered by Merrill Lynch and now available in similar formats from other brokerage houses. In these plans, $20,000 (or more) is invested in a money-market fund, which can then function as collateral for loans of up to 90 percent of the value of your shares in the fund. In addition, you're issued a special VISA card with which you can obtain cash advances up to the amount of the collateral in your account (though limited to $5,000 in certain banks) at any of 80,000 locations worldwide. Checks imprinted with your name give you instant access to your funds.

CMA loans have the same disadvantages as any other collateral-secured loans, and their interest rates are even higher than regular personal loans from brokers.

3. FINANCE COMPANIES, SECOND-MORTGAGE COMPANIES, AND INDIVIDUALS WHO SPECIALIZE IN HOME-EQUITY LOANS

When you borrow from these sources, the equity in your home, condominium, or cooperative serves as collateral.

4. PAWNBROKERS

Most medium-size or large cities have at least one pawnshop—that often overlooked but enduring institution that makes personal loans on the security of personal property in their keeping. When my grandmother came over from the old country, her one prized possession was a string of coral beads. Whenever she needed cash, she took them out of her locked drawer, dressed in her best outfit, walked to the streetcar, and paid a visit to the pawnbroker. For her, the pawnshop was—as it still is to hundreds of thousands of people in this country—the "poor person's bank." In Mexico it actually has official status as such. The government-controlled pawnshop, Monte de Piedad, lends money each year to 5 million people at interest rates ranging from zero, for loans under the equivalent of about $12, to 4 percent per year for loans on jewelry.

In general, the modern pawnbroker will lend you only a small percentage of the value of the item you pawn. If you leave, say, an $800 stereo as collateral, the pawnbroker may loan you as little as $80. In most states, ceilings are fixed on pawn loans, usually at about $2,000. Even so, the typical loan is less than $200.

Here's how a pawnbroker calculates the amount of a loan: Let's say you bring in a diamond ring appraised at $18,000. Jewelry appraisals are customarily overvalued by about 20 percent. (Appraisers earn a percentage of the value they set on a piece, so it's in their interest to boost its value.) Deducting 20 percent from the appraised value leaves $14,400, the retail price of your property. The wholesale value, the price at which the pawnbroker can sell the piece should you default, is half of that, or $7,200. The pawnbroker will then offer you a maximum of 25 percent of the wholesale value. So, on a piece of jewelry appraised at $18,000, the most you can expect to borrow is $1,800.

There are some other disadvantages of dealing with pawnbrokers. For instance, interest rates are high, sometimes as much as four times greater than what banks charge. (Some pawnshops, though, match bank rates.) Also, loans are only short-term, ranging from thirty days to a year. During the term of the loan, you lose possession of your property; a pawn ticket is the sole documentary evidence of the transaction.

If you're unable to pay your loan on the due date, you lose your property, and the pawnbroker then has the right to sell it. Thus, if you know in advance that there's a chance you will default, it would be wiser for you to *sell* your property rather than pawn it. You can sell a piece of jewelry appraised at $18,000 for about $7,200 (the wholesale value), but you're not likely to get more than $1,800 when you pawn it.

Despite the disadvantages, pawnbrokers satisfy many people's needs for small, short-term loans, made without credit checks. Interestingly, even the wealthy are often no strangers to pawnshops. People with money don't always have ready access to it and sometimes find themselves temporarily low on cash. "I'd be too embarrassed to ask my banker for just $1,000 or so," a prominent television actor once confided in me. "So I take a ring or one of my other prized possessions to the pawnshop, and my problem is solved." When the Beverly

Hills Pawnshop was located on Beverly Drive at Wilshire, some of Hollywood's notables were known to pass through its doors. When liquid cash is scarce, the pawnshop is a haven for rich and poor alike.

5. SMALL-LOAN COMPANIES

Small-loan companies will accept your color TV, refrigerator, stereo, furniture, and other household goods as collateral for a loan. The loan is secured by what is called a chattel mortgage, which permits the borrower to retain possession of the goods but gives the lender the right to seize them in case of default.

"The _last_ thing we want to do is seize them," the manager of a small-loan company told me. "We are seldom able to sell household goods for enough to cover the loan. We place a chattel mortgage on the loan primarily for its psychological effect. People will scrimp and save to meet their payments if they think they're in danger of losing their TV or their furniture."

"But _do_ small-loan companies ever actually seize household goods?"

"Very, very rarely," I was told. "What we prefer to do is say, 'Look, normally you pay us both principal and interest on every installment. For now, just pay us back the interest—that's not much—until you get back on your feet again. Then start paying off the principal as well.' It works." And it's profitable to the loan company, because interest payments could continue indefinitely.

An architect named Thomas was unexpectedly laid off his job, and within a month he had fallen behind in his loan payments to a small-loan company. He had used his furniture as collateral, but rather than taking possession of these items, the loan company asked him to make at least the monthly interest payments until he

found a job. Consequently, although Thomas was forced
to keep up his $18-a-month interest payments, he was
given a temporary respite from the $111 monthly princi-
pal payment.

A small-loan company that turns you down for
a signature loan may often approve a chattel-mortgage
loan. And unless you're unable to make the most minimal monthly payments, you need not be afraid of losing
your household goods.

6. PRIVATE LENDERS

Loans for a variety of reasons, both personal
and business, are made by private parties. Brokers often
act as the go-between, and many individuals advertise
money to loan in the classified section of the _Wall Street
Journal_ under the heading "Business Connections."
Private lenders who make these collateralized loans do
so primarily because they see them as good investments.

In summary, if you need a loan larger than one
you can obtain on your signature alone, investigate and
evaluate the possibility of borrowing, using the following
as collateral:

- a bank savings account—you borrow against money
  that you've deposited in the bank without having to
  withdraw those funds
- home equity—the real estate you own
- stocks and bonds, ranging from securities that are
  traded on various stock exchanges to Treasury bills
- diamonds, gold, and other valuable assets, although
  only rarely will a bank accept them as collateral
- life-insurance policies, a simple means of borrowing
  from the "cash value" of whole-life protection
- personal belongings like TVs and furniture, which can

be borrowed against at small-loan companies, although at only a small percentage of their value.

To avoid a credit check, consider the following sources:

- life-insurance policies; a written request is all you need to borrow from a whole-life policy
- brokerage houses, which evaluate only the value of your securities, not your credit history
- home-equity loans, granted exclusively on the basis of the market value (minus your indebtedness) of your real estate
- pawnshops, in which interest is usually high and the loans are short-term
- small-loan companies, which allow you to maintain possession of your property unless you seriously fall behind on your payments.

No matter where you obtain a personal loan—and whether it's a signature or a collateral loan—there is a price tag attached to it. It's essential to carefully calculate in advance what your loans will cost you. You will probably be surprised at the significant difference a single percentage point of interest can make, particularly on a long-term loan. In the next chapter I will explain just how important factors like interest rates and repayment schedules are, and I will show you how to choose the most economically advantageous loan for your individual needs and circumstances.

CHAPTER 4

HOW TO SAVE
MONEY—AND MAKE
MONEY—ON PERSONAL
LOANS

During a lecture at Purdue University, I posed this question to the audience: "When you think of taking out a personal loan, what is the first question that comes to mind?"

Ninety percent of the students responded, "How much are the monthly payments?"

That answer is an expensive trap in which many people get caught. Although monthly payments are important, the overall cost of the loan is even more critical; in fact, it should be your primary consideration. Rarely—if ever—would you buy anything without asking the price. So why shouldn't you also determine the total price when buying a loan?

Actually, the lender expects you to and has the answer ready. The federal Truth in Lending Act, passed in 1969, makes it mandatory for the lender to make full disclosure of all the costs. One look at any borrowing disclosure statement, however, is enough to discourage the most ardent math wizard.

If you're a seasoned borrower, getting a simple answer from the lender won't satisfy you. You'll want to know how the lender arrived at the numbers and exactly what they mean. Depending on the way interest rates are calculated, and whether any additional administrative fees are added, you can either save a significant number of dollars or be charged quite a bit more than may really be necessary.

A good friend of mine who is a former banker once commented, "I don't think any lender sets out to kite the price, but as you know, there are many ways to figure the cost of a loan." He is a believer in the prizefighter's motto, "Protect yourself at all times." He says, "No one should go into a deal blindly; it's always good to know what the bankers know." What they _do_ know has for too long been obscured by the "math mystique"—the belief that calculating interest rates is so complex and labyrinthine that it's beyond the grasp of everyone except Harvard M.B.A.'s. This is simply not true.

In this chapter I'll cut through that math mystique by showing you the four methods of interest-rate calculation: the "added on," "discount," "spread-out," and "rule-of-78" methods. Armed with this information, you will be able to determine the best buys in personal loans and what you'll save when you pay off your loan before the final due date. I'll also compare the basic interest rates of all personal-loan sources to guide you to the least expensive lending institutions. Finally, I'll show you how to take advantage of some low interest rates to turn a personal loan into a moneymaking tool.

THE INS AND OUTS OF INTEREST

When the terms of a loan are quoted to you, pay particular attention to two factors: the interest percentage rate and the total cost of the loan. From the borrower's viewpoint, interest is actually a part of the total loan cost, calculated as a percentage (say, 18.5) of the money borrowed (say, $2,400) over a period of time (say, one year). In this example, the interest charge is $444 (18.5 percent times $2,400) per year. The rate of interest expressed in percent per year is known as the annual percentage rate (APR).

When an interest rate is quoted by the month, you can convert it to the APR by multiplying by 12. For example, the Chase Manhattan VISA card rate is 1.5 percent per month on the unpaid balance. That works out to an APR of 18 percent (1.5 times 12). APRs, of course, can vary from one type of lending institution to another. For example, the APRs offered at commercial banks are typically lower than those of small-loan companies.

So, using the APR of commercial banks as a

standard of comparison, the accompanying chart shows how other loan sources typically compare to it. (The standard APR for commercial banks is designated as S.)

COMPARATIVE APRs OF PERSONAL LOAN SOURCES

LOAN SOURCE	APR
Commercial banks	S*
Savings banks	S*
Savings-and-loan associations	S*
Credit unions	S* less ¼ to 3 percent
Family and friends	S, but subject to negotiation
Employer	S less ¼ to 100 percent
Credit-card companies	S
Small-loan companies	S plus 6 percent to $2S$
Executive loan services	S plus 6 to 8 percent
Life-insurance companies	S less 9 to 18 percent
Securities brokers	S plus 1 to 5 percent
Merrill Lynch CMA	S plus 2¾ to 7¼ percent
Pawnbrokers	S to $4S$
Private loan sources	S, but subject to negotiation

* On signature loans only. Collateralized loans are S to S minus ¼ to 1 percent; and APRs for savings-backed loans can go as low as 1 percentage point above interest paid on the deposit account (but rarely do).

Current rates on consumer loans are listed in the financial pages of most major newspapers, typically under a heading like "Consumer Loan Rates." These rates fluctuate in response to changes in the prime rate and also may vary from bank to bank depending on each institution's desire for business. (If a bank's officials want to increase their volume of loans, they tend to make their rates more competitive.)

No matter where you're considering obtaining your next loan, remember to ask the lender specifically about the *total* cost of the loan. If you borrow *x* dollars and pay back *x*-plus dollars over the term of the loan, the "plus" is the cost of a loan. Interest makes up most of this cost, along with any fees the lender may add for services—a common device to circumvent—legally—the ceilings on interest rates. To determine the *total* cost of a loan, or what is often called the finance charge, add these fees to the interest charge.

The extra fees, incidentally, are quite commonplace, but they can seem particularly confusing. Although states do set a ceiling on the amount of loan interest that can be charged—the so-called usury laws— lenders are permitted to add "points" or service charges when the interest rates throughout the industry are at or above usury limits.

Interest-rate calculations can also seem perplexing because of the different methods financial institutions use to compute them. By choosing the most advantageous one, you can save hundreds of dollars.

In some cases, for example, you can pay the interest *at the end* of the loan period, if that's the lender's policy. In the example presented earlier, the $444 interest on $2,400 could be paid at the end of a year. This is known as the "added-on" method of interest payment, because the interest payment ($444) is added on to the principal ($2,400).

Another approach is to pay the interest *at the start* of the loan period. This is called the "discount" method of interest, but that term is deceptive because there is no discount on the interest rate, but rather on the amount of money you get. The check you are handed for your "$2,400" loan at 18.5 percent interest will actually be for only $1,956 ($2,400 minus $444).

As you can see, the added-on method is a better deal; you pay $444 for a loan of $2,400, whereas the discount method costs you $444 for $1,956. You save $444 with the added-on method.

To translate this into APR terminology, the added-on APR is 18.5 percent; the discount APR is 22.7 percent ($444 divided by $1,956)—quite a difference!

I call the third technique for calculating interest payments the "spread-out" method. In this approach, the interest is spread out in equal installments over the term of the loan; the $444 interest on a $2,400 loan is spread out over twelve installments of $37 each. The total monthly payment is $237 ($2,400 divided by 12 plus $37).

Many people conclude that the spread-out method is as advantageous as the added-on method, and it sometimes appears that way. But interest-rate calculations are funny. Yes, it does seem as if you're paying $444 on $2,400. But on a spread-out loan, because of the decreasing amount of loan money you have available to you each month as you gradually repay the loan, the APR *is* quite high. After the final payment on this 18.5 percent spread-out loan, the average APR over twelve months is actually 33.6 percent!

The fourth method of loan calculation is called "the rule of 78." Although it is not widely used today, you should be familiar with it in case you encounter it. Here's how it works:

The figure 78 is determined by adding the month numbers of a twelve-month loan period (1 + 2 + 3 + 4 + 5 + 6 + 7 + 8 + 9 + 10 + 11 + 12 = 78).

The rule states that the amount of each monthly interest payment is calculated according to a formula:

$$\frac{\text{months to go on loan}}{78} \times \text{total interest}$$

So on total interest of $444, for example, here's how the formula works out over twelve months:

Month number	Months to go	Rule of 78	Monthly interest payment
1	12	12/78 × $444 = $68.30	
2	11	11/78 × $444 = $62.62	
3	10	10/78 × $444 = $56.92	
4	9	9/78 × $444 = $51.23	
5	8	8/78 × $444 = $45.53	
6	7	7/78 × $444 = $39.85	
7	6	6/78 × $444 = $34.15	
8	5	5/78 × $444 = $28.46	
9	4	4/78 × $444 = $22.77	
10	3	3/78 × $444 = $17.08	
11	2	2/78 × $444 = $11.39	
12	1	1/78 × $444 = $5.69	

78/78 × $444 = $444.00

If you pay the loan in full after you've paid six installments, you'll save the interest on the last six months (months 7 through 12), which amounts to only $119.54—$102.46 less than 50 percent of the total interest. The longer you let a rule-of-78 loan ride, the less you'll save by paying early. The sooner you pay off a loan of this type, the more you'll save.

Remember, although calculations like these may be intimidating, the lender is required by law to make them available to you *before* you sign for the loan. Also, at any time during the course of a loan, you can call the bank and ask, "If I pay off my loan today (or next week or next month), what will the total cost of my loan be?" They will be able to provide you with an exact answer to that question after a few moments of computation.

If interest calculations have begun to intrigue you, and you want to learn more about them, write for "The Arithmetic of Interest Rates" to Public Information Department, Federal Reserve Bank of New York, 333 Liberty Street, New York, NY 10045. This illustrated pamphlet is free.

Once again, before you sign for *any* personal loan, remember to ask about the APR as well as the total cost. Every sophisticated borrower does. But there are other elements to weigh as well.

FACTORS TO CONSIDER WHEN CHOOSING THE BEST LOAN FOR YOU

When you shop around for a loan, ask at several loan sources for the total finance cost and the APR for the loan you require, and compare them carefully.

1. Buy the loan with the lowest finance cost.

2. If two or more loan sources quote the same or only slightly different finance costs, choose the loan with the lowest APR.

3. The shorter the term of the loan, the lower the cost. Everything else being equal, if you have to choose between a one-year loan at Bank A and a three-year loan at Bank B, choose the one-year loan (provided that you can handle the higher monthly payments).

If you have already begun to build a solid, long-term relationship with a bank, however, it may be wise to apply for a loan from that institution, even if you end up paying more. Doing so could be worthwhile in terms of continual access of loan funds. (It's a good idea, of course, to shop among banks *before* you begin to build a long-term relationship with one.)

SHOULD YOU REPAY THE LOAN EARLY?

Is it worthwhile to repay a loan early, say, in six months instead of a year? Yes, if it's an added-on loan or a spread-out loan; you'll save 50 percent. But *don't* repay a discount loan early; you've already paid the interest up front. You've seen how, with a loan calculated according to the rule of 78, when you repay a one-year loan in six months, there will be some savings, but not a full 50 percent. You now know how to evaluate, in each case, whether paying early will save you money.

At some time or another, almost everyone applies for and receives a loan. If you have a good reason for borrowing, there is nothing wrong with doing so. Just be sure you can afford to pay it back. You now know how to figure out—or find out—what the *real* cost of your loan will be, and you're equipped to find the kind of loan you need at the lowest possible cost.

BORROWING FOR INVESTMENT PURPOSES

People borrow money for many reasons—to pay medical bills, to buy a car, to take a vacation. If you use your loan to make purchases or travel, of course, you won't make any money on it. But if you use the loan to make investments, you can cut the cost of the loan, or even end up with a profit.

Let's assume that you are taking out a loan against your savings account, perhaps to help establish your credit rating. If you invest this borrowed money in a certificate of deposit or a money-market fund, you can earn about 12 to 15 percent (as this book goes to press). Depending on the cost of your savings-account loan, this strategy could net you a profit, because you will probably be earning more in your new investment than the loan is costing you.

When you're trying to decide where to invest your loan money, keep in mind that money-market funds earn more than C.D.'s. You can buy into a money-market fund with as little as $1,000 to $2,500 and then have access to your investment by means of checks. Some money-market funds are insured for up to $100,000 (by the Securities Investor Protection Corporation), but some aren't insured at all.

You can buy a C.D. for as little as $2,500, but you'll receive maximum returns only if you invest at least $10,000. You can then withdraw all but $1,000 to $2,500 of your investment, but you pay a penalty of 1 percent per year on the amount withdrawn. On some C.D.'s, however, there is no easy-access privilege, and your funds are locked in until maturity, unless you're willing to pay *severe* penalties for early withdrawal.

On balance, I would say that an insured money-market fund, or a money-market fund of U.S. government securities, is preferable to a C.D. For the names and addresses of money-market funds look through the ads in the financial section of local newspapers or the *Wall Street Journal.* Send for prospectuses, and read them carefully before you buy. For detailed information on C.D.'s, contact an executive at your bank.

As a common-sense guideline, use a loan for investment purposes only when the interest you pay is less than the interest you earn. That means that only low-cost loans such as savings-account loans, life-insurance loans, and loans from friends, families, and employers can be profitably used for investment purposes.

A final word of caution: if you borrow to invest, invest only in safe securities.

CHAPTER 5

MAXIMIZING THE
VALUE OF YOUR
CREDIT CARDS

Not long ago, at a barbecue in California's San Fernando Valley, the conversation turned to the news that bank credit cards had raised their rates and imposed a monthly or yearly fee. I listened to a round of irate comments, "can-you-believe-it" remarks, and vows on everyone's part to rid themselves of plastic forever. Then I asked a few questions.

Most of the partygoers admitted that even with the higher costs, they wouldn't be able to make ends meet without credit cards. Not only had credit cards become financial IDs necessary for cashing checks, traveling, and generally validating one's existence; they had simply become an essential, taken-for-granted supplement to the weekly paycheck.

One guest made the point graphically. He took a stack of credit cards from his wallet, spread them out on a table, and exclaimed, "That's $3,500 anytime I need it."

Credit cards—those 2-x-3½-inch pieces of plastic—are in fact yet another way of borrowing money. When you buy goods and services with these cards, the companies that have issued them pay the merchants for the items. With many credit cards you have several months to pay back the money that has been "loaned" to you (if you are willing to pay the interest).

With the exception of big-price-tag items—houses, medical degrees, boats, planes—there's virtually no commodity that you can't charge with plastic. You can buy a weekend at the Waldorf, or a clown for your child's party. You can buy hamburgers, diamonds, sweat shirts, roses, and a night at the opera. You can even charge the purchase of money.

There are two general categories of credit cards: bank cards (VISA and MasterCard), department-store cards, and oil-company cards are the most common kind; travel and entertainment cards are the other type. Cards of the first type allow you to pay off your credit-card charges over a period of time. Most bank cards have begun to impose an annual service fee of about $15 to $20 for use of the cards, in addition to any interest fees that may be levied. If you shop around, however, you may still be able to find a bank that offers the cards free of charge. Incidentally, department-store and oil-company cards (thus far) almost never charge a fee.

T & E (travel and entertainment) cards are offered by American Express and Diners Club and require a membership fee each year. Unlike bank-card charges, the charges made on T & E cards must be paid *in full* shortly after billing.

In this chapter I will tell you about ways to save money with your credit cards, how to extend the number of "free money days," when to use your credit card instead of getting another type of loan, the types of cards that extend loans in cash, and other ways to use your credit cards. Let's begin by discussing some of the strategies you can use to get the fullest financial advantage from your credit cards.

THE CONCEPT OF "FREE MONEY DAYS"

You can actually get *free* use of the bank's money for up to fifty-five days with *bank* credit cards. Here's how it's done:

With these credit cards (VISA and Master-Card), as well as with department-store and oil-company cards, you have a certain number of days to pay for the goods and services you've charged—*without additional interest costs.* During that time, all you owe is the x dollars you charged, not x dollars plus 18 percent or more interest. In essence, this is "free money time," because the credit-card company has already paid the merchant for what you charged. You're getting free use of the card company's money and will be charged interest only if you don't pay the amount due by the designated date.

Now let's see how long you can stretch out that free money time. Every credit card has its own "monthly billing date," which is clearly printed on your statement. This is, very simply, the date each month on which you get billed. With bank cards you are allowed twenty-five days _after_ this billing date to pay the amount due before interest is levied. Thus, you automatically have twenty-five free money days.

Now here's where you can utilize your first credit-card strategy: charge your purchases _on_ your billing date. You won't be billed for those items until the _next_ billing date, which is another thirty days away, giving you an extra month of free money time. Once you add to that the initial twenty-five days of free money time, you have a total of fifty-five free money days.

Note: You can request a specific billing date from the card issuer—on the first of every month, for instance, rather than the twentieth, which might have been arbitrarily assigned you.

Keep in mind that different rules apply for T & E cards. With these cards, payment is due on receipt of the bill, so you don't get an initial twenty-five free money days. But if you make your purchases on the billing date, you'll still get thirty free money days before you receive the bill.

INSTANT CASH WITH YOUR PLASTIC

In Chapter 2, I mentioned that T & E cards can be used to obtain short-term loans. Your bank credit cards can play a similar role, although the terms are not quite so attractive. With a bank credit card, you can automatically qualify for a cash advance just by going to the issuing bank and filling out the required papers. You can usually borrow up to the amount of the unused credit that the bank has assigned to your account, based on your credit history. Thus, if your VISA card has a $1,000 credit limit, and you have already charged $200 to the account, you can still receive an $800 cash advance.

With these types of credit-card loans, you are instantly charged "loan fees" that are often 2 percent of the loan amount. Also, interest charges begin to accumulate immediately at the normal credit-card rate of 18 percent or more per year.

Overdraft checking tied to your bank credit cards provides loans similar to those of cash advances, but usually with less expensive loan charges than direct credit-card loans. With overdraft checking, if you write checks for more than the amount in your checking account, your credit card automatically "loans" your checking account the funds to cover the checks, in multiples of $50 or $100. You will be charged a loan fee of about 1½ to 2 percent on the amount transferred into your checking account, plus the standard interest that is immediately charged.

PAYING YOUR CREDIT-CARD CHARGES

When your bank credit-card bill arrives—no matter how many free money days you've managed to get—I strongly suggest that you pay it in full on the due date. If you don't, you'll begin paying interest on the unpaid balance, starting the next day, at an annual rate of at least 18 percent.

If you're like many people, you become irritated when you make a purchase and find yourself paying an additional few cents—or dollars—in sales tax. Well, on a typical $10 purchase, the credit issuer may charge you another $1.80 for interest—if you don't pay your bill on the due date. You *have* to pay the tax, but you *don't* have to pay the interest, if you pay on time.

Incidentally, interest is not ordinarily charged on T & E card purchases, but don't try to get away with late payments consistently. Chances are your card will be canceled. Some T & E cards do accept installment payments for ship and air travel and certain kinds of merchandise. My advice is not to rely on these installment payment plans; you could end up paying exorbitant amounts of interest. Instead, pay up on your due date.

As with most rules, however, there *is* one exception to this pay-off-your-credit-card-bill guideline. It may actually be advantageous in certain circumstances to pay bills in installments. Say you're in the market for a home computer, and you see one you like: "Regular Price: $2,000. Marked Down—Special Today Only: $1,300."

But what if you don't have $1,300 to spare, and you won't be able to save that amount for three months? In a case like this, it makes sense to use your bank credit card to buy the computer. Even in the worst possible billing situation, you will still come out ahead. Let's assume that your billing date is the day after your purchase. That gives you twenty-five free money days until the due date if you're using a bank card. If you take two months to pay off the purchase, you will have paid perhaps only about $40 interest on the $1,300 bill. So, with the use of your credit card, the cost of the computer will come to $1,340 ($1,300 plus $40) instead of $2,000—and you never could have saved that $640 *without* a credit card.

One added note about T & E cards: although they do charge an annual membership fee (approximately $30 per year), they still may have a particular advantage for people who travel extensively and, in the process, run up large monthly bills for airlines or hotels. If you're not in town to pay your T & E bill on time, you *won't* be levied an interest fee on the unpaid balance as you would on a bank card. So for the frequent traveler, a T & E card can be a good investment.

CREDIT CARDS AND INSTALLMENT CONTRACTS

There are other ways to use your credit cards that you may never have considered. For instance, since you can borrow money with your credit card (via a cash advance), it often makes sense to use borrowed funds to pay off other loans, particularly retail installment contracts. These contracts—also known as time-purchase agreements or conditional-sales contracts—were the most popular means of buying merchandise on time until 1965, when bank credit cards went "on the air" (that's bankers' slang for "distribute them by mail whether consumers want them or not"—a practice now forbidden by law). Some major stores and many smaller ones still offer the installment contract, however.

On an installment contract, you pay an average of 6 percentage points more interest than you would on a credit-card cash advance. I suggest that you take out the credit-card loan, pay off the installment contract, and keep the excess 6 percent in your savings account. There is an additional factor to keep in mind, however: almost all installment contracts are repaid by the rule of 78, which was described in Chapter 4. Unless these types of loans are paid off early, it's probably not worthwhile to pay them off until the due date.

In the future, if you have a choice of purchasing an item with your credit card or with an installment contract, opt for your credit card. Not only will you save money on interest charges, but you will gain these other advantages:

• *You will save more should you repay your credit-card loan early.* Interest on credit cards is calculated as a percentage of the unpaid balance, rather than by the rule of 78.

• *Your credit-card purchase cannot be repossessed even if you never pay a cent for it.* What you buy becomes yours the moment the transaction is completed. By contrast, what you buy on an installment contract remains the property of the seller until the last cent is paid. Should you default on the latter, the seller can repossess the property, even though you may have paid all the installments except the last.

TRAVELING WITH A CREDIT CARD

Whenever and wherever you travel, your credit cards should be as essential as your luggage and airline tickets. Some people insist that as long as they have traveler's checks, no credit cards (or even cash) are necessary; however, I recommend credit cards for several reasons.

Traveler's checks *usually* cost from 1 to 2 percent of their value (though certain brands of traveler's checks are available free of charge—be sure to ask about them). There's never an extra charge for using credit cards when you travel.

When you pay for something with traveler's checks, whether you're traveling domestically or abroad, it's really tantamount to paying with cash. When you pay with a credit card, your cash goes right on earning interest in your deposit funds until you make your credit-card payment.

When you cash traveler's checks in a foreign country, you seldom get the best exchange rate. That isn't a problem when you make purchases with your credit cards.

For these reasons, it's actually cheaper to travel with credit cards than with traveler's checks. (As a practical matter, however, you do need a small sum in traveler's checks to cover purchases that cannot be made with a credit card.)

But what about security? It's true that traveler's checks are safer than credit cards, but they are only marginally more secure. In case of loss, traveler's checks are 100 percent replaceable. With credit cards, you have *no* liability on a lost card if you notify the card issuer prior to the time any illegal charges are made with your card. That is, you are not responsible for any charges made with that card after you've reported its loss. Even if you notify the issuer *after* some charges have been made, you are responsible only for a maximum of $50 per card.

If you're a frequent traveler, I think it's wise to pay a small yearly sum to register your cards with an organization like the Credit Card Service Bureau. If your cards are lost or stolen, you can make one toll-free call to the bureau anytime, day or night, and the bureau will promptly notify each card issuer. That ends your liability for any purchases subsequently charged to your account, and a new set of cards will be issued rapidly (often in twenty-four hours).

What's more, if you're stranded anywhere in the world because you've lost your credit cards and your wallet, a call to the bureau's toll-free number, (800) 336-0220, will get you an airplane ticket home (it will be waiting for you at the airport) and $100 in cash (it will be wired to you). The cash and the cost of the airline ticket need not be repaid for thirty days, and no interest is charged.

OTHER USES FOR CREDIT CARDS

Sometimes it seems that the uses of your credit cards are limited only by your imagination. How many of the following have you considered?

• *Order by mail with credit cards without sending a check or money order.* A money order costs money, and a check usually does, as well, when the balance in your account falls below a certain limit. (Banks typically levy a monthly fee for maintaining your account. Divide that fee by the number of checks you write, and you get the cost per check. It can be surprisingly high.)

Many mail-order products can be ordered by phone with a credit card, which costs you nothing since the number is toll-free. Ordering by mail costs you next to nothing (the price of an envelope and a stamp), and only your credit-card number and your signature are required. In the meantime, your money remains in the bank, continuing to earn interest for up to fifty-five days.

• *Get discounts with your credit cards.* Credit-card companies themselves offer certain goods and services to their customers at special prices. The offers usually come in the same envelope as your monthly bill. One of the biggest bargains is VISA's group

life insurance. For details, write National Benefit Life
Insurance Company, National Security Trust Administrator, P.O. Box 1227, Providence, RI 02701.

• *Receive free services.* American Express
offers free traveler's insurance (under certain conditions) and free check-cashing privileges. Investigate
your T & E, bank, and other cards (oil company, air-
lines) and ask for a list of giveaways.

• *Use your credit cards to get some of the tax
deductions to which you are entitled.* Have you ever
stopped to think about how much excess tax you're paying just because you don't keep records of tax-deductible
expenses? "But it's such a nuisance," so many people
say. Not when you make purchases with credit cards.
You get a receipt at the time of purchase and a monthly
statement from the card issuer. Save them for tax purposes.

• *Get discounts when you offer to pay cash instead of using a credit card.* Did you know that when
you pay for retail-store purchases with a credit card, the
store pays 8 to 14 percent of your bill to the credit-card
issuer? Knowing this, thousands of consumers have
begun offering to pay cash, which saves the store this 8
to 14 percent. In return, the shop owner gives the buyer
a reduction in the selling price, usually equal to about
half of what the store would have paid to the credit-card
company. Many store managers are already agreeing to
this arrangement.

Credit cards, despite their costs, then, can be
far more than just a convenience. They can provide you
with significant financial savings and benefits if you use
them wisely. They can become an important ally in
achieving overall monetary well-being.

But as helpful as credit cards may be, they are

not a financial panacea. Some people, in fact, become so heavily indebted, not only through using credit cards but also through personal loans and unexpected expenses, that they need to be rescued fiscally, often by a debt-consolidation loan. The following chapter will equip you with the information you'll require to identify your need for one of these loans, as well as guidance on how to obtain one.

CHAPTER 6

DEBT-CONSOLIDATION LOANS TO PAY ALL OF YOUR CREDITORS AT ONCE

Perhaps you know the feeling of being so harassed by creditors that you're afraid even to open your mailbox or answer your phone. A fast-growing number of Americans find themselves overwhelmed by a burdensome stack of debts that at times seems insurmountable.

Some debt-ridden people have gotten into fiscal difficulties because of unexpected medical bills. Others have lost their jobs and consequently have fallen behind on monthly payments. Still others have slipped into financial trouble because of overuse of their credit cards or in the aftermath of a divorce.

Although anyone in any age group can get stuck in the debt quagmire, it is most commonly those in the twenty-seven- to thirty-five-year-old group—those who are starting families and buying and furnishing homes—who fall into the insolvency trap.

CONFRONTING YOUR DILEMMA

When faced with staggering indebtedness, some people simply bury their heads in the sand. For too many, it's much easier to pretend the problem doesn't exist than to confront it stoically.

Most of these individuals have simply refused to recognize that, as painful and hopeless as their situation may seem, there *is* a way to escape it. Michael Todd, the former movie producer, once proclaimed, "Poor is a state of mind; broke is a temporary condition." Unfortunately, too many people believe that "broke" is their permanent lot in life and take no positive steps to improve the situation.

Not long ago I interviewed a married couple on "Hour Magazine." The husband, a machinist, had lost his job, and the chain of events that followed had devastated him. He had become angry at the world, had lost all sense of self-worth, and had even become sexually impotent—all because of the pressures of unemployment and mounting bills. He felt helpless and hopeless, convinced that there was no way out.

He was wrong. There *are* solutions to indebtedness, no matter how severe your circumstances may be. You simply have to take responsibility for initiating some positive action that can make the situation more livable and eventually pull you out of the cycle of debt completely.

When the stack of bills becomes too immense, you might start thinking about a debt-consolidation loan—a large loan from a single source that will allow you to pay back all your existing creditors at once, leaving you with just one big loan to pay off. This is in fact one of the most common reasons people take out personal loans these days. Typically, this sort of loan *lowers* your overall monthly payments, because the payments on the new loan are usually spread out over a longer period of time.

As useful as debt-consolidation loans have proved for many thousands of people, they are certainly not a magical cure-all, particularly if you soon find yourself unable to meet the new monthly payments. A debt-consolidation loan doesn't relieve you of your financial obligations, but rather transfers them to a new format. No wonder a business associate recently lamented to me, "Paula, what the world needs are debt-consolidation loans for debt-consolidation loans!"

In the following pages you will learn how to make debt-consolidation loans work for you, how to avoid the pitfalls that can accompany them, and the best way to create a solid money plan to keep you from falling back into severe debt for a second or third time. You will also learn about the nationwide network of non-profit services that can provide you with help for your money problems, and the bankruptcy laws that you can use to your advantage.

EXPLORING YOUR OPTIONS

First, contact your creditors. Force yourself to overcome any fear you may have of doing so, then honestly let them know the problem you're facing and try to work out a payment schedule. Most often, they will be willing to arrange a realistic payment plan; they may even accept amounts as low as $5 to $10 per month until your bill is fully paid.

If a reasonable program can't be agreed upon, a debt-consolidation loan is worth exploring. These are obtained primarily from banks, credit unions, finance companies, and savings-and-loan associations.

Lenders, however, rarely label these transactions debt-consolidation loans, even though your intent may indeed be to use the money to pay your existing bills. Instead, these loans carry the names discussed in Chapters 1 and 2: signature loans, personal loans, collateral loans, and so on. Refer back to the opening chapters for a detailed explanation of how to obtain them.

Another popular path to debt-consolidation funds is to take out a second mortgage on the equity in your house. You have probably seen the ads for firms like the Money Store and Aames Home Loan that promise "quick, easy, big cash." It sounds fine, but keep in mind that such loans are backed and guaranteed by your most important asset, your own home. You will also have to pay relatively high interest rates.

Until a few years ago, serious money investors and institutions stayed out of the second-mortgage market. Now, however, major banks from coast to coast have found it a lucrative field, and their rates are better than those of finance companies.

So if you choose a second mortgage (or second trust deed, as it is often called) as a source of debt-consolidation funds, don't automatically run to the finance company that recently advertised on your local television station. Compare rates from finance companies and major banks. Look back at Chapter 3 for additional information on equity borrowing.

DEBT-CONSOLIDATION MONEY: IMPORTANT POINTS TO KEEP IN MIND

Many of the rules that apply to signature and other types of loans are also relevant to debt consolidation. But there is some specific information that you should take into account when you intend to use the money you borrow to pay off your bills. Keep the following points in mind.

HOW PAINLESS ARE THEY?

Debt-consolidation loans are a deceptively simple solution to your money problems. The lump sum you borrow from a bank, credit union, or other loan source *will* allow you to satisfy all your current creditors at once. But your new loan, to be paid off over a much longer time period than any of your individual smaller debts, will end up costing you much more in interest charges. Even so, many people choose debt-consolidation loans, because they do offer some obvious advantages: you get instant cash; you keep your creditors off your back; and you gain a sense of financial control.

Since it may seem relatively easy to pay off this

stretched-out loan, it can then be tempting to make new purchases you cannot truly afford. This will of course sink you right back into the morass of debt. So proceed with caution once you obtain a loan.

IF YOUR CREDIT RATING IS POOR

If you find yourself saddled with heavy debts, your credit rating probably isn't too healthy. This might make it pretty difficult for you to obtain a debt-consolidation loan. After all, credit ratings are an important evaluation tool when loans are being granted. If yours has an excessive amount of negative information in it, the bank loan officer might be hesitant to approve your loan application.

Before you become overly concerned, however, I suggest that you obtain a copy of your credit report, using the procedure described in Chapter 1. When you examine it closely, you might be pleasantly surprised by what you see. Not all creditors report to credit-reporting agencies, so your credit rating may, in fact, be better than you suspect.

Even if the credit report looks discouraging, apply for the loan anyway through normal channels. Explain to the loan officer, as favorably as you can, the reasons you've been having financial problems. Then try to persuade him or her that you'll be able to meet your new obligations if this loan is granted. If, despite your recent financial difficulties, you can successfully demonstrate that you will be able to repay the loan, your chances of obtaining it will be significantly improved. Having a co-signer who is willing to assume responsibility for your loan should you default will also enhance your standing.

But if banks, credit unions, and savings-and-loan associations turn you down, investigate some of the other sources of loan money as well—an employer, family or friends, or an insurance company. When you turn to these sources, your credit report is not considered and thus will not weigh against you.

THE TERM OF YOUR LOAN

No matter where you obtain your debt-consolidation loan, apply for the shortest possible term that you realistically think you can handle. Meeting the larger monthly payments of a short-term loan will help you stay in control of your urge to spend and charge. Also, the shorter the loan, the less it will cost you overall.

ONCE YOU'VE OBTAINED THE LOAN

After you've received approval for your debt-consolidation loan, use that money wisely—and avoid saddling yourself with the same financial problems over and over again. Follow these guidelines:

1. Before you actually receive your debt-consolidation loan, make out a personal budget. Clearly account for all your income and all your expenses. This should help you manage, understand, and improve your money behavior.

2. The day the loan money comes through, pay off the most urgent and highest-interest bills first. Then pay off the rest as soon as possible.

3. Take the credit cards out of your wallet, wrap a rubber band around them, and put them in a dresser drawer—out of sight, out of use. When you switch to using cash exclusively, you will gain a more realistic sense of what you are spending.

4. For at least a few weeks, play penny pincher. Forget about any moneymaking schemes you may hear about, and don't spend any unnecessary cash.

5. Consider moonlighting or working overtime until you can pay off your debt-consolidation loan.

6. If possible, begin a payroll-deduction plan. Under this system, a portion of your paycheck—as little as $10—is channeled directly into your credit union or bank savings account. Learn to contribute to your own savings program first, even before your paycheck is handed to you. What you don't see you won't miss.

7. Although you should never take your financial problems lightly, don't let yourself be overwhelmed or depressed by the seriousness of your circumstances, either.

One noted financial strategist recently explained how he once made a game of getting out of debt. He sold all possessions he knew he could repurchase in the future. He trimmed his life-style and challenged himself to reduce his debts a little each day. Such a game concept can effectively help you to counteract any feelings of remorse, shame, and guilt over being in debt. Try to view your situation as an opportunity to improve your life, rather than as an insurmountable obstacle. Think of your debt-consolidation loan as a first step toward keeping your finances under control and learning to make your money work *for* you.

CONSUMER CREDIT COUNSELING

Marie Elber, a twenty-seven-year-old saleswoman, discovered the "magic" of credit cards at the age of twenty-three. She applied for a local boutique credit card and in quick succession also acquired a gas-company card, a VISA card, and four other cards.

Unfortunately, Marie's ability to obtain credit was greater than her income-producing ability. She fell deeper and deeper into debt. Finally, one afternoon, Marie went to a local pet shop to buy a puppy. When she was ready to pay for it, the store clerk asked, "Cash or charge?" As usual, Marie instinctively went for her VISA card. But this time she stopped. "It was my moment of truth," Marie told me later. "I was $4,000 in debt, and somehow buying a pet with a credit card suddenly seemed absurd. It made me realize how drastic my problem was."

A friend referred Marie to Consumer Credit Counselors, a nonprofit organization that helped her outline a money-management and repayment plan. Within two years, Marie had completely cleaned her credit slate.

If you consistently find yourself in debt, you are a prime candidate for this type of financial counseling. Most cities have nonprofit credit-counseling agencies that offer guidance on how to get out and stay out of debt. A counselor studies your family's life-style, determines how much of your income is needed for day-to-day living, and shows you how the remainder can be used to pay outstanding bills. The service is free in most states, and only a nominal fee is levied in others. To locate the credit-counseling agency nearest you, write to the National Foundation for Consumer Credit, Inc., 1819 H Street, N.W., Washington, DC 20006.

BANKRUPTCY—WHAT ARE YOUR OPTIONS?

At a meeting recently, I ran into Charlene Robbins, a friend of mine who has her own public-relations agency. She had been in a severe automobile accident and had finally recovered fully after weeks of hospitalization and physical therapy. But in the process, she had run up $40,000 in medical bills for which her insurance company refused to reimburse her.

Feeling hopeless in the face of her staggering

debts, Charlene asked me, "What about bankruptcy? Do you think I should consider it?"

I told Charlene that another, less harsh alternative was available—Chapter 13—and that she should consider it.

CHAPTER 13

Chapter 13 is part of the bankruptcy law, but it is *not* bankruptcy.

Under Chapter 13, you notify the U.S. Bankruptcy Court of your income and your debts. With their guidance, you create a monthly schedule to pay off your creditors gradually, over no more than three years' time. The court will even arrange with your creditors to reduce some of your debts—say, holding you liable for only 50 cents on the dollar. This is a relatively routine procedure, and rarely is there a need to hire a lawyer to ensure that your interests are protected.

Once the court and your creditors agree to the plan, the court protects you in the following ways:

- All legal action against you is stopped, and future legal action related to those debts already incurred is prohibited.
- Your creditors are forbidden to contact your employer.
- Wage assignments and wage deductions cannot be made against you; if they have been made, they are terminated.
- A restraining order issued by the court prevents your creditors from dunning you, harassing you, or contacting you in any way.
- Late charges, service charges, and sometimes interest charges are discontinued.
- A great many of your assets cannot be touched in fulfillment of your debts.

To obtain the forms you need to file for Chapter 13, call the clerk of the nearest U.S. Bankruptcy Court. (Check the white pages of your telephone book under "U.S. Federal Government—Courts.") The clerk will direct you to a nearby legal stationer (the court itself does not supply the forms). Buy the forms and fill them out.

The only other costs of a Chapter 13 are a filing fee of $60, plus a fee to a court-appointed trustee of 10 percent of your monthly payments. The $60 is amortized over the period of repayment; for example, over three years the payments would be $1.67 a month. The 10 percent on, say, a $400-per-month payment would amount to $40 a month.

As part of Chapter 13, the court appoints a trustee to your person—an official who will administer your debts. You send the trustee a bulk payment each month, which he or she disburses to your creditors. Your creditors will be invited to attend your first meeting with the trustee—at least that's the theory; in practice, creditors almost never show up.

After this initial meeting, your petition is usually processed routinely and granted within three months. In some courts you may be asked to be present when the petition is granted, but most often the good news comes by mail.

After you've completed payments—usually at the end of three years—you may be asked to return to the court to be discharged from Chapter 13. After that, you have no further obligations to your creditors, even if you have paid them only one cent on the dollar.

Even though this kind of arrangement was once called the "wage earner's plan," you don't have to be a wage earner to apply—the unemployed can also qualify. Under Chapter 13, your bills will ultimately be paid off, without your ever having formally declared bankruptcy.

True, your credit history will indicate the filing under Chapter 13, but that is a much less damaging entry than bankruptcy.

BANKRUPTCY

Should your debts become completely unmanageable, you can wipe them out by declaring bankruptcy. At the same time you (and your spouse) can take advantage of "exemptions" to retain your home and various other possessions. That's the law as Congress enacted it in the Bankruptcy Reform Act of 1978, which became effective on October 1, 1979.

I don't advocate bankruptcy; I think it's a last-resort action only. But if you can find no other way to extricate yourself from your financial woes, it's your legal right to utilize it.

According to one study, debts in the average bankruptcy total 9 percent more than the person's gross annual income. So if you make $20,000 per year, you would be a typical bankrupt if you have $21,800 in debts.

Depending on the state you live in, you're entitled to retain certain possessions after declaring bankruptcy. In most states these exemptions include a share of your earnings from the thirty to sixty days preceding bankruptcy, a portion of the equity in your home, all your clothes, some furniture, part of your personal savings, life insurance (if your spouse or a dependent relative is the beneficiary), and some of the tools of your trade.

The clerk of the nearest Bankruptcy Court can tell you where to obtain bankruptcy forms. Fill them out, listing all your debts and assets (even the money in your wallet). Then file them with the clerk. The filing fee is $60.

Caution: When you fill out the forms, be certain that you list *all* your debts. Debts not listed will not be discharged. On the other hand, it won't do you any good to list alimony and child support; when your petition is granted, you'll still have to pay these, as well as house and car debts and federal and state taxes.

With the filing of the petition, you're protected from your creditors, just as you are with Chapter 13. The court will set up a meeting for sometime between twenty and forty-five days after you file your petition. You as well as your creditors and your trustee will be asked to attend. As with Chapter 13, your trustee is a court-appointed official who will administer your bankruptcy. The meeting is usually a formality; the creditors are aware that they can do nothing about your petition and seldom appear.

Your nonexempt property is sold by the trustee, usually at auction. The proceeds are added to your nonexempt cash, which has already been seized. The total is then distributed proportionally to your creditors. The sale and distribution of funds takes place within weeks after your meeting with your trustee.

Within ninety days of filing your petition, the court will discharge all your debts. You may be requested to attend court to receive your discharge. More likely, you will receive your notice of discharge in the mail. Bankruptcy is discreet, swift, and efficient.

You *can* file a petition for bankruptcy without a lawyer. For complete details on the filing process and fees, contact your local Legal Aid office, a bankruptcy attorney, or the Bankruptcy Court in your area. From any of them you can obtain the necessary information on forms and filing fees. A competent bankruptcy lawyer will typically charge you about $500 and can handle all the procedures for you. I believe it's worth the fee.

Keep in mind that a record of your bankruptcy

will remain on your credit history for ten years. Consequently, reestablishing a good credit rating after bankruptcy is not easy; many banks and stores simply refuse bankrupts who apply for loans or credit.

A good way to start reestablishing your credit rating, if you have any money at all in a savings account, is to apply for a passbook loan. This is an easy loan to obtain; your savings account is held as collateral until the loan is paid back. Repay the loan quickly, and you will have an important positive entry on your credit history to begin offsetting the record of bankruptcy.

If you're mired in debts, you may find yourself choosing one of the options discussed in this chapter: debt-consolidation loans, Chapter 13, or bankruptcy. Julius Caesar once advised his staff, "Before every battle, the wise general plans his retreat." In a sense, any of these three options is your chance to retreat—and retrench. They also give you the opportunity to come back and fight again. Make it a victorious return.

CHAPTER 7

NEW ALTERNATIVES
FOR FINANCING
THE CAR YOU BUY
OR LEASE

In a computer store recently, I overheard a customer muttering, "I'm trying to decide between buying a computer and buying a new car." The salesperson responded, "Buy the computer; it's cheaper."

As the current Detroit sales figures indicate, the cost of buying and maintaining a car has tarnished the attractive image of the American Dream Machine. As of 1981, the average cost of a new car was $9,800, and the typical down payment was $2,000. The down payment plus the monthly payments, of course, are only the tip of the iceberg in a series of costs that include insurance, registration, gasoline, maintenance, parking, and depreciation. The total annual cost of owning and operating a car now averages 44.57 cents for every mile you drive.

Those facts have forced many people to look into alternative methods of car financing and to reevaluate the basic concept of transportation and how to buy it.

Buying is still the traditional means of obtaining an automobile, but a growing number of Americans are turning to leasing instead. Part of this chapter is devoted to this increasingly popular alternative to buying. I'll also provide you with an evaluation of the relative merits of buying and leasing and a comparison of the monthly out-of-pocket costs of the two. You'll also learn about the ways to finance a car, as well as the contract options available to you when you lease one.

BUYING A CAR

Let's assume that you've found the perfect car, and you can hardly wait to park it in your driveway. You've always purchased your cars in the past and would like to buy this one, too. But you may be worried about financing this time, particularly if the car is higher-priced than any you've bought before.

First, keep in mind that the best way to buy a car is with cash. Few of us can afford to, of course. Most Americans continue to buy their cars on time—fixed monthly payments, usually extending from thirty-six to forty-eight months on a new car and from twenty-four to forty-eight months on a used one.

The car becomes collateral for the loan, and under the terms of the typical installment contract it remains the property of the lender (or of whomever the lender assigns it to) until the loan is paid in full. Even when you owe just one last dollar on your loan, the car does not belong to you. Should you default on payments, the lender can repossess your car and sell it to pay off the loan.

But you don't have to finance your car with a traditional car loan. There are other options, including an insurance loan or a deposit-account loan. In these cases, your car is _not_ used as collateral. Instead, you receive the loan money, you hand over the cash to a car dealer, and the car is yours. It can never be repossessed.

Most sources of car loans also lend money for many other reasons as well and have already been mentioned in Chapters 2 and 3. Those sources often find car loans particularly appealing, because they are short-term, high-interest loans and are usually backed by an asset: your car.

Here are the seven most common sources for loans that may be available to you for financing your car, listed in the general order of preference in two categories: collateral loans and noncollateral loans.

COLLATERALIZED CAR LOANS

When a loan is collateralized by an automobile, the car becomes security that is pledged for the repayment of the loan. You do not legally own the car until the final loan payment is made. In the event of default, the lender can repossess your car.

CREDIT UNIONS

Interest rates are usually the lowest at credit unions and are calculated in a way that results in the least cost to the borrower. Credit unions tend to make many car loans, and loan requests from members are seldom rejected.

BANKS

Rates are higher than at credit unions (by about 1 to 3 percentage points). Interest is usually calculated by the so-called added-on method (see Chapter 4 for an explanation of interest-calculation methods). Frequently, holders of bank car loans find that when they're ready to trade in their car, a substantial portion of their principal is still unpaid.

DEALERS

Most car dealers provide some type of financing, either through their parent companies (such as GMAC, Chrysler Credit, Ford Motor Credit) or through a local financing outlet. In such cases you negotiate the terms of the loan directly with the dealer, including interest rate and repayment conditions. You will probably pay a higher interest rate here than you would on a loan obtained from a bank. Once the arrangements are finalized, the dealer may sell your contract to a finance company or a bank, to whom you then make your payments. In essence, the dealer acts as a go-between, making arrangements for you to borrow money from a third party.

FINANCE COMPANIES

Most people view finance companies as last-resort lenders because of the unattractive rates they typically offer. But they can provide a valid alternative if all other sources have turned you down. You can deal directly with finance companies, but their rates are often two to three times as high as a bank's.

NONCOLLATERAL LOANS

DEPOSIT-ACCOUNT LOANS FROM BANKS

These are not direct car loans; instead, the bank lends you an amount of money up to the balance of your account. Your savings must remain on deposit while you repay the loan, but they still earn interest during that time. Interest rates for these loans are very good, usually just 2 percentage points higher than what your money earns in the savings account.

INSURANCE COMPANIES

If you have a life-insurance policy called "whole life," you can borrow money from its "cash value" at rates that are about half the commercial car-loan rate. The insurance company will bill you for the interest, but you can repay the principal at your own speed. If you should die before the loan has been repaid, however, the amount you still owe is deducted from the face value of the policy before the company pays your beneficiary.

SIGNATURE LOANS FROM BANKS

Like deposit-account loans, these are not direct car loans but rather unsecured loans with which you can purchase a car. The interest rates for these loans are often higher than the rates the same banks charge for new car loans.

GETTING THE FACTS

Louis Cheresh, a physical therapist, knows more about cars than most people and can pick the best car off a dealer's lot just by listening to its engine hum. But he admits that until recently, he probably allowed himself to be ripped off many times, simply because he never asked the right questions about car financing.

"I always bought the best car for me, but probably didn't get the best financing, simply because I didn't know anything about it," Louis told me.

Today, Louis realizes that it's just as important to shop around for car financing as to shop for the car itself. Now that you've been introduced to the *sources* of automobile financing, spend some time acquiring the information you'll need to find the most advantageous financing terms available.

Although credit unions generally offer the best rates for traditional car loans—banks, car dealers, and finance companies are next in line—it's still wise to shop around. Here are the facts you need to gather in order to evaluate your options:

• *The total finance cost.* This means exactly what it says—not in percentages but in dollars. I prefer this standard of cost comparison to the APR. It tells you *exactly* what you're going to pay to finance your car, and *that's* the bottom line. Choose the loan with the lowest total finance cost.

• *Annual percentage rate (APR).* This is the cost of the loan expressed as a yearly percentage of the amount still unpaid and is a useful statistic to have at your fingertips when comparing loans of the same amount and duration. If you are comparing loans with the same repayment period, the loan with the lower APR is your best bet.

• *The repayment period.* The shorter the period, the lower the finance cost. With a shorter repayment period, however, the monthly payment is larger. Examine your budget and decide.

• *The down payment.* Be careful here. The dealer is likely to quote a percentage figure. You may think it's a percentage of the price of the car, but it may be a percentage of the price of the car plus sales tax and license and registration fees. Ask so that you know the exact dollar amount.

Watch out for car dealers who offer you a "no-down-payment" loan. Ordinarily, this means that the down payment is financed under a separate agreement, or the down payment is added to the cost of the car. In both cases you not only *do* pay a down payment, but you also pay interest on it.

• *The monthly due date.* Request a payment date that puts the least strain on your budget. You probably don't want to pay all or most of your bills around the same time of the month.

• *Penalties for late payments or prepayments.* Find out now whether you will have to pay an additional fee if any of your monthly payments are late, or if you decide to pay off the loan ahead of schedule. Many auto-loan contracts specifically include a penalty fee for both circumstances. Shop around for a loan *without* a prepayment penalty and with as low a late fee as you can find.

• *Insurance requirements.* Some loan sources demand that you take out credit life and disability insurance, which would pay off your loan if you were to die or become disabled during the course of the loan. The insurance offered by the finance source may be more expensive than what you can get elsewhere, so shop for it. *Warning:* If you do buy insurance from your finance source, it will probably be added to your monthly payments, and you'll pay interest on it.

CAR BROKERS

So-called car brokers are independent business people who have licenses to buy and sell automobiles but do not have their own car lots or showrooms. Instead, they have contacts through whom they obtain cars (often dealerships in the community), which they in turn sell to you.

Some automobile buyers purchase their vehicles from these brokers, reasoning that the middlemen can spare them all car-financing hassles. But that's not always how it works out.

True, the broker can provide a car for you, with all the options you desire, for an average of about $125 above dealer's cost (the fees vary from broker to broker). Many brokers are listed in the Yellow Pages; others sell through ads in car magazines, and through credit unions and such organizations as PTAs, alumni associations, and veterans' groups. You order from a computer print-out and do not have an opportunity to test-drive or even see the car before it's delivered. The broker usually arranges for you to pick up the car through a dealer in your neighborhood, where you can also have it serviced.

The right broker can put you in the right car at the right price and protect you with the right kind of warranty. But with the wrong broker, you can go very wrong.

Gina Pascal, an interior decorator, has bought her cars through brokers for more than two decades, initially because it was such a carefree route to take. She simply told the broker what she wanted, and about ten days later she picked up her car.

But Gina never analyzed the credit terms that the broker routinely offered her—at least not until her banker suggested that she could probably obtain a better deal through the bank. That's when she began comparing numbers and found that through the broker's financing, she was paying an interest rate that was 10 percent higher than what her bank could offer her.

"I still buy my cars through a broker," says Gina, "but now *I* arrange for the financing. I've probably saved thousands of dollars over the years by having the bank, not the broker, do the financing for me."

Some brokers *require* you to finance the car with them at very profitable rates and insist that you purchase equally profitable life, accident, and health insurance. They also may demand that you buy an even more profitable extended warranty. The "bargain," in these cases, is really a very poor deal.

Before you decide on a broker, check with your credit union or other finance source, and talk to people who have bought cars from the broker you're considering. Yes, that broker may be able to handle your financing, but sometimes the price is too high.

CAR LEASING: IS IT FOR YOU?

There was a time when leasing a car was considered advantageous only for doctors, lawyers, or other professionals—or for corporations—for whom the leasing cost could be used as a tax deduction. But those days are over. More and more Americans are now leasing cars. Already in California, 40 percent (as of 1981) of all new cars are leased, not purchased. General Motors estimates that by 1984, 50 percent of the cars in the country will be leased.

Why the growing interest in leasing? Some people lease for convenience. With leasing, you can take care of many things at once—from license plates to insurance—right in the leasing agreement. You can also add a maintenance contract to the lease, which covers most repairs, ranging from oil changes to complete overhauls.

Leasing also requires little or no down payment. As the prices of cars continue to soar, leasing will become an increasingly attractive alternative to buying for this reason alone.

In essence, when you lease a car, you are entitled only to its *use.* You do not own it. The ownership of the vehicle remains with the dealer or leasing company with whom you've made the agreement. You may also have a mileage-per-year limit imposed upon you, or the requirement that you service the car only at a particular garage.

Whatever the limitations, some people find them quite acceptable. Although the initial cash requirements are nonexistent or minimal, however, credit guidelines are strict. In fact, you need a stronger credit history to lease than you need to obtain a car loan. If your credit rating is excellent, you can expect to lease with no down payment. If it is good but not superb, you'll probably be asked for a small down payment, usually equivalent to two of your monthly payments.

If your credit rating is just fair, you'll have to put up a more substantial down payment. The leasing company calls this a "capitalized cost reduction." Capitalized cost is the amount the leasing company paid for the car (including options) plus expenses and profits. Your down payment reduces capitalized (sometimes referred to as "cap") costs and lowers your monthly payments. Some leasing companies waive a down payment but tack the capitalized cost reduction onto your monthly payments. In that case you'll be paying the down payment *with interest,* which is hardly a good deal.

CHOOSING YOUR LEASED CAR

You can order your leased car from a car dealer who handles leases, or from specialized leasing companies that may also lease computers, machinery, and other products. The dealer or leasing company buys the car you want and then leases it to you.

Although it is possible to obtain a mechanically defective car through leasing, the chances are less than when you buy a car. This is because the leasing company will have to sell the car in a few years, after you have used it, so the firm will give your car a tough inspection before buying it. Should your car develop severe mechanical problems, the leasing company will usually replace it.

If you have a maintenance clause in your contract, the leasing company will agree to service the car and handle all malfunctions, major and minor. It's to the leasing company's advantage to keep the car in A-1 condition; remember, it will be up for sale in a few years. With this maintenance contract, your only costs (aside from your regular payments) are gasoline and insurance.

THE LEASING CONTRACT

As with any other legal contract, be sure you (and your attorney) read the leasing agreement carefully before signing it. Make certain that you understand all its clauses, and ask questions if anything seems unclear.

Most leases last from one to three years and can be negotiated as either closed-end or open-end. Here's the difference between the two:

In a *closed-end* agreement, you lease the car for a specified time—say, two years. Once that period expires, you agree to return the car to the leasing agency. At that time your obligation ends.

With an *open-end* lease, the leasing company gives you an assessment at the time the lease is signed of what the car will sell for at the end of the lease period. This estimated amount is called the "bring-back value." When you return the car at the end of the lease, the lessor will attempt to sell it on the wholesale market. If the car brings less than the dealer originally estimated, you (the lessee) are responsible for paying the difference; if the car brings more, however, you are entitled to a refund.

As a general rule, an open-end lease costs a few dollars less per month, but because of its higher risk, it is considered a lease for gamblers. Even so, it is the most prevalent type of leasing arrangement.

Leasing contracts contain other clauses that can often be negotiated, including:

- *The amount of the down payment (if any).*

- *The amount of each monthly payment.*

- *The period of the lease.*

- *The bring-back value (if applicable).*

- *The penalty if you drive over a specified number of miles.* It's up to you to inform the lessor how many miles you expect to drive during the period of the lease. So err on the high side if there's a penalty attached to overmileage. If a penalty exists, try to have it apply after the first 1,000 miles over the limit, not after the *first* mile. Also, ask for a rebate at the end of the lease if you've driven fewer miles than estimated.

- *The meaning of "unreasonable amount of wear."* This phrase is often used in leasing contracts, frequently referring to excessive mileage. But it has been interpreted in many other ways, from habitual use in hilly country or on potholed city streets, to occupancy by large families with dogs. Ask for a schedule of definitions and penalties.

• *The limit of your responsibility if you don't have a maintenance clause in the contract.* Every contract states that it is your responsibility to keep the car in good working order throughout the period of the lease. Find out specifically what the lessor means by "good working order" and what penalties will be imposed if those standards are not met.

• *A guarantee that the car will be replaced if it is defective.*

• *A service center that must be used.* The lessor may designate a particular garage where the car must be serviced, but this could be inconvenient if you're out of town when your car needs repairs. If your contract has a maintenance clause, find out who pays in such a case. If you don't have a maintenance clause, find out if you're penalized in any way for repairs you have made.

• *The car insurance that may be required by the lessor.* You usually can get insurance relatively inexpensively from the lessor's group plan, but shop around anyway.

• *At the end of the lease, your option to buy the car.* Open-end leases often include this option, and it might be to your advantage to purchase the car for your own purposes. Or, if you have a buyer lined up who will pay more than the bring-back value, it might pay to buy the car to resell.

• *Renewal of the lease.* If your credit is poor, renewal avoids having to make another down payment.

If renewal is permitted, see if you can get a reduction in monthly payments. After all, the car *has* depreciated.

• *Breaking the lease.* Usually *you* can't break a lease. It is sometimes permitted, though, after some penalties are imposed. Find out what those penalties are; they should be spelled out in the contract. The lessor, however, usually *can* break the agreement. Find out the conditions under which your car must be returned whether you or the lessor terminates the contract.

LEASING VERSUS BUYING

As I mentioned earlier, some people choose leasing because of its convenience, or for its tax advantages (the cost of leasing and operating the car can usually be deducted if it is used for business purposes). Others are attracted by the ability to "move up" to a nicer car with leasing. As a general rule, you can afford the next-higher level of car when you lease rather than buy.

But from a purely dollars-and-cents standpoint, which has the lower overall cost—buying or leasing? If you traditionally keep your cars for five years or more, you're better off buying. If a shorter time period is the rule, leasing is generally only a few hundred dollars more expensive then buying. You may choose leasing in order to avoid making a down payment. Even if you could afford a down payment, you might decide that there are wiser ways to spend that lump sum of money—on education, medical bills, home repairs, starting a business, or a better investment.

Here is a typical cost comparison between leasing and buying a car. The chart on page 118 shows the calculations that a banker prepared for Elaine Wardlaw, a magazine editor, when she recently decided to acquire a $7,000 car. Although she had presumed that leasing would be much more expensive, the numbers showed a relatively small difference between buying and leasing.

By leasing rather than purchasing, Elaine would avoid making a significant down payment ($1,484), as well as paying required sales taxes ($420). Also, her monthly payments would be less for a lease— $162.42 versus $204.46—and thus her payments over thirty-six months would be less.

Overall, when she considered all factors, Elaine discovered that it would cost only a little more to lease than to buy—in her case, $252.56 more. On a closed-end lease, it would cost an additional $10 per month for thirty-six months; thus, the difference would be $612.56 after three years.

Whether you ultimately decide to lease or to buy, you'd be wise to understand beforehand all the intricacies of acquiring a car. It takes some creative thinking; you should consider not only the type of car you want, and the best way to finance it, but also how your choices affect the _entire_ picture of your current and future money needs. Some people will continue to buy their cars in the upcoming years, but others will decide that they can make better use of their money by leasing. Evaluate each money source that's been discussed in the previous pages and what it can offer you in relation to the others. When you make your decision as to how you will obtain your car, and where the financing will come from, it should be a fully enlightened judgment. Be sure to make the most of your options.

LEASING COST (open-end lease)—36 months

List price of car	$7,000
Value of car after 36 months	3,500
(also depreciation amount)	(½ of $7,000)
Monthly payments of lease	162.42
Total amount of payments over 36 months	5,847.12
Plus value of car after 36 months	+ 3,500
Cost after 36 months	$9,347.12

PURCHASE COST (20 percent down)—36 months

List price of car	$7,000
Cost of car including 6 percent sales tax	7,420
	(sales tax varies from state to state)
Value of car after 36 months	3,500
Down payment of 20 percent	1,484
Amount left to be financed	5,936
Monthly payments	204.46
	($42 more than monthly lease payments)
Total amount of payments over 36 months	7,360.56
Plus down payment	+ 1,484
Total cost after 36 months	$8,844.56
Plus money you would have earned had down payment been in a savings account at present interest rates (over 36 months)	+ 250 (roughly)
Total cost of car at end of 36 months	$9,094.56

SUCCEEDING IN THE
HOME-FINANCING
MARKETPLACE

Everyone, it seems, has a real-estate tale to tell these days. My favorite story was related to me by a Pan Am stewardess, Eve Henson, whom I met after a seminar I gave at the Ambassador Hotel in Los Angeles on personal investment strategy.

Eve hadn't given much thought to becoming a homeowner before attending the program that day. But the talk brought home to her the effect inflation would have upon her future financial security, and she knew she had to take action.

When another Pan Am stewardess invited Eve over to see her new condominium the next day, Eve decided what kind of action she wanted to take. Inspired, and a bit impulsive, she set out that very afternoon to locate a condominium of her own, which she planned to buy and then rent out. She selected a $105,000 unit in Culver City, California. She had thus far given little thought to the finer details of financing.

But Eve was forced to confront the financial facts soon enough. The down payment on the condominium was $12,000. Searching for a way to come up with the cash, she first checked with a Pan Am personnel manager. She was told that all her lines of credit there—the credit union and retirement program—were either used to capacity or not available. But when she dug a bit further, her personnel manager discovered a second retirement program to which Eve was contributing that *did* afford her borrowing rights. She obtained a $6,000 low-interest loan and was halfway to her down-payment goal.

Eve then decided to approach her more well-to-do friends to see if they might be interested in forming an investment partnership with her. Two of them agreed, and each anted up $3,000 to help buy the condo. Two months later, the escrow closed and the unit was theirs. Eighteen months later they sold the unit at a $12,000 net profit, which enabled Eve and her partners to then buy separate homes.

The story may sound as if it came straight out of a book of fairy tales, but Eve employed a method of creative financing that many people are using to get a start in the real-estate market.

The general partnership method, which I call "team investing," is particularly popular among some first-time homeowners, although it is also increasingly popular among sophisticated investors. For a minimal investment, it allows each partner to learn the ropes of ownership—from financing to maintenance to resale.

Partnerships are by nature somewhat compli-cated, and there are some points you should consider before you enter into a deal of this kind. Each party should be represented by an attorney. The agreement between the partners should clearly spell out what each person's responsibilities will be. And there should be a well-delineated contingency plan that covers the possi-bility of any one of the partners' wishing to sell out to the others. It is helpful, too, if one of the partners is in a stronger financial position than the others. If partner-ship agreements are drawn up with thorough attention to detail so that all parties are covered in all situations that can arise through the purchase of real estate, they can turn out to be quite profitable for everyone involved.

THE STATE OF THE MARKETPLACE

For many potential home buyers, this may seem like a particularly difficult time. In early 1982, for example, building starts were half of what they should have been, relative to other economic growth factors. In some parts of the country $100,000-and-up homes are now the rule, not the exception. Mortgage interest rates are well into the double digits (about 17 percent in mid-1982), and an increasing number of people feel that they simply cannot afford to purchase their own house. Many are having to find alternatives to conventional bank financing.

If you've been looking for a house lately, you may have been shocked by what you've found. Financing, though always a major concern in the purchase of a home, is now the primary issue. Most Americans can no longer qualify for the traditional, fixed-rate, thirty-year bank mortgage that their parents and grandparents relied upon for half a century.

More than ninety percent of the first-time home buyers in the United States, according to the National Association of Realtors, cannot qualify for today's average mortgage of $50,000. Consequently, whereas a decade ago one out of every three mortgages went to first-time buyers, today that figure is no more than one out of five. High down payments and interest rates are viciously eroding our reliance on the fixed, low-rate, long-term mortgage—that brilliant financial invention that made this a nation of homeowners.

My research into the current market has convinced me, however, that you *can* still get financing that will take the bite out of your down payment and keep your monthly payments at a tolerable level. What has become known as "creative financing" has made home buyers out of many people who once believed that ownership of a house was beyond their means. Families who only recently felt they would have to settle for renting have found ownership to be a valid financial option. There are several innovative types of loans, almost unheard of even a decade ago, that have reopened the door to home buying for those with limited cash.

This chapter is aimed not only at the potential home buyer, but also at the current homeowner who plans to sell his or her property sometime in the near future. If you're about to leap into the marketplace as a buyer, you'll learn here how best to weave your way through the maze of options, about the various money sources for real-estate loans, and about the many methods of creative financing. You will also learn the importance of working with an attorney to protect your interests. You'll find out about governmental financing sources: the Federal Housing Administration (FHA), the Veterans Administration (VA), and the Farmers Home Administration (FmHA). And if you're a homeowner who is considering selling, you will discover several different effective ways of shaping the deal.

LENDING SOURCES FOR REAL ESTATE

Whether you're buying or selling a house, the money required to finalize the deal almost always has to be borrowed from somewhere. As with other loans, mortgages are available from a long list of sources besides the traditional savings-and-loan associations. But let's start there.

SAVINGS-AND-LOANS

S & L's are set up specifically to service the housing business: builders, developers, buyers, and sellers. S & L's only occasionally make bigger loans than banks, offering primarily thirty year loans, typically for 80 percent of the value of your home. (In certain cases they will go as high as 90 percent, but only when the loan is covered by private mortgage insurance.) Different S & L's will be partial to making loans in different

parts of your community. Your real-estate broker or the
S & L's loan officer will quickly tell you whether a particular S & L is making loans in your area. As a general
rule, S & L's charge borrowers 2 percent more than what
the money cost them to obtain.

COMMERCIAL BANKS

Another source of mortgage money is the commercial bank. Although often overlooked, because they
are better known for short-term loans and personal and
business loans, they _are_ involved in the home-mortgage
field. Federal and state regulations usually prevent
banks from lending more than 90 percent of a house's
appraised value and limit loan periods to a maximum of
thirty years.

INSURANCE COMPANIES

Some insurance firms are presently active in
the mortgage market. They have a constant stream of
funds arriving from policy premiums, and a few insurance companies consider prime real estate an excellent
investment for that cash. A percentage is typically set
aside for residential funds. If you are arranging your own
financing, contact the lending division of major insurance companies within your city. You may be pleasantly
surprised by their relatively low interest rates.

Insurance-company paperwork, however, is no-
toriously slow, and thus loan approval may take several
months. When insurance-firm funds _are_ available for
real estate, they are typically offered for thirty-year
terms.

MORTGAGE BANKERS

Brokers are conduits for a variety of funds, including real-estate money. They function as "match-

makers," putting people like you together with pension funds, trusts, endowments, and even rich individuals who are searching for quality investments. They are actually not banks, but rather brokers—that is, go-betweens. Because they are in constant contact with money sources, they can frequently find a better loan for you than you could arrange by yourself. For their services they charge a fee, commonly referred to as "points," ranging from 1 to 5 percent (or percentage points) of the total loan amount.

Check the Yellow Pages under "Mortgage Bankers" for the firms in your city.

FINANCE COMPANIES

Businesses such as Aames Home Loan and the Money Store are primarily in the second-mortgage business—that is, they make loans based on the equity built up in a home. These loans, which are for periods of up to ten years, carry higher interest rates than most other lending institutions offer. If you are looking for a second mortgage on your home, be sure to shop around, checking with banks as well as finance companies.

CREDIT UNIONS

If you belong to a credit union, particularly a large one—either through a labor union, an employer, or a professional organization—you may be able to tap that organization's mortgage funds. Although the interest rates are quite reasonable, the loan ceiling is low—generally around $35,000. Credit unions also usually insist that the loan be repaid more quickly than loans from an S & L or a bank.

It can be easier to borrow from a credit union than from any other lender, because you are treated as a "member of the clan." Call your credit union to check out its terms. If your needs are fairly modest, its terms might be just right for you.

PRIVATE INVESTORS

Often contacted through mortgage bankers, private investors also sometimes advertise in the _Wall Street Journal_ (under "Business Connections") or in major newspapers such as the _Los Angeles Times_ and the _New York Times_. Private investors are rarely interested in first mortgages, because these are such long-term arrangements. Most are looking instead to make second-mortgage loans, often at better rates than you could get from a bank or any other lender.

Whenever you deal with a private lender, an attorney experienced in real-estate law should represent you. With a lawyer's guidance, the transaction can be made as simple as a signed note backed by your property, with payments made monthly.

UNCONVENTIONAL PRIVATE LENDERS

Real-estate brokers and appraisers are not routinely thought of as sources for real-estate loans, but real-estate brokers, for example, not only have excellent money connections; they themselves occasionally may even be interested in lending you money. The same is true of real-estate appraisers. By the very nature of their business, appraisers constantly come in contact with buyers and sellers—including people who have money and people searching for it. If they are not interested in investing in your real-estate venture themselves, they can be an excellent source of both information and introductions to other money sources and potential partners.

HOW TO USE UNCLE SAM TO CUT MONTHLY PAYMENTS AND DOWN PAYMENTS

When most people think of home financing, their thoughts often turn to the sources already mentioned. But they sometimes overlook the fact that the government might very well be able to help them. In fact, the federal government makes available various mortgage plans for which you may qualify. Here are the basic facts about each:

THE FHA MORTGAGE

One of the best potential sources for home-buying funds is a Federal Housing Administration (FHA) loan. The FHA doesn't make the mortgage loans itself, but it does _insure_ them. You apply for and obtain an FHA mortgage from a bank, S & L, or mortgage company, and if you default, the government will bail out the bank. (The government, however, will make an effort to obtain the debt from you.)

FHA loans are offered under some of the most appealing terms you'll find anywhere. Their primary advantage is that the down payment may be less than that of a conventional loan. You will be required to make a down payment as small as 3 percent on the first $25,000 of appraised value, plus 5 percent of the remainder.

The loan period is thirty to perhaps even forty years. That reduces monthly payments considerably (the longer the mortgage, the lower the monthly payments). The interest rate on FHA loans is 1 to 3 percentage points less than the average conventional mortgage rate. (FHA rates, like all others these days, are to some degree subject to change. For current FHA rates, write or phone the FHA, Department of Housing and Urban Development, 451 7th Street, S.W., Washington, DC 20410.)

Although bankers like the FHA's guarantee, they don't appreciate those low rates; so they get around them by adding points. Even so, the lender is limited to adding just one point (that is, 1 percent) to the buyer's FHA loan, which is usually labeled the "loan origination fee." The *seller* can be charged additional points, however.

If your credit rating is poor, you may have particular difficulty obtaining an FHA loan. The government doesn't want to get stuck with bad debts, particularly under the Reagan administration, so you'll have to undergo a complete credit check.

There are other problems associated with obtaining an FHA loan, which is why most mortgage hunters scurry around trying to get conventional and creative finance mortgages. Here are some of the difficulties you'll face if you apply for government financing:

• *The FHA appraises the house.* Let's say that you agree to buy the house from the seller for $72,000. You know it's overpriced, but for a laundry list of reasons you want that particular house anyway and decide to buy it at the inflated price. The FHA appraiser says that you *shouldn't* have agreed to pay more than $65,000, however, so you don't get the loan, unless the seller is willing to lower the selling price to $65,000.

• *The FHA inspects the house.* I know of some cases in which the *buyer* has had the house inspected, found a few things wrong with it, and agreed with the seller to have them fixed. But the FHA inspectors proved tougher; their standards are considered among the highest in the building industry. They were unhappy with what they saw, and the buyer didn't get the loan.

• *The FHA insists you put up your* own *money for the down payment.* If you have to go to a bank—or your Aunt Nellie—for even just a few hundred dollars toward the down payment, you probably won't get the loan, unless Aunt Nellie signs a statement that the money is a gift.

• *The FHA mortgage is inflexible.* If you require a single change in the FHA contract, your request may be turned down.

• *The FHA insists that you pay your property taxes and home insurance according to its guidelines.* You're required to hand over one-twelfth of those payables *to the bank* with each monthly mortgage installment. The bank puts the non-mortgage money into an escrow account (which means the money is untouchable until the bank pays your tax and insurance bills on their due dates). If you object to this arrangement, you won't get the loan.

• *The FHA wraps its mortgages in red tape.* Unlike conventional bank loans, FHA financing may require several weeks of paper processing before final approval is granted. So be prepared to wait for your funds.

THE VA MORTGAGE

All U.S. military veterans who served at least 180 peacetime days or 90 wartime days are eligible for VA loans. These loans are guaranteed by the Veterans Administration and can be used to finance a house as well as for many other necessities. Like FHA loans, they are made by banks, as well as by S & L's, mortgage bankers, and credit unions.

The terms of VA loans are even better than those of an FHA mortgage. In most cases, for example, *no* down payment is required, although some lenders do insist on it.

Most VA loans have a repayment period of up to thirty years. If you want to pay off your mortgage sooner (your total cost is less that way), you can do so without a penalty. (By contrast, there *is* a penalty—a percentage of the total value of the mortgage—for early payment on conventional mortgages.) Also, if you have trouble meeting the payments on a VA loan, and you want to decrease the amount of each monthly payment by extending the period of the loan, the VA may be able to make such an arrangement with the bank. The VA will typically guarantee the lender 60 percent of your loan up to $25,000.

Interest rates for VA loans are usually about the same as for FHA loans. (For current interest rates, write Veterans Administration, Washington, DC 20420, or call your local VA office.)

If you qualify for a VA loan, first get all the information you can from the Washington or local VA office. Then pay a visit to your bank or other lending institution and fill out an application. Just as with a standard loan application, you will have to prove you are credit-worthy—and can make the monthly payments while covering your other living expenses. The application processing is done through your local lender. The amount of red tape and time then depends on the strength of your application and the willingness and ability of the lender to speed the process along.

The loan guarantee can be made only on the appraised value of a house, not on its selling price; the VA will appraise the property before the loan can be approved. So be prepared for a delay while the appraisal is being made.

Even though you will have to put up with government red tape, VA and FHA loans are still worth considering. Their terms are excellent, making the extra paperwork and delays well worth your while.

THE FMHA MORTGAGE

If you live in a rural area, the Farmers Home Administration is yet another good source for government-backed loan money. It serves people who can't obtain a loan through traditional sources, but who can nonetheless afford monthly house payments. In general, the government guidelines will find you eligible if you live in a small town or rural area or if your income is below the national average.

You obtain the FmHA mortgage through a bank, in the same way as an FHA or a VA mortgage, and the Farmers Home Administration guarantees the loan. The terms are excellent. The down payment, for instance, is usually minimal; sometimes there's none at all. Repayment can be extended for up to thirty-three years, and interest rates are very low, perhaps the lowest you can get. These rates do vary, however, depending on your income and how many dependents you have. For details, write Farmers Home Administration, Department of Agriculture, Washington, DC 20250.

Government-backed home financing is certainly still available to those who qualify for it, but the fact is that fewer people qualify for it these days, simply because of tightening restrictions and limited funds. For most of us who want to live in our own homes, creative financing is the best alternative.

MORTGAGE INNOVATIONS THAT HELP YOU AFFORD THE HOME YOU WANT

By my count, there are more than a hundred new kinds of mortgages offered in the current real-estate market, and dozens more are on the drawing board. Without these creative financing packages, the average family no longer able to qualify for a traditional thirty-year, fixed-rate mortgage, would be closed out of the home market. In mid-1982, over 80 percent of the real-estate deals being made involved creative financing techniques.

The *structure* of a real-estate deal now often means the difference between making or not making the purchase of the house you want. Let me describe several creative financing methods that have become common-place:

1. THE VARIABLE-RATE MORTGAGE (VRM)

Four out of ten bank mortgages in 1981 were variable-rate mortgages; as you're reading this book, the ratio may have climbed even higher.

VRMs are long-term loans for which the interest rate (and thus the monthly payments) may rise or fall over the years, in response to a formula written into your contract, often connected to the Federal Home Loan Bank's monthly "national average mortgage rate." In general, your own loan's interest rate can change as often as quarterly, but usually there is a ceiling on the total interest increase (typically, 2.5 percent) over the term of the loan.

Lenders frequently prefer this type of mortgage, because it doesn't tie up their money at a fixed interest rate for twenty-five to thirty years, particularly when they presume that interest rates will rise. And it's acceptable for many borrowers as well, especially if they do not plan to stay in their home for an extended time and thus will not have to worry about where interest rates will be in ten to twenty years. If interest rates are presently high, and thus are likely to drop, a VRM may be a wise choice. It may present problems, however, for families on fixed incomes who plan to stay put.

Sometimes an adjustable-rate mortgage is made more attractive by starting off 1 to 2 percentage points *under* the prevailing interest rate and by extending the term to forty years, which cuts monthly payments appreciably. The total cost of the loan, however, would increase under such an arrangement.

2. THE WRAPAROUND MORTGAGE

Also called the All-Inclusive Deed of Trust (AIDT), the wraparound is a financing arrangement that not only makes it easier for a buyer to finance the purchase of a home, but also makes the sale more profitable for the seller. Frankly, it's a confusing loan method that should be entered into only with legal guidance. Here's an example of how it might work:

Let's assume you want to buy a $100,000 home, on which the seller currently holds an existing loan of $50,000 at 9 percent interest, payable at $500 per month. With a wraparound arrangement, you pay a $20,000 cash down payment to the seller, who then carries a so-called wraparound deed of trust for the remaining $80,000 of the sale price, at terms the two of you have agreed upon (say, a 12 percent interest rate, payable at $900 per month). The seller continues to make the original $500 payments on the $50,000 existing loan, but you pay $900 per month to the seller, who keeps the $400 difference.

The wraparound loan benefits sellers—they sell their property and make money on the loan arrangement, too. Buyers come out ahead as well. They may be able to get into the home marketplace at a lower interest rate than banks and S & L's currently offer. Buyers also avoid the new-loan fees an institutional lender charges.

3. THE LEASE-OPTION PLAN

In a lease-option agreement, the prospective buyer agrees initially to lease the property, but has an option to purchase it at a later time. Individuals who are not interested in team investments or in exploring the other financing options described above sometimes choose this arrangement. Here is how it worked for a friend of mine:

Janet Caron, a designer, recently made a lease-option arrangement on a condominium in West Los Angeles. The selling price was $135,000. After evaluating her current and future financial situation, she decided that she could afford payments of $1,200 a month—but not the additional $21,000 for a down payment.

The seller suggested a lease-option arrangement, whereby Janet would pay $1,200 a month in rent, with the option to buy in one year; that year's rent money would be applied toward the ultimate purchase of the condominium. In addition, she would put down a $5,000 nonrefundable option payment, which would "hold" the property for her for a year while she rented it. The deal also clearly defined what the selling price of the property would be in one year, based on three independent appraisals that both the buyer and seller agreed to have done. (The appraisers estimated a 5 percent increase in value in twelve months, or a total value of $141,750.)

Janet accepted this arrangement. She has calculated that she should realistically be in a position to buy a year from now. If she then chooses *not* to purchase the condo, the seller will keep the option money and, of course, the lease payments. If she buys, all the lease payments will go toward the purchase price (depending on how the contract was originally negotiated); the option money may be deducted from the selling price as well.

True, this type of arrangement primarily benefits the seller, but the option money bought Janet just that—an option—and it provides her with a realistic chance at a real-estate deal that would otherwise be beyond her means. For her, it is an important foot in the door.

4. THE GRADUATED-PAYMENT MORTGAGE

This is an attractive package because the first year's monthly payments are set at $100 to $200 _less_ than those of a conventional bank mortgage. Payments increase year after year for the first five years, until they are equal to conventional bank mortgage payments. It's a particularly appealing arrangement for couples who are just starting out.

After the first five years, though, the payments are _greater_ than those of a conventional bank mortgage. And over the full course of the mortgage (usually twenty-five to thirty years) you'll have paid out many thousands of dollars more than you would have with a traditional mortgage.

Before you choose a graduated mortgage, ask yourself, "Am I willing to pay a higher-than-normal rate for most of the life of the mortgage in order to afford the house I want _now_?" If money is particularly tight for you now, and you can be sure of being able to afford those high payments later, go ahead.

5. THE EQUITY-SHARING MORTGAGE

The bank agrees to give you a mortgage at a reduced rate, provided you sign over a portion of the equity. In essence, the house is yours, but when you sell it, the bank gets its share of the cash profits. Interest rates are subject to negotiation, but they could be 6 to 8 percentage points below prevailing levels. If you don't mind having a silent partner, this could be a worthwhile arrangement for you.

Incidentally, the amount of equity that the bank retains varies. The average bank equity is about one-third (in return for lowering interest rates by at least one-third of their current rate). The bank then agrees to wait, say, ten years, or until the house is sold, whichever comes first, before it cashes in its equity (even though the mortgage runs for thirty years). If you don't sell within ten years, the bank will demand that you purchase its share of the equity, and then it will refinance your mortgage.

THE NEGATIVE-AMORTIZER MORTGAGE

Amortization means paying the principal on a loan, that is, the basic amount you've borrowed excluding the interest on that amount. Negative amortization means that a portion of the interest is treated as principal.

A negative-amortizer loan is a two-stage loan. During the first period of the loan, usually five to ten years, your monthly payments are calculated based on a below-market interest rate. Your payments, during this initial term of the loan, are lower than they would be if you had taken out, say, a bank loan at current market interest rates. The interest schedule is structured, however, in such a way that during this entire initial term you will be paying off only interest, and not principal.

For example, let's say you need a $60,000 mortgage, and the current interest rates are 19¾ percent. You've determined that you can't afford the payments on a conventional thirty-year mortgage, which would be about $1,000 a month. But a private mortgage company offers you a negative-amortizer loan with terms that cut the interest rate, in the initial term, to 14¾ percent. Your monthly payments, during this period, would be about $750, which is within your means.

It's during the second stage of this kind of mortgage that things really start getting expensive. The mortgage is re-amortized at this point; new—and much higher—monthly payments are established. This is how it's figured: The difference between the current interest rate when you took out the mortgage and the rate the mortgage company actually gave you (the difference between 19¾ and 14¾ percent), which was figured at $250 per month, is added up for the entire first term of the mortgage. This would total $30,000 for a ten-year period for the $60,000 mortgage described above. This $30,000 would be added to your original principal of $60,000 (remember, none of your principal was actually paid off); you would then refinance the total of $90,000—remember, it's now ten years after you first took out the mortgage—at the going market interest rate.

The only advantage to this type of mortgage is the lower interest during the initial term. Overall, you'll pay *much* more in interest, since your principal itself will be increased. You should consider this an acceptable alternative only if you're desperate for a house and you can't get a mortgage by any other method. It should be considered last-resort financing.

SOME IMPORTANT HOME-BUYING ADVICE

No matter how you ultimately decide to finance your home, there are a couple of vital points that you should always keep in mind.

1. As I mentioned earlier, hire an attorney to read any sales agreement before you sign it. Some tricky

and confusing clauses can be incorporated into such agreements, particularly with the creative financing methods now being utilized. Many lawyers specialize in real estate, and their ability to spot problems in your contract will prove invaluable.

2. Keep in mind that commissions for real-estate agents and brokers are not bound by hard-and-fast rules. Although they have traditionally been set at 6 percent, they _are_ open to negotiation. Some brokers, for example, have agreed to fees as low as 3 percent, particularly when selling higher-priced houses. Others have deferred part of their commission, taking one-third at the time of the sale and having the buyer pay the rest at a specified future date. Try to negotiate this point.

As you can see, even in hard times, it is still possible to buy your dream house (or co-op or condo) for monthly payments you can afford. And though you will often face some hurdles before landing the real-estate deal that is right for you, you'll find it's well worth the effort. The financial advantages of homeownership are significant—from accumulating equity to interest-payment tax deductions—so look into every option that can make house-buying a reality for you.

Once you have your home, of course, it may need some fixing up—either as soon as you move in, or several months or years down the road. Fortunately, financing can usually be obtained for home improvements; the next chapter is devoted to the subject of renovating your house and where to get the money to do it.

CHAPTER 9

HOW TO OBTAIN AND MAKE THE MOST OF HOME-IMPROVEMENT LOANS

Valerie Franklin, a Los Angeles art dealer, and her husband, Tim, a noted contemporary painter, decided it was time that they became homeowners. After scouring the market from one end of Los Angeles to the other, they decided to buy a "fixer-upper" and remodel. The decision, they realized, would entail considerable expenditure of both time and money. But they found it was cheaper to buy and renovate than to pay twice the money for the "perfect" home. The task ahead involved knocking down walls, installing a new kitchen, rebuilding a fireplace, renovating the bathrooms, painting, buying new carpets, and putting on a new roof—no small task, but as Tim now enthusiastically comments, "It was all worth it."

This scenario is not an uncommon one. Valerie and Tim are part of a nationwide do-it-yourself renaissance. Many people are becoming urban pioneers, rehabilitating houses and lofts in both inner cities and suburbs, and even participating in the renovation of entire city blocks.

A CREATIVE TWIST ON THE AMERICAN DREAM

The current economic conditions may encourage you to renovate, whether you're interested in fully remodeling a turn-of-the-century Victorian mansion or simply adding a room to your ranch-style home to give your family more living space. High housing prices and mortgage interest rates have made "staying put and adding on" an attractive and growing trend. In 1980 the Department of Commerce stated that "for the first time, expenditures for alterations and repair [remodeling] will equal or exceed new construction spending."

Michael Sumichrast, chief economic adviser for the National Association of Home Builders, verified this phenomenon, reporting recently that "for every dollar going into new construction ... $1.10 to $1.20 is being spent on remodeling." The result is that in 1982 alone, a record $33.5 billion will be put into 3 million bathrooms, 2 million kitchens, and more than $5 billion worth of replacement windows and doors.

Don Logay, editor of *Qualified Remodeler* magazine, predicts that by the end of the decade homeowners will be spending as much as $100 billion annually to fix up old houses or to add onto newer houses. "Fixing up," then, has become the creative solution to a tight and expensive housing market.

But home remodeling also costs money, which usually has to be borrowed. Fortunately, there are several places to which you can turn for these funds. In the following pages you will learn about the six sources of financing for remodeling. You will also read where to put those improvement dollars to increase the value of your home and when to avoid the expensive temptation of overimproving relative to your surrounding neighborhood. Later in the chapter, you will learn about the various government programs specifically designed to aid in renovation, as well as the new tax laws that benefit those who are willing to improve or enhance older structures—including homes, commercial buildings, and warehouses.

SOURCES OF MONEY FOR HOME IMPROVEMENTS

If you will need a loan to finance your home improvements, start your loan comparison shopping as soon as you know the specific costs of the improvements and/or additions—preferably as much as three to six months before you want to begin construction. The more time you allow for comparison shopping, the better your chances are for fully evaluating your options and lowering the cost of the loan.

As you talk to each lending source, ask in advance what documents will be required in addition to the basic loan application. Don't be surprised if you're asked to submit a copy of the contractor's estimate or contract, as well as copies of the city or county building permits. If you're doing the work yourself, you may also be quizzed about your ability to complete the job.

Some lenders may also require a deed of trust on your home to secure the loan, plus a title report and property appraisal (all of which you must pay for). If you're self-employed, they may also ask for personal financial statements, plus references and tax returns for the previous few years.

1. LOW-INTEREST GOVERNMENT LOANS—START HERE

Government agencies are the last remaining source of cheap home-improvement money. The Federal Housing Administration (FHA) Title I program offers federally guaranteed home-improvement loans made through "approved" lending institutions such as banks and savings-and-loan associations. Not all lending institutions are approved, however, and some lenders simply aren't interested in the low-interest, government-guaranteed loans. Check directly with the FHA in Washington, DC, for the institution in your area that offers these loans, or start by calling the largest banks and savings-and-loan associations near you. If they don't offer these loans, they probably know who does.

The FHA sets the interest rates, repayment period, and loan amounts for these transactions but provides the lender with some room for adjustment. For example, a bank may set lower dollar limits or tougher qualifying restrictions than the FHA.

The FHA Title I funds currently carry the following stipulations: you can qualify if the improvements you wish to make include room additions and kitchen and bath remodeling, but you are out of luck if you want money for luxury additions such as a tennis court or a sauna. The federal guidelines are strict about frills. The FHA is also touchy about fire and burglar alarms, which don't qualify either.

2. DIRECT GOVERNMENT LOANS FOR VETERANS

Direct government loans differ from FHA loans in that they are made by the federal government directly, not through local money outlets—and they are exclusively for veterans. The primary sources are both the federal and state governments. For example, funds are available in California from the state's Department of Veterans Affairs, through a program called Cal Vet. Interest rates and funding vary according to current legislation and market conditions.

Don't second-guess what funds may be available or the current status of the law. If you are a veteran of the armed forces, it's worth calling your local VA office to find out if you can qualify for these special funds and how the rates compare with the rates from traditional lenders. (The VA's interest rates are typically relatively low.)

3. PERSONAL SIGNATURE LOANS

If you need less than $5,000 and can repay the money in a relatively short time (one to three years), a personal loan may be an excellent source of home-improvement money. You can apply to your bank, savings-and-loan association, or credit union. (Refer to Chapters 1 and 2 for complete details on personal signature loans.)

The advantage of taking out a personal signature loan for remodeling is that the loan is not backed by or tied to your property—that is, it is not collateralized by your home and your equity in it. Assuming your credit is good, personal loans can also be approved quickly. Typically, there is no need to specify that the funds are to be used for home improvement.

4. INSURANCE-POLICY LOANS

If you have a whole-life insurance policy that contains a cash-value portion, you can borrow money at a relatively low interest rate and use it for any purpose, including home improvements. Repayment is at your own pace, but if you die before the loan is repaid, the remaining balance will be deducted from the face value of your policy before your beneficiaries are paid.

5. BANK HOME-IMPROVEMENT LOANS

Let's assume that the cost of your home-improvement project is greater than $5,000, that you have no whole-life insurance policy, and that you can't qualify for government programs. Your next option is to explore a home-improvement loan from a bank. These are collateral loans backed by the equity in your house and based on your credit rating. In general, loan amounts of $15,000 and more are available, with longer repayment periods and frequently lower interest rates when the funds are earmarked for home improvement. The reason: the lender has the security of your home as your guarantee of repayment. If for some reason you can't repay the loan, the lender's recourse is obvious: foreclosure on the house.

Most lenders (banks, savings-and-loan associations, credit unions, and finance companies) offer home-improvement loans. This is a competitive type of financing for which it is worth your while to compare terms at a minimum of five different sources, beginning with your current mortgage holder. Be sure to stipulate that you want only a home-improvement loan and are not interested in totally refinancing your existing mortgage (more about that soon).

Note: As I mentioned previously, begin your comparison shopping early, even if you won't need the loan money for many weeks. You can fill out your application, have it approved, and ask to have the rate and loan guaranteed in writing for up to ninety days. This will protect you in the event that interest rates increase between signing and the time you need the money.

6. REFINANCING YOUR EXISTING MORTGAGE

If your remodeling project will cost $15,000 or more, you might consider refinancing your existing mortgage. This requires extreme caution, however.

John and Pat Martin had lived in their Santa Monica home for twelve years when they decided to make a major addition to it, nearly doubling its square footage by adding a new kitchen, family room, and darkroom. They received an estimate of $40,000.

The Martins' current home mortgage was at 7½ percent, and to finance the remodeling project their mortgage holder offered to refinance the existing mortgage totally, plus the $40,000 remodeling fee, at 14 percent for twenty-five years. The net effect was that they would be taking out a new loan for $60,000 ($40,000 plus the amount still due on their existing 7½ percent mortgage).

The advantage of such an arrangement would be lower monthly payments over the twenty-five-year period. But instead, the Martins chose to retain their 7½ percent loan and to finance the home-improvement loan separately—at 14 percent for fifteen years. The monthly payments of the remodeling loan seemed relatively high, but the overall cost of both this loan and the existing mortgage was cheaper.

Refinancing your entire mortgage may be valuable, however, if you have purchased your home within the last few years at a relatively high interest rate, or at one close to the current home-improvement-loan rate. In most cases it will reduce your monthly mortgage payments by spreading out the new loan over a longer period.

Should you choose to refinance your mortgage totally, be sure to investigate _all_ the costs involved, including any charge for early repayment of your primary mortgage, as well as other fees, such as points—each point equals 1 percent of the loan—and new-mortgage costs. Have your lender calculate your options both ways, and ask for the annual percentage rate (APR), monthly payments, and total cost before making your decision.

7. CONTRACTOR-AIDED FINANCING

If you work with a contractor, ask whether he or she has financing connections, either with traditional sources or with any of the government-sponsored programs mentioned earlier. If so, certainly consider them, but keep in mind that contractors are not lenders or money people. They most commonly act as middlemen between you and their financial sources. Here is how a typical contractor financing arrangement works:

The contractor provides you with the loan application, which you complete and return. If the contractor approves the loan, he or she usually "assigns," or sells, the contract to a third party, thereby making money on the transaction. You then make your loan payments to that third party. This type of arrangement is beneficial to you only if you are having difficulty getting loan approval on your own. You will more than likely end up paying *more* for this kind of loan.

If possible, keep the areas of construction and financing separate. Not only will you get a better loan deal that way, but you'll also keep your working relationship with the contractor on a clear-cut business basis.

WHERE TO PUT YOUR HOME-IMPROVEMENT DOLLARS FOR TOP RESALE VALUE

Expecting automatic increases in resale value, homeowners have poured thousands of dollars over the years into gourmet kitchens, kidney-shaped swimming pools, and other major additions to their houses. Most of these improvements were made on the dual assumption that the improvement would increase livability and automatically increase the property value.

This is no longer true, however. Recent changes in the economy have forced most home buyers to shift their housing interest from "frills" to "no frills." Thus, if you're making improvements primarily for resale purposes, your remodeling decisions should be different from those you would make if you plan to stay in your house for a period of years.

IMPROVEMENTS THAT ADD VALUE

High energy and maintenance costs have caused significant attitudinal changes among home buyers. According to the National Association of Realtors, today's buyers are primarily interested in more living space—specifically, functional rooms such as bedrooms and bathrooms. The most popular home in the nation today is the three-bedroom, two-bath house. Overly equipped kitchens don't have nearly the appeal they once did.

Most overly improved. The kitchen is the most excessively improved area of the house as well as the most energy-draining. A more valuable improvement (with resale in mind) than conveniences such as a trash compactor would be replacing incandescent lighting with fluorescent fixtures and wiring. Since fluorescent lighting is four times more efficient than incandescent, it is a more attractive selling feature.

Curb appeal: outside improvements. "Curb appeal" refers to anything that can be seen from the curb or street, including landscaping, siding, roofing, and painting. Virtually anything that enhances that first impression makes the not-so-subtle statement that a house is special. Thus, this type of improvement has a good chance of enhancing the resale value of a house.

The over-improvement trap. Ironically, you can often "overimprove" for your neighborhood. On many steets you've probably seen that one unique house that stands out from the others. It may have a front-yard gazebo or a tennis court. When it comes time to sell, appraisers and buyers may be impressed with the house's appearance, but the value of the house is ultimately based on comparable houses in the area and their current selling prices. Because most appraisals are based on factors like square footage and the number of bedrooms and baths, the front-yard gazebo doesn't count for much. The object, then, is not to overimprove relative to the rest of your neighborhood unless you are planning to stay for many years and are making the improvement simply for personal satisfaction.

Other additions that fall into the questionable category include swimming pools, special-purpose structures (such as greenhouses), and luxuries such as finished basements. These may, in fact, add *no* market value to your house. In the case of a swimming pool, negative factors like maintenance and high energy expenses can in fact make the "improvement" a liability when you want to sell.

Spend some time studying the chart on pages 150-153. It indicates not only what various remodeling improvements cost (as of 1982), but also what their resale value will be at the time the house is sold. As you can see, most remodeling jobs are good investments if you're planning to stay in your present home for a while. If you plan to sell very soon, your best investments are probably adding a full bath and/or adding a fireplace.

REHABILITATION AND RENOVATION FUNDS FOR MAKING THE OLD NEW AGAIN

Many parts of the inner cities of Baltimore, Los Angeles, Cincinnati, New York, and other major metropolises are being rebuilt and many historic buildings are being restored. From individual homes and buildings to entire blocks, this renovation movement is in full bloom; it's been said that the bulldozer blitz of the sixties has given way to the urban reinvestment of the eighties.

This rejuvenation involves a cooperative financing effort among the federal government and local businesses and residents, prompted by the new tax incentives of the Economic Reform Act of 1981. If you are of sufficiently hearty spirit to take on the rehabilitation of a Victorian home or a brownstone, there may already be specially earmarked monies available to help you accomplish your goal. In the next section you will learn

COST VS. VALUE

This chart is based on an "average" American home. The house is a 17-year-old single-level ranch home—with 1600 sq. ft. of living area, including three bedrooms and one bath—in a suburban midwestern location. It is valued at $90,000 before any improvements.

These figures are intended to give homeowners a relative relationship of cost vs. value based on a limited sampling of remodeling projects, expert opinions, homeowner planning. Regional differences will raise or lower the cost/value and should be taken into consideration.

TYPE OF JOB	REMODELING COST		RESALE VALUE		FINANCE VALUE		COST vs. VALUE
Estimate is based on prototype home	Estimated cost to present owner by leading remodeling contractor		Estimated value to future owner by realty expert		Amount of increase to actual finance value by savings & loan		
	Range	Average	Resale Value	%	Financial Value	%	Conclusions
ROOM ADDITION	$18–$24,000	$21,000	$12,000	57%	$11,000	52%	
400 square feet of additional living space	Gives you "new home" benefits without having to sacrifice existing low-interest mortgage.		Resale value range: 55–60%. How room is used affects the resale value.		Represents a good investment if most homes in your area have room additions.		Good investment if you plan on staying. Short-term recovery in 55–60% range.
	Estimate by: J.W. Construction Company, Arlington, TX						
REMODEL KITCHEN (MAJOR)—Including all new appliances, new cabinets, counter tops, flooring, and decorating.	$6–$16,000	$10,500	$ 8,000	76%	$5,000	48%	
	Makes kitchen more useful overall. More efficient appliances (dishwasher/microwave) offer energy benefits and greater convenience.		Resale value range: 75–80%. Women buyers value a good kitchen design much higher than men. Room size affects value also.		Should be considered if kitchen is in poor condition or truly inadequate.		Good investment if you plan on staying. Short-term recovery in 75–80% range. At time of resale, accrued energy savings from new appliances can be added to recovery percentage.
	Estimate by: St. Charles Kitchens of Oakbrook, Oakbrook, IL						
REMODEL BATHROOM	$2,700–$7,000	$3,300	$1,000	30%	$1,000	30%	
5' x 7'—complete with new fixtures, walls, and flooring. (Waterproof Sheetrock used.)	Total renovation is less costly than piecemeal replacement as needed. A remodeled bath both beautifies and updates your home—adding to its value.		Remodeling becomes more important in larger baths where custom features can be included (double sinks, dressing areas, etc.) and has a higher resale value.		Good investment if in extremely poor condition.		Good investment if you plan on staying. On small 5x7 bath, short-term recovery is 30%. For resale, do what is needed to bring room up to standard.
	Estimate by: Creative Home Improvements, Merrick, NY						

TYPE OF JOB	REMODELING COST		RESALE VALUE		FINANCE VALUE		COST vs. VALUE
Estimate is based on prototype home	Estimated cost to present owner by leading remodeling contractor		Estimated value to future owner by realty expert		Amount of increase to actual finance value by savings & loan		
	Range	Average	Resale Value	%	Financial Value	%	Conclusions
ADD A FULL BATH	$3,500–$8,000	$4,200	$3,500	83%	$5,000	119%	
Tub/shower, toilet, vanity/sink, medicine chest, tile, and flooring. *Location of the ventilating stack is an important cost factor.	An extra bath offers improved household efficiency and serves to balance your home (as in this instance, with three bedrooms and one bath). The home is also more attractive to a buyer.		Resale value range: 80–100%. A very strong selling feature, especially in a three-bedroom home. Location is important to value—whether on first floor, or a master bath off master bedroom.		Viewed as a particularly good investment, especially if one bath can be used as a master bath in conjunction with the master bedroom.		This is a good investment—whether you plan on staying or selling. Short-term recovery in 80–100% range, with high finance value: 100% +. A master bath off master bedroom is a resale plus.
Estimate by: Creative Home Improvements, Merrick, NY							
WINDOWS AND DOORS	$6,300–$10,500	$7,500	$2,000	27%	$3,000	40%	
Exterior replacement using 18 vinyl prime windows with insulated glass, two vinyl storm doors, and two wood prime doors.	Energy-saving benefits provide an investment payback of approx. 10–12 years. Also offers greater convenience (cleaning and maintenance) with improved security and gives home a better appearance.		Resale value range: 25–30%. Will run higher with buyers who are energy-cost or maintenance-free minded.		Good investment especially when condition of existing windows and doors warrants replacement.		Good investment if you plan on staying. Short-term recovery in 25–30% range. Full investment payback period about 10 to 12 years. Offers maintenance and security benefits. Accrued energy savings can be added to recovery percentage at resale. If over eight years, can actually result in profit.
Estimate by: Retsye Industries, Inc., Des Moines, IA							
SIDING	$3,350–$5,000	$4,300	$3,000	70%	$2,000	47%	
1500 sq. ft. of aluminum siding with ¼" insulating board underneath.	New siding is 2 or 2½ times the cost of painting, giving an estimated cost recovery period of ten years. Besides improved appearance, it offers energy savings and maintenance benefits.		The improved appearance and maintenance-free feature are an obvious plus, but the energy-saving insulating benefit must be pointed out to a potential buyer.		New siding is a good selling point, and is worthwhile if a current owner plans to stay a few years.		Good investment if you plan on staying a few years. Short-term recovery in 70% range. Accrued energy and painting cost savings could represent full profit recovery after five years.
Estimate by: L.A.S. Enterprises, New Orleans, LA							

TYPE OF JOB	REMODELING COST		RESALE VALUE		FINANCE VALUE		COST vs. VALUE
Estimate is based on prototype home	Estimated cost to present owner by leading remodeling contractor		Estimated value to future owner by realty expert		Amount of increase to actual finance value by savings & loan		
	Range	Average	Resale Value	%	Financial Value	%	Conclusions
ADD INSULATION	$650–$1,700	$1,000	—	—	$500	50%	
Increase level to R-42 using 8" of blown wool fiber in attic, blown insulation in sidewalls, and batt insulation under floors.	(This estimate is for ceiling and walls.) The payback period, through energy savings, is from three to five years. At time of resale, an energy-efficient home is a definite selling plus.		With consumer awareness currently on the rise, this will become highly important in the years ahead.		Additional insulation can be a good selling point. It is an even better investment if the owner plans on staying a few years and could well pay for itself within five years or less.		Good investment if you plan on staying four or five years. Short-term recovery estimated to 50%. After energy-saving payback period is completed, extra insulation becomes a moneymaker until time of sale

Estimate by: Momper Insulation, Ft. Wayne, IN

ADD PATIO OR DECK	$2,500–$5,000	$3,850	$1,500	40%	$2,000	52%	
16′ x 20′ (320 sq. ft.) deck using cedar or pressure-treated pine. Steel pole support, and includes handrail and built-in seat. *Redwood deck adds 60% to total pricing.	An outdoor deck offers comparative low-cost additional space for six to twelve months a year depending on your location. Makes home more livable and more marketable.		Value is based on a Midwest home. Selling in warm weather would bring percentage higher.		Good selling feature regardless of geographic location. Owners in warm climates should base investment level on similar properties in their area.		Good investment if: (snow-belt states) you plan on staying, or (sun-belt states) you plan to sell within a few years. Short-term recovery for colder climates is in 40–50% range and is substantially higher for warm areas.

Estimate by: Homework By Dugan, Atlanta, GA

TYPE OF JOB	REMODELING COST		RESALE VALUE		FINANCE VALUE		COST vs. VALUE
Estimate is based on prototype home	Estimated cost to present owner by leading remodeling contractor		Estimated value to future owner by realty expert		Amount of increase to actual finance value by savings & loan		
	Range	Average	Resale Value	%	Financial Value	%	Conclusions
ADD A FIREPLACE	$2–$3,000	$2,500	$2,500	100%	$2,500	100%	
A factory-built 42" or 43" zero clearance energy-efficient model with glass doors. Floor-to-ceiling brick or stone face 7' wide. Raised hearth and 6' mantle	Energy-efficient fireplace will save you money as long as you own your home and is a key sales feature at time of resale. A fireplace holds universal appeal regardless of climate.		The aesthetic value adds to the resale dollar value every time. When showing a property in cool or cold weather, we ask the seller to have a fire going.		Good investment for as long as owner plans to stay, and a strong future selling point.		Good investment if you plan on selling. Short-term recovery estimated at 100%. Finance value also 100%. An even better investment if you plan on staying long enough to accrue energy savings, beauty, enjoyment.

Estimate by: Bilt-Rite Construction Company, No. Little Rock, AR

TYPE OF JOB	REMODELING COST		RESALE VALUE		FINANCE VALUE		COST vs. VALUE
ADD SWIMMING POOL	$10–$20,000	$12,000	$2,000	17%	$2,000	17%	
16' x 32' in-ground	A pool is a true luxury addition for any home. Besides the leisure and social aspects for entertaining, it also meets the needs of today's health- and exercise-oriented society. Particularly good for families with children.		Resale value range: 10–20% in colder climate areas. In warmer climates, the value increases greatly. Resale value depends on time of year sold, climate, and location of home.		Should be considered a "personal" investment.		A good investment, particularly for those who plan on staying. Short-term recovery ranges from 10% in colder climates; 60–75% in warm climates. An investment for those who want a luxurious and social lifestyle.

Estimate by: R.E.K. Industries Inc., St. Louis, MO

about the various government programs that exist to support renovation and where to find out which ones may apply to you and your community.

TAPPING LOCAL SOURCES: COMMUNITY INVESTMENT FUNDS

For mature communities such as New York and Boston, the Federal Home Loan Bank has allocated $2 billion a year nationally for redevelopment or rehabilitation. At last count, 700 savings-and-loan associations in more than 250 cities can borrow mortgage and construction money from the Community Investment Fund (CIF) at below-market rates and lend it at standard rates. Some S & L's, however, pass along the low-interest money *directly* to the borrower without raising the rates. Remember, this is for urban projects only, and only in *big* cities.

This law went into effect in 1978, specifically to channel loan money into rehabilitation rather than new housing. The Federal Home Loan Bank oversees the program, ensuring that these low-interest monies are made available by all savings-and-loan associations for urban renewal. By law, a certain percentage of an S & L's loans must go to renewal projects. If the associations do not comply, the FHLB often applies pressure, particularly when that S & L requests new branches, mergers, or expansions.

Funds *must* be loaned under this plan, and that means opportunity for you. If you're in the market for rehab money, see if your lender is *eagerly* participating in this program.

When you make inquiries at particular S & L's about CIF funds, ask each one about its own policies in administering the plan. If they vacillate over your inquiries, don't hesitate to let the FHLB know.

THE ALL-IN-ONE LOAN—BUYER/FIXER-UPPER PLAN

If you're buying, say, a brownstone with well-thought-out plans for revitalizing it, the Federal National Mortgage Association (FNMA) has a combined "buyer/fixer-upper" plan.

Let's assume that the house you're considering costs $20,000 (don't laugh; some in Baltimore were sold in the 1970s for $1 if the purchaser agreed to renovate them!). This $20,000 house, however, needs $20,000 worth of improvements. A loan, called a "Fannie Mae" loan (a charming and affectionate term heard frequently in financial circles, derived from the initials FNMA), is available to cover most of your total of $40,000; these loans are available from lenders who are FNMA members. Here's how they work:

If the loan package you need is for, say, $40,000, you put $2,000 down and borrow $38,000 from an FNMA-affiliated lender, including many banks and S & L's. The first $20,000 (your $2,000 and $18,000 from the loan) buys the house. The remaining $20,000 is placed in an interest-bearing account at the bank, to be drawn from as the construction progresses. Contact local banks and S & L's for more information.

HUD SECTION 312 LOAN PROGRAM

If you qualify, the U.S. Department of Housing and Urban Development can provide you with a construction loan of up to $27,000 at the giveaway interest rate of 3 percent! In 1979, 270 million federal dollars went into 700 cities through this program, and in 1980 the total amount was higher. Even if this program's funding tapers off somewhat, the program is likely to

continue in some form, as long as the cities are in need of
fixing. Here's how you qualify for this loan program:

1. The money you borrow must be used first to
make the house comply with building codes (wiring and
plumbing, for example) and beyond that to enhance its
value, according to HUD's published guidelines.

2. The house must be located in a designated
revitalization area—which means an area that the city,
state, or federal government wants to "save."

The quickest way to find out if Section 312
funds are available in your area is to call the regional
HUD office, or check the white pages under city government listings for the community development office or
the housing rehabilitation agency.

HUD TITLE I

HUD's Title I program is designed to improve
the "habitability" of houses in urban areas. With a good
credit rating, you can get up to $15,000 for fifteen years
at varying (but still below-average) interest rates. (*Note:*
"Habitability" applies to the basics, rather than to frills
like swimming pools and tennis courts.)

HUD does not make the loan directly, but the
agency acts as guarantor on the loan to the bank, backing 90 percent of it. This program is strictly voluntary on
the part of the lender, but you will probably find one or
more participants by calling several banks or S & L's, or
by contacting HUD directly.

BLOCK GRANTS

If you are ambitious, or one of an enterprising
group of people who are enthusiastic about redeveloping
an urban neighborhood, you can apply for federal Community Development Block Grants (CDBG). These dollars come through local agencies which distribute the

funds. They are offered in the form of actual grants (in essence, "free money"), low-interest loans, subsidies, or a package combining all of these. The grants are narrowly aimed toward so-called essential repairs, improvements that make houses more livable. The funds are approved locally, so someone at City Hall can direct you to the person or department that administers the CDBG program in your area.

I've found that home improvements can be one of the most rewarding investments, not only in terms of their psychological and emotional value but from the fiscal point of view as well—if you choose them and finance them wisely.

CHAPTER 10

RAISING FUNDS FOR
YOUR EDUCATION

When Charles Lyon returned to college as an adult to obtain a master's degree at Stanford University in 1971, he paid $2,610 for tuition and required fees in his first year. "The costs seemed high back then, but somehow we managed," Charles recalls. "But when my daughter applied to Stanford for the 1982 school year, she was told that those same fees would total $8,220 in her freshman year alone."

Charles and his wife had started setting aside money years before for their daughter's higher education, "but we never dreamed how expensive it would eventually be," he says. "We finally decided we would need some help over the four years—a loan or perhaps a grant. So we began looking around to see what was available."

Paying for college has never been easy, but these days a growing number of people are becoming convinced that the cost of higher education is now beyond their means.

One recent study predicted that by the end of the 1980s, a $60,000 price tag for a four-year college education will not be unusual. In the 1982–83 school year alone, the tuition and required fees at Princeton University amounted to $8,380; even at a public institution like the University of California, these costs totaled $1,194. And these figures don't include all the personal costs that living away from home entails.

Before throwing up your hands in frustration, however, consider this: there is a total of $9 billion available annually for student aid, which in 1981 was distributed to 6.1 million people. Literally hundreds of sources exist for this financial assistance, ranging from corporate grants to government loans.

It is true that, as of this writing, the Reagan administration is seeking to limit or even eliminate certain government-supported programs. Such measures are particularly tragic at a time when tuition costs are rising faster than inflation. But although the doors to student aid are no longer as wide open as they have been, money is still available for those who are willing to pursue it.

Whether you are a student yourself, or the parent of a college-age child, you might be surprised by the many financial-aid programs still available. In the following pages I'll describe the most important types of available loans and grants and the student-aid plans with which you should be familiar, and I'll explain how you can participate in those plans.

WHO QUALIFIES

Perhaps the single most important point to keep in mind is that college funds are available to all kinds of people, not just the poor. Most programs are open to the middle and upper-middle classes, too. Until 1978, federal programs had family-income limits of $25,000. At that time, however, Congress _raised_ the income ceiling to $40,000, thus allowing many thousands of additional students to qualify. Today, the single most common error that keeps people from getting a slice of the multibillion-dollar pie is _not_ applying for funds.

WHEN TO APPLY

If you'll be needing some financial help, be sure to begin the application process early, immediately after you or your child has been officially accepted in college. If you wait until school starts in September to apply for student aid, you may find the financial coffers empty. Funds are typically allocated on a first-come-first-served basis, so it's wise to start the financial-aid wheels in motion as early as possible. Contact the financial-aid office at the school you or your child will be attending for information and an application form. Unfortunately, most people treat these applications like tax returns, waiting and postponing, not sending them back until the last hour. Make it a point to be early on this one.

If you are applying for a scholarship that requires Scholastic Aptitude Test scores, schedule your SAT testing date early. Make all the necessary preparations for smooth processing of the papers.

THE MOST IMPORTANT CONTACT

They key person who will assist you in getting the money you deserve and for which you qualify is the financial-aid officer at the college or university you or your child will be entering. He or she should be up-to-date on the various federal, state, and private programs that can make or break your financial link to college.

The financial-aid officer is typically highly motivated to help students get as much funding as possible, since in many cases students can't attend college without such financial assistance. They are on your team, working to ensure that you can afford your education. Even so, the quality and capability of financial-aid officers vary, and thus it is important for you to know the basics of the various available programs. You should have your own informed overview, so that you will be able to double-check as you go along. A recent Carnegie study, for example, found that only 22 percent of entering students were told of _all_ the programs for which they could qualify. So it pays to know the basic structure of the programs if you need to prod the financial officer along.

In most cases, though, the financial-aid officer is an excellent, in fact your best, ally. To give you an example of how he or she can help you, I'll describe, step by step, the process that you might go through.

After receiving notification that you or your child has been accepted at a particular college, you would immediately contact that school's financial-aid officer (FAO). In your first meeting, you will be given information packets and forms to complete. Often, these forms request copies of your family's tax returns from recent years.

Once you fill out the forms and return them to the FAO, they are sent to one of several "scoring" centers around the country. There, they are evaluated to determine the amount of money for which you are eligible, based on income and other factors. Three to four weeks later, when the processing is completed, the evaluated forms are returned to the FAO, who then works on matching you to the appropriate grant or loan program.

COMMITMENT TO REPAY

As you consider the loans and grants to which you may have access, you should approach this loan commitment as seriously as you would any other and promise yourself that you'll repay all the money you succeed in borrowing. Grants are, on the other hand, outright gifts, and thus repayment is not expected. But student loans are money that is advanced to you and must be returned according to an agreed-upon payment schedule. Whether you are a parent or a student, most student loan programs are available at extremely low cost and frankly, to anyone who attended college even twenty years ago, a luxury rate. If you take out a loan of this kind, it is important to repay it, no matter how long it takes.

In fact, these days many students take a cavalier attitude toward their loans. At one time during the 1970s, nearly 10 percent of student loans were defaulted or were made part of personal bankruptcy proceedings. Such actions, however, are duly noted on credit reports, which will be examined the next time you apply for any kind of loan or seek a home mortgage.

If you find yourself in a serious cash crunch, arrange a repayment plan with your college or bank—say, $5 or $10 per month. Any amount will demonstrate that you are earnest in your desire to pay off the loan.

STUDENT LOANS

"Student loans may be the cheapest money around today," one amazed parent told me. She was not far off. The student-loan program, much in the news because of defaults and bankruptcies on the part of former students, is still alive and functioning and continues as an important source of college funds.

There are basically two types of federal loan programs—one processed by the colleges, the other primarily by local banks.

NATIONAL DIRECT STUDENT LOANS

The college-administered program, called National Direct Student Loans (NDSL), is available for both undergraduate and graduate students. The terms of NDSL loans are superb—no interest until graduation, even if you're only a half-time student. Upon graduation (or departure from school), the interest starts accumulating, but at only a 5 percent yearly rate. Repayment must begin six months after you graduate (or drop below half-time status), and you usually have up to ten years to repay. The amount of your monthly payments depends on how much you borrowed, but it will be at least $30 per month.

Under the NDSL loan program, the amount you can borrow depends on your particular circumstances. For example, you can borrow up to $3,000 if you're enrolled in a vocational program, or if you've finished two years of your schooling aimed toward a bachelor's degree and are presently in your third year. This total includes any amount you borrowed under NDSL during the first two years of your college education.

For graduate or professional education, you can borrow a total of $12,000, which includes any amount you borrowed under NDSL for your undergraduate education.

Contact your college's financial-aid officer for more information about NDSLs.

GUARANTEED STUDENT LOANS

The Guaranteed Student Loan (GSL) program requires that you complete a loan-application form, not at school but at a bank, credit union, or savings-and-loan association. The application must then also be signed and approved by your college's financial-aid officer, to verify that you are indeed a student.

You can apply for any amount of money up to the limits described below, and as of 1982, the interest rate for new loans was 9 percent, set by federal law. (The federal government or a government agency in your state guarantees these loans.)

If you're an undergraduate, you can borrow up to $2,500 a year with a GSL, but no more than a total of $12,500 during your undergraduate college career. If you're a graduate student, $5,000 a year is the ceiling, but your total loan, including any loans made at the undergraduate level, cannot exceed $25,000.

GSL loans also require an origination fee of 5 percent of the amount you borrow, which is deducted from the amount of the loan. So if you borrow $2,500, a fee of $125 will be deducted to help the government finance these low-cost loans. Thus, you will actually receive only $2,375, but you will pay interest on the full $2,500.

In general, you qualify for GSLs when your family's adjusted gross income (salary plus interest and dividends) is less than $30,000 a year. However, exceptions are occasionally made for families with more than a $30,000 adjusted gross income if the student can claim extenuating circumstances that make a loan necessary. In such cases a need-analysis form must be filled out.

The GSL program is not an open window for money. Because it involves a bank loan, albeit a very-low-interest one, the loan application must still go through the same channels—including credit checks—as any other kind of loan application and be reviewed by college and government officials. In certain cases, students are also asked to put up collateral for the loan. Filling out several sets of forms and waiting for the requisite responses takes a considerable amount of time; these loans cannot be obtained overnight. They usually require four to six weeks to be fully processed.

Repayment of GSL loans begins six months after you leave school, and you usually have at least five years to repay, sometimes as long as ten. The minimum monthly payment is $50.

PLUS LOANS

In addition to the government-backed loans discussed above, PLUS loans are available to an undergraduate student's *parents*. They may borrow up to $3,000 for their child under this plan. Once the student enters graduate school, he or she can apply for one of these same loans on their own, also for up to $3,000.

Apply for PLUS loans at a bank, credit union, or savings-and-loan association that participates in the program. As of 1982, the interest rate on these loans was 14 percent, and repayment could be spread out over ten years. There is no need requirement for a PLUS loan, and no family-income restrictions.

PLUS loans, however, are not available from every bank, credit union, or savings-and-loan association. In fact, few but the largest can afford to lend money at 5 percent when the going rate of regular loans may be three times as high. Banks that participate in the program do so as a community service. To find the banks in your area that offer them, telephone several local banks or check with your FAO.

LOANS FOR PRECOLLEGE EDUCATION

Even *before* college, some families need financial assistance for children who attend private prep schools. Tuition and board at these schools is now soaring as high as $8,000 a year. Fortunately, loans are now being offered by 120 of the 800 members of the National Association of Independent Schools, a Philadelphia-based organization. The typical interest rate is 5 percent; interest payments begin after graduation, but payments on principal don't start until after the student leaves college. The average loan is about $650, with a ceiling of about $2,000. The pay-back period is normally eight years.

FINDING A LOAN ON YOUR OWN

Many students seek educational loans on their own, *without* any government guarantee behind them. But they rarely find such attractive terms this way.

Loans from conventional financial sources have high interest rates, the repayment duration is six to eight years, and the payments begin within a month of the time you receive your money.

Educational loans may also be available from your church or synagogue, your employer, your labor union, and/or your club (Kiwanis, Rotary, and so on). Loans of this type are usually low-cost; repayment doesn't begin until after you leave school; and payments may be spread out over as long as ten years. Your financial-aid officer can tell you what private loans are currently available in your area and how to apply for them.

COLLEGE GRANTS

Each year, thousands of students have their college education supported by one of the nation's grant programs. Once again, keep in mind that this type of financial assistance does *not* have to be repaid. Here is a description of the various grant opportunities now available:

PELL GRANTS

The federal government administers the Pell Grants program, also sometimes called the Basic Educational Opportunity Grant (BEOG) program. It is the country's largest financial-aid plan, for use at any accredited college, university, nursing school, or vocational school. One million undergraduate students a year qualify for these grants; application forms are available from high-school counselors or college financial-aid officers.

Students in families with incomes of up to $25,000 a year have received Pell Grants, but the eligibility standards are complex. The computer determines eligibility on the basis of a "needs-analysis formula" which takes into consideration such factors as family size, the number of children in college, discretionary income, assets, and the cost of education at your particular school. Should you be eligible, the needs-analysis formula determines exactly how much you will get. You will receive this information in a Basic Educational Opportunity Grant Student Eligibility Report (BEOGSER), which comes to you in the mail after you've submitted the application forms.

About 80 percent of these funds go to families with incomes of less than $12,000 a year. In this program, the lower your family income, the better your chances of getting a grant. The average Pell Grant in the 1981–82 academic year was for $901; the _maximum_ grant for 1982–83 was set at $1,670.

SUPPLEMENTAL EDUCATIONAL OPPORTUNITY GRANTS

Other aid for undergraduates is offered by the federal government in the form of Supplemental Educational Opportunity Grants (SEOGs). They are intended for particularly needy students; you can qualify for them when your family can contribute less than half of the total cost of your college education. The less their ability to contribute, the better your chances of obtaining a grant.

In the SEOG program, the college itself, rather than the government, is the decision maker, determining who will and won't receive funding. Grants can be as high as $2,000 a year and are typically matched by additional funds provided by the college's own sources. Contact your school's financial-aid officer for more information.

STATE STUDENT INCENTIVE GRANTS

Since the early 1970s, State Student Incentive Grants have become an increasingly significant source of student funds. Requirements for SSIGs vary from state to state, as do the application forms. In New York State, families must have an annual income of less than $25,000 to qualify, and the maximum grant is $2,500 a year. In most other states the ceiling on the size of the grants tends to be less.

For requirements and award maximums in your state, as well as application forms, check with your high school counselor or your college's financial-aid officer.

SOCIAL SECURITY BENEFITS

If you are a student and have a non-working disabled parent, or one who is retired or deceased—and who is covered by Social Security—you may be eligible for a monthly educational grant. To qualify, you must be eighteen through twenty-one years old and a full-time student. Exactly how much you will receive depends on a Social Security Administration formula. Check with your nearest Social Security office.

SCHOLARSHIPS

There are hundreds of other "free money" sources—namely, scholarships. Many are awarded on the basis of need, but others are based on outstanding personal qualities, such as academic merit, proficiency in a sport, artistic or musical ability, and so on. Scholarships are offered by institutions of higher education; by local organizations such as corporations, civic clubs, churches, and synagogues; by the National Merit Scholarship Corporation; by the National Negro Achievement

Scholarship; by the Jaycees and the American Association of University Women; and by many other groups. For a list of available scholarships, eligibility requirements, and dollars awarded, see your high school counselor or your college's financial-aid officer.

Some commercial firms will help you search for a scholarship as well, including Scholarship Service (New York City), Student College Aid (Houston), and National Scholarship Research Service (San Rafael, CA). But even though their fees are modest, you may do just as well with the free assistance of the available school personnel.

VETERANS ASSISTANCE

Another important source for "scholarships" should be mentioned. If you were on active duty in the U.S. military between February 1955 and January 1, 1977, you are automatically eligible for the GI Bill, which offers educational aid as well as many other benefits. Under this law, you will receive a monthly stipend for up to forty-five months. For details, check with your local VA office, or write: Veterans Administration, 810 Vermont Avenue, N.W., Washington, DC 20402.

For men and women who entered the military after January 1, 1977, a separate program is available, called the Veterans Education Assistance plan. Under its provisions, you can have a certain amount of money deducted from your military paycheck each month and placed in a special education fund. Once you leave the service and enter college, the government will give you $2 for every $1 you put into the account. The Veterans Administration can supply you with more information.

Despite federal budget cuts and other current economic uncertainties, the dream of a higher education for most American youth is far from fading. There's still plenty of money out there—and golden opportunities for getting your share of it. On the basis of the guidelines in this chapter, plan your educational fund-raising strategy _now_. If you find there's still a fiscal shortfall, raise the dollars you need with some of the other money-getting methods described in this book. The big advantage of being a money pro is that you can always raise money for anything—and that includes schooling.

Education is an investment in the future—and one of the best investments you can make for yourself and your children. It is well worth your while to explore all your financing options and to take advantage of the ones that can work best for you.

CHAPTER 11

WHERE THE GRANT MONEY IS AND HOW TO GET IT

Andy Lipkis is an idealist who turned his dreams into reality. Concerned with the deteriorating state of the environment and how to improve it, Lipkis founded a nonprofit enterprise in 1975 called the Tree People. The organization is devoted to planting smog-resistant trees in California's forests and urban areas, as well as conducting educational classes on the environment.

One of the first things Lipkis thought of when he conceived the initial plan for the Tree People was that the organization would be an excellent candidate for grant money. After all, its activities would ultimately save taxpayers and local fire departments millions of dollars and man-hours by replanting saplings.

Lipkis decided to make his funding needs known in a roundabout fashion, by alerting the news media to his financing requirements, in hopes that the publicity would act as a catalyst. His approach worked. Today his organization is funded through a combination of money from private corporations, the Environmental Educational Fund, the California Division of Forestry, and private donations.

Grants are regularly obtained for a wide variety of projects, from cancer research and civil-rights promotion to television shows, sculpting, and growing soybeans. Magazines have been launched with grants, as have projects that investigate the future of multinational corporations and the fate of women in military academies. Last year alone, 1,400 government agencies dispensed more than $80 billion in grants, and more than 30,000 private, corporate, foundation, and community sources contributed another $60 billion.

In the following pages you will learn about the world of grants—what types of projects are most likely to be funded, how to find potential grant dollars with one phone call, and how to increase your chances of obtaining a grant. I'll also highlight the most important factors of a grant proposal—whether you write it yourself or utilize a professional grants writer. And you will learn about the key sources of additional grant assistance and information.

WHAT IS A GRANT?

In essence, grants are monies made available by the government, private foundations, and corporations, in exchange for your contractual agreement to carry out projects that are generally considered to be in the public interest and for the public good. Since the WPA programs of the Depression era, the lion's share of grant money has been channeled to state or local governments and private nonprofit organizations. Even so, some grants are available to private parties. Individual grants from the National Science Foundation, the National Endowment for the Arts, and the National Endowment for the Humanities presently account collectively for about 2 percent of the total federal budget for grants.

Corporate and foundation philanthropy is most often directed toward groups and organizations. But the doors are not closed to you as an individual—if you have a good project and excellent credentials.

GRANT-GETTING—HOW TO PLAY
AND WIN THE GAME

Many people and organizations have taken a stab at grant-getting, but the failure rate is dismally high—about 95 percent of all applications are rejected. The primary reason for this high refusal rate is the fierce competition for the grant dollar. When you apply, you, as individual, are vying against nonprofit groups and

state agencies, as well as some corporations that have
full-time grants people on staff. With such sophisticated
competition you need to be very well equipped in the ri-
valry for money. If you are thoroughly prepared, your
chances improve significantly.

THE CREDIBILITY FACTOR

I recently asked Norton Kiritz, executive director of the Grantsmanship Center in Los Angeles, what
he felt was the most important factor in winning a grant.
His answer: credibility. The money is there, but before
foundations or government agencies will grant it to you,
Kiritz says, they want to make sure that you or your organization has a history of proven achievement, that you
are committed to your endeavor (with or without a
grant), and that you have staying power.

According to Kiritz, a lot of naive people have
the illusion that there are huge quantities of grant
money out there just waiting for the right, bright idea.
But it doesn't work that way. In fact, getting grant
money is every bit as difficult as raising venture capital.

Thus, some of the best advice I can offer is that
you be willing to "pay your dues." The more time you
put into building a solid reputation and track record in
your field of endeavor before applying, the better your
chances of succeeding at grantsmanship. The grant-giving agency must be convinced that you have the experience and the know-how to implement your project
successfully.

MOTIVATIONS FOR GIVING

The list of potential grant donors seems almost
endless. Oil companies, one of the largest and most prof-

itable of U.S. industries, have become significant grant-givers in recent years, their money going to local community-service organizations, colleges and universities, and the arts. Other corporations—from Xerox to American Honda—have not only given both large and small grants to fund specific projects completely, but have made smaller token contributions that recipients have been able to channel into areas of their own choosing.

Norton Kiritz recently confirmed my understanding of why so much money is granted. He said that for corporations and foundations, the motivation is threefold: grant-giving results in a genuine feeling of fulfilling social responsibility, it provides a tax advantage, and it is an excellent public-relations tool. The IRS, for example, allows corporations to donate up to 10 percent of their pretax income for good causes. If they don't give away that 10 percent, it is taxable, and much of it will have to go to Uncle Sam. Despite this specific motivation, however, corporations give, on the average, only around 1 percent, rather than the allowable 10 percent, largely because some business executives still believe that corporations should not act as philanthropies.

The public-relations benefits of these gifts, however, are enormous and widespread. You've heard TV announcements like "This program has been brought to you by a grant from the Ford Foundation" and similar statements dozens of times if you're a viewer of PBS programs, from "Masterpiece Theatre" to "Sesame Street."

Foundations and corporate offerings, however, are only poor second cousins to the "big daddy" of the grants game: the federal government. Its money is channeled through various federal sources, targeted for research, educational programs, the arts, and the sciences.

The government's motives for giving grants are

clearer. First, this is one way the government can take direct financial action to solve problems in the realms of health, welfare, and other social services. In other cases, however, the grants arise through old-fashioned politicking. Lobbyists who represent various organizations (educational, private-interest, and so on) pressure individual senators and representatives to help pass funding legislation, and in a sort of back-scratching maneuver the members of Congress often acquiesce.

THE GOLDEN AGE OF GOVERNMENT GRANTS

There is also a long *tradition* of government support in particular areas, including the arts, which began with the nobility of Germany, Austria, and Italy during the nineteenth century, when orchestras and opera companies found support among the leaders of their new nations. Today, France pours between $15 million and $25 million a year into the Paris Opera alone.

In the United States, the "golden age" of grants for artists and writers was in the 1930s under the Works Projects Administration, which gave artists and writers financial support. The artists, for example, were offered a small room in a warehouse as a studio, cheap supplies, a monthly stipend (say $150), and an easel. At the time, some members of Congress complained that the WPA seemed like a dolled-up bread line, but many artists who survived because of government support ultimately became the leaders in American art.

The WPA ended in 1938, but not before it had funded some 11,000 artists. During World War II and the McCarthy era, arts funding declined, only to be revived as part of the "Great Society" of the Johnson administration. Many of those 1960s programs still exist, including the National Endowment for the Arts and the National Endowment for the Humanities, although their funding has been reduced under the Reagan administration.

GRANTS IN OTHER FIELDS

Of course, the arts are not the only areas that receive government attention, but the United States is a relative newcomer in other fields. The Soviet Union, Germany, England, France, and Japan have subsidized their inventors for decades, but this country began inventor-subsidy programs only a few years ago. Japan, which has probably gone farthest with such a program, has provided a variety of incentives over the years to encourage innovation; Japanese cars and electronic products are no doubt the direct results of such support.

In recent years a growing proportion of both government and private funds has been distributed to women's groups and organizations, to support their programs and philosophies. Catalyst, a women's employment and career-development agency, is among the most successful solicitors of funds from corporations and foundations, as are Abused Women's Aid in Crisis, the Coalition for Medical Rights of Women, and the Committee to Defend the Reproductive Rights of Women.

THE BASIC STEPS FOR OBTAINING GRANTS

If you are serious about pursuing a grant for yourself or your organization, I suggest that you adhere to the following guidelines:

1. Examine your institution (or yourself) to de-

termine the type of funds you might qualify for and be most capable of raising. What is your particular sphere of expertise? What projects interest you, in areas in which you already have a proven track record?

2. Conduct a search for possible funding sources from among the 26,000 foundations in the United States and the hundreds of government agencies. Grant consultants are available for such purposes, but they usually charge large fees. Instead, you can turn to resources like the Foundation Center, a nonprofit organization based in New York and San Francisco. The center, which is supported by foundations, maintains libraries around the country and lists all foundations and the grants each offers. For a reasonable fee, the center will even conduct computer searches to identify organizations that can provide funding for a particular area or idea.

If there is no specialized foundation library near you, most public libraries also have lists of foundations. The New York Public Library, for instance, has one heavily used shelf in its reference section that contains lists of grant-giving institutions. Information on government grants can readily be obtained simply by asking the reference librarian.

3. Determine the ideal way to approach the foundation, corporation, or government agency you have in mind. When you solicit any agency, your goal is to *make its staff at least as interested in your proposal as you are in its grant.*

If your background reading is extensive enough, you will probably discover what impresses particular sources most. For example, private foundation executives, such as those from the Ford Foundation, tend to give money to well-known institutions or groups armed with references from people "known to the foundation." In dealing with the government, however, a compelling written application can significantly boost your chances, since government applications are read carefully and graded by outside readers.

4. Be willing to invest time and energy in obtaining the grant you desire. Grant-getting is a serious, time-consuming activity, and you can substantially improve your chances of success by knowing the guidelines that should be followed—and following them.

WRITING FOR DOLLARS

Proposals are to grants what credit applications are to loans: they are an essential element in obtaining funding. If you are interested in being financed by a government agency or foundation, you are certainly battling the odds without a carefully prepared proposal.

Who should write it? When some people are faced with the task of preparing a grant proposal, they instinctively rush to the nearest grant writer or consultant for help. Because of the growing interest in grants, the number of grant consultants has burgeoned in recent years, to a present total of over 10,000 full-time professionals. About 2,500 of them are consultants; the rest are staff members of institutions or government bodies. More than thirty major fund-raising firms now exist in the country; they charge anywhere from $250 to $1,000 a day.

Norton Kiritz of the Grantsmanship Center recommends that even with all this talent available to you, it is still usually preferable—if you're allied with an organization—to do it yourself, by adhering to the guidelines on the following pages. Not only are grant writers expensive, but the entire consulting field, says Kiritz, is full of hustlers and rip-off artists. So, even in the best of circumstances, if you hire a grants proposal writer, you will have to wend your way carefully through a buyer-beware market.

There's one other important point: the skills you need to become a good grant writer are often the same skills required of a good organizational manager. So if you're involved in fund-raising for a nonprofit organization, you (or someone in your organization) should already have the knowledge you need to construct a viable proposal.

If you're an *individual* applying for a grant (without the support of an organization), outside help could prove worthwhile. Not all visual artists, for example, or inventors, would be capable of writing effective grants on their own, or would want to take the time to learn how to do so.

Regardless of who writes your grant proposal, the language should be clear, simple, and to the point. "Too many people think that there's a special grant-writing jargon, a bureaucratese," says Kiritz, "but this is just not so. Language that is unclear and indirect will kill a grant proposal as quickly as anything else."

I believe that the Grantsmanship Center (1031 South Grand, Los Angeles, CA 90015) is your best contact for information about proposal writing. It offers low-cost courses on proposals in many sections of the country. All the elements of a successful grant proposal are also outlined in an excellent forty-seven page booklet, "Program Planning and Proposal Writing," available from the Grantsmanship Center. The following suggestions for the points that all proposals should contain are the highlights of that booklet.

1. *A summary.* Because a brief summary is the first item the reviewing committee will read, it should be carefully and concisely written, covering who you are, what your project is, and what it will cost. The proposal

reviewers at the corporation or foundation will read the summary before anything else, and thus you should make certain that it is as compelling and interesting as possible. In general, it should be no more than two to three paragraphs.

2. *Introduction.* In this section you describe who you are, which will satisfy the committee about your ability to undertake and successfully complete your proposed project. Mention how and when your organization was founded, the past achievements of the group, and who has supported you in the past. You can also include quotes from letters of support from your clients, public officials, or noted individuals in your field.

3. *Problem statement.* Describe the particular problem(s) you plan to research and solve through your project. Document the facts and figures of the problem(s) with statistics and statements from authorities. The problem(s) should have reasonable dimensions— that is, they should be of a scope that can realistically be dealt with.

4. *Program objectives.* Explain what you foresee as the outcome of your program. For example, will it feed poor people or help police departments better understand the reasons for crime? Will it prepare children for various types of learning situations or teach them more confident self-expression? Often you can define your objectives by beginning your statements with phrases like "to increase . . . ," "to decrease . . . ," and "to improve . . ." Also state the time frame within which your objectives will be met.

5. *Methods.* What activities and procedures will you employ to achieve your objectives? Why is the approach you've chosen a particularly rational one? Are these methods well tested, and are the people who work with you experienced? How will your staff be selected?

6. *Evaluation.* Describe how you will evaluate

the success (or failure) of your program. For example, will you seek opinions from professionals in the field or members of the community? If you will use an outside firm or consultant for the evaluation, how much will it cost, and what are the credentials of this source? Will the evaluation be used to improve your program in the future?

7. *Future funding.* Explain how you will continue funding your programs in the years ahead after the grant has run out. If you are asking for funds to establish a particular program, your grant source would logically want to know how the program might be perpetuated in the future. So, will you be able to fund it yourself in the upcoming years? What money-raising efforts do you have in mind for the future, and why are they likely to be successful?

8. *Budget.* What will this project cost—including salaries, supplies, travel, rental of office space and equipment, and telephones? Be as specific as you can, but be aware that the grantor realizes that you are only making estimates. Plan for various contingencies in your budget, such as cost-of-living salary increases.

OTHER SOURCES

I talked recently with Doris Siegal, who described her longtime dream for a "We Care" Club House—a twenty-four-hour center for compulsive overeaters. It sounded to me like an ideal project for grant funding, and I suggested that she try to obtain it.

Seeking this kind of outside funding had never occurred to Doris. Yet grant money is regularly given for drug-addiction, alcohol-recovery, and similar types of programs. In light of what I knew about grants—both federal and private—her idea seemed like a natural.

Doris's first question was how to find possible sources for funds. I referred her to the Grantsmanship Center in Los Angeles and then suggested that she read the following books, many of which are available at public libraries. They should be helpful to you as well.

About Foundations: How to Find the Facts You Need to Get a Grant. This is a simple, step-by-step guide to the research process for finding a grantor. You can order it from the Foundation Center, 888 Seventh Avenue, New York, NY 10019.

Catalog of Federal Domestic Assistance. This is a must for seekers of federal funds—a comprehensive guide to whom to contact and how to go about getting U.S. grants. You can get price information and order it from the Superintendent of Documents, U.S. Government Printing Office, Washington, DC 20402.

The Corporate Foundation Directory. Listed in this directory are corporate foundations and officials, indexed by state, field of interest, and types of grants offered. Order it from Taft Corporation, 1000 Vermont Avenue, N.W., Washington, DC 20005.

The Foundation Center National Data Book, Volume One and Volume Two. These volumes contain material on thousands of smaller foundations not listed in *The Foundation Directory.* You can order it from the Foundation Center, 888 Seventh Avenue, New York, NY 10019. Price: $40.

The Foundation Directory. This guide contains 2,818 entries on foundations that contribute about 80 percent of all private grants in the United States. It is available from Columbia University Press, 136 South Broadway, Irvington, NY 10533. Price: $36.

Foundation Grants to Individuals. If you decide to go it alone, this is your bible. It's a specialized directory of about 1,000 foundations that have awarded as much as $96 million to over 40,000 individuals. You can order it from the Foundation Center, 888 Seventh Avenue, New York, NY 10019. Price: $15.

Researching Foundations: How to Identify Those That May Support Your Organization—Part I and Part II. This directory is available from the Grantsmanship Center, 1031 South Grand Avenue, Los Angeles, CA 90015. Price: $1.55 per part.

Grant money can be gotten if your project is worthwhile, and if you or your organization is equipped to carry it out. If you're involved with a top-notch non-profit program or are an artist, inventor, scientist, or writer, it is well worth your while to take a closer look at the world of grants. You may find a viable source of funds to make your valuable dream a reality—just as Andy Lipkis did. Although, as this book goes to press, Congress is debating the amounts of government monies that will be available for grant-giving, funds are still accessible. Following the guidelines in this chapter will increase your chances of getting some of it.

SOURCES AND STRATEGIES FOR OBTAINING BUSINESS CASH

The American entrepreneurial spirit is still strong and growing stronger. Even in hard times, increasing numbers of people are deciding they want more out of life than a paycheck at the end of the week and a pension program that may materialize one day. But too often the dream remains a dream when cash can't be found to turn it into reality.

Even if you begin working nights on your dining-room table (the starting place for more good ideas and companies than you might imagine), it takes some initial capital for such basics as stationery supplies and the telephone; if you want to manufacture a product, you'll need to finance equipment, shipping, and, of course, personnel. You'll also need to be able to pay your own salary to keep yourself afloat during those first crucial and challenging eighteen months of getting established.

If you are already one of America's 13 million small-business owners, you probably learned long ago that even a profitable business does not necessarily put hard cash into your pocket in its initial stages. Contrary to popular belief, the more successful your company becomes, the more cash you need to support its growth and continued success.

It becomes a bit of a Catch-22. You would think that as your business flourishes, you should become less dependent on outside financing sources. Yet most small-business people quickly learn that success and growth cost money—money for expansion, personnel, facilities, inventory, and equipment. So, whether you're starting out or the owner of a seasoned, mature company, you'll discover that a continuing supply of outside financing is often necessary.

When I was a partner in a small manufacturing firm, we used several different financing methods, relying primarily on bank loans and receivables financing. In the following pages you will learn how to use these financing techniques and several others. You'll learn about the private and government sources for business cash. And I will introduce you to the business plan that I have developed and tested, a crucial element in obtaining business financing.

GETTING YOUR BUSINESS BACKING FROM THE PRIVATE SECTOR

There are four major nongovernment loan sources for small businesses: commercial banks, investment banks, growth-capital companies, and venture-capital companies. "Factors," financial companies that purchase your accounts receivable, are a fifth source. Though they're not resorted to quite as frequently as the others, they can prove very helpful.

Here is some basic information about these private-sector sources of business financing.

1. COMMERCIAL BANKS

Known in the financial community simply as banks, these are the primary business-loan source in the nation. They vary in the kinds of financing they offer, in the interest rates charged, in their willingness to accept risks, and in their attitudes toward small businesses. It is your responsibility to first size up each individual bank and decide which are most likely to authorize your loan. You should determine which type of bank financing will best satisfy your needs. Then you must be prepared to present your request in a professional manner.

Many banks have set up venture-capital divisions that enthusiastically pursue good business ideas, particularly those that appear to have potential annual sales of $5 million to $20 million. For example, they are at present keenly interested in the high-technology fields of medicine and electronic products such as semiconductors, but they are also intrigued by any new concepts that offer tremendous profit potential.

Sometimes a bank might require that you provide an endorser in order to obtain a loan, particularly if there's a reason to doubt your own credit-worthiness. If you can come up with backing from another company or individual that the bank regards as financially sound, you'll probably get your loan.

An endorser—most commonly one of your suppliers or investors—guarantees your loan in writing, ensuring that if you don't repay the loan, he or she will. For instance, let's assume that you're planning to buy $250,000 worth of widgets from Widgets, Inc., in the next twelve months. But you tell the president of Widgets that you can't get the loan to buy them unless Widgets, Inc., will guarantee it. In order to get the sale, the president may agree to do so.

2. INVESTMENT BANKS

Investment banks service only existing businesses; they are excellent providers of expansion capital. These banks do not make loans but arrange for loans to your company from other sources, such as pension funds and insurance companies. In essence, they are middlemen between firms needing capital and sources for this money. Loans of up to $10 million, payable in monthly installments for as long as fifteen years, are available. Unfortunately, rates are higher than prime, and a 2 percent fee is added.

3. GROWTH-CAPITAL COMPANIES

Growth-capital companies supply hefty amounts of money (from $100,000 to millions of dollars) to small companies that other loan sources have turned down. They generally look for businesses with a pattern of steady growth that can convincingly project a net income of 50 percent above what is required to repay the loan. If a loan is to be repaid in installments of $100,000 per year, for example, a growth-capital firm will generally insist that the projected annual net income of the business be at least 50 percent higher than that, or $150,000. Also, the business must be run by a skilled and trustworthy management team. Three- to five-year loans are available at about six percentage points over commercial-bank rates.

4. VENTURE-CAPITAL COMPANIES

These companies actually buy equity in businesses, unlike growth-capital companies, which merely make loans. The venture capital itself comes from investors such as industry executives, institutions, and wealthy families who are interested in taking risks on new ideas for which they see a profit potential. In return for their money, venture capitalists want "a piece of the action." They usually like to get 50 percent of the business in exchange for providing the initial working capital; additional sums are promised to them when a predetermined milestone has been reached.

In short, a venture capitalist becomes your silent partner, unlike a growth capitalist, who simply loans you money that you must eventually repay. The terms of each deal are different, of course, but it is virtually a definition of the term _venture capitalist_ that these parties become owners along with you and typically want control if you will give it to them. This can be a major emotional hurdle for many entrepreneurs and is something to be considered very seriously. But the participation of the _right_ venture capitalist can prove rewarding and profitable for your business.

5. FACTORS

Factoring companies, or factors, are financial firms that can supply you with operating capital when every other money source turns you down. They are *not* moneylenders; rather, they purchase your accounts receivable (unpaid invoices to your clients). Instead of waiting thirty, sixty, or ninety days to be paid, cash is in your hands the day your invoices go into the mail. Here is how factors function:

Before mailing your invoice to a client, you send it to the factor. If the client is credit-worthy, the factor will advance to you up to 80 percent of the face value of the invoice on the date of invoice. The factor then forwards the invoice to your client, requesting that payment be made to the factor. When payment is received, the factor sends you the remaining 20 percent, less the factoring fee. The drawback is that the fee is large, making this an extremely expensive type of financing.

YOUR BEST FINANCING SOURCES

Which of these sources should you turn to?

Obtaining money from the bank is the traditional way of funding a business, and one of the best. In the uncertain economy of the 1980s, banks have preferred to make loans to businesses that involve tangible property—manufacturing, real estate, and retailing, for example. It is difficult to get a loan for a new service business—say, an advertising agency—but if you can convince the banker that you can repay on time, you can usually get a loan for *any* kind of business. One powerful "convincer" is a flawless record of repaying previous loans, personal as well as business.

Unless you have a strong personal relationship with a given bank, you will need collateral for a business loan. A bank will accept, among other things, machinery, securities, real estate, and cash-value life insurance.

But even the heftiest collateral will not *guarantee* that you will obtain a loan. If your equipment is not profit-producing (typewriters, mimeograph machines, air conditioners, and so on), your loan application could be rejected. And if your credit rating is poor, the bank may still consider you a bad bet.

Even though commercial banks may be your best loan source, the venture-capital route is often worth exploring; using someone else's money to get your business going can be a very intriguing proposition. Sacrificing 50 percent—or even more—of the control (and profits) to the venture capitalists is acceptable to many entrepreneurs; it's often a worthwhile trade-off for an initial—and essential—supply of funding.

I had an opportunity to be on the venture-capital side of the desk several years ago. After a publicly held company that I had co-founded was sold, my partners and I began to search for new ventures in which to invest. We placed an ad in the *Wall Street Journal* to solicit currently operating companies in need of cash and management, and we received an impressive number of responses. My partners and I interviewed and evaluated nearly 250 companies and start-up opportunities. We told all the applicants that in exchange for our working capital, we wanted controlling interest in the firm. In the course of those 250 interviews, the issue of control was the most common stumbling block for both sides. Finally, we found an electronics company that met our criteria and agreed to our terms. We channeled our capital into it and turned it into a moneymaking enterprise.

GETTING YOUR BUSINESS BACKING
FROM UNCLE SAM

In addition to private funding sources, there are five major sources of *government* money for small businesses. One, the Small Business Administration, is well known. The four others may surprise you, however; they are Local Development Corporations, Small Business Investment Companies, Minority Enterprise Small Business Investment Corporation, and the Environmental Protection Agency.

1. THE SMALL BUSINESS ADMINISTRATION (SBA)

Congress established the SBA in 1953 to help small businesses. By SBA definition, a small business doesn't refer only to the carpentry shop you set up in your basement; it also includes certain kinds of firms with up to 1,500 employees and annual sales of up to $22 million.

When you're making your initial plans for going into business, contact your nearest SBA field office. It may be able to provide you with a loan if at least two banks have said "no" to your loan request, and if you meet its other requirements. In any case, you'll receive an answer from the SBA within two weeks of filling out your application.

The Reagan administration has cut deeply into SBA funding, thus making this agency a less reliable loan source than it once was. At its best, the size of the average SBA loan is about $75,000, although guarantees can range as high as $500,000. In most cases, the SBA does not make its loan directly. Instead, the majority of its loans are bank loans which it guarantees.

If you're not able to obtain the full amount you

need from a bank, the SBA may lend you up to $150,000 to make up the deficit. Or the SBA may elect to lend _the bank_ up to $150,000, with the understanding that the bank in turn will lend the money to you. This is known as a participation loan.

Most SBA loans are given for a period of up to ten years. On real property or construction loans the length may be increased to twenty-five years; however, on working-capital loans, the limit is six years. You will find that interest on direct loans varies according to a statutory formula (check with your SBA field office), but it's low compared to conventional business loans. Rates on SBA-guaranteed and participation loans are set by the banks within the framework of SBA regulations and differ little from rates on direct SBA loans. I've also found that rates on both direct and indirect SBA loans can vary from state to state.

QUALIFICATIONS FOR AN SBA LOAN

The SBA has specific loan requirements for each business category. Your SBA field office will tell you what those requirements are for your particular business. In general, though, here is what the SBA will look for if the loan is for your first business:

- _A credit rating of 1._
- _Proof of good character._ Testimonial letters from your current and former employers, your account-ant, your clergyman, your lawyer, and so on can be helpful.
- _Proof that you can operate your new busi-ness within your projected budget._ Rely on your accountant to help draw up the budget.
- _Previous business or managerial experi-ence._
- _The ability to invest some of your own money_

in the venture. In 1982 the SBA was looking for a 30 to 40 percent investment by the owner.

• *Reserve capital of your own.* With a reserve you can weather any unforeseen business setback.

• *Proof that you can make monthly repayments out of profits, not capital.* This is the payoff line.

Even if you meet every other requirement, your request is likely to be rejected unless the bank and/or the SBA is convinced that you will repay the loan on time. Have your accountant prepare a realistic cash-flow projection sheet.

SPECIAL SBA LOANS

If there are unique extenuating circumstances surrounding your business-loan needs, ask the SBA if it can help. Special kinds of loans are available under certain unusual conditions. To name just a few:

• If you're in a seasonal industry—toys, for example—and you need working capital to tide you over, the SBA treasury might be able to help with a loan of up to $150,000.

• If your company is fully owned by handicapped people, or if 75 percent of your employees are handicapped, you're entitled to a direct loan from the SBA of $100,000 or a guaranteed loan of up to $350,000.

• Should a government construction project harm your company economically, the SBA will provide you with a low-cost, thirty-year, no-limit loan.

• If your facilities are damaged by a major physical disaster, so designated by the President of the United States, and if you cannot qualify for bank financing, the SBA will come to your rescue with a loan of up to $500,000, with payments at low interest, spread out over thirty years.

2. *LOCAL DEVELOPMENT CORPORATIONS (LDCS)*

These are SBA-sponsored private corporations that help small businesses obtain facilities or capital equipment by means of a unique borrowing-leasing arrangement. Here's how an LDC works:

Let's say that your plant is located in a small community. You need to computerize your assembly line and house the control unit in a new temperature-controlled building. Cost: $450,000. You project profits of 125 percent over the next five years, but the local bank and the SBA field office look at your projection skeptically. They feel Japanese imports could price you out of the market. You're a high-risk investment in their eyes, and they won't back you.

So you go to an LDC. It is composed of local residents and has been set up to create jobs in the community and handle money supply for high-risk ventures. But it does not make loans. Instead, it borrows $450,000 from the SBA and the local bank and uses that money to buy the equipment, computerize your assembly line, and build your new control building. It then *leases* the renovated assembly line and the new building to you.

The SBA and the bank gain because the business (and thus the loan money) has the support and guidance of the LDC. Also, in case of default, the LDC, as owner of both the equipment and the building, can sell them. *You* gain because you get what you need with lease payments, spread over thirty years, which are the equivalent in cost of installment payments on a thirty-year SBA loan. In some cases you can even assume ownership of the equipment after the lease expires.

For information on how you and other business people in your community can form (or contact) an LDC, write the Small Business Administration (addresses on pages 254–258) for details.

3. SMALL BUSINESS INVESTMENT COMPANIES (SBICS)

When both your bank and the SBA have turned you down, and there's no LDC in your community, there may be another excellent loan source to which you can turn. SBICs are privately owned companies licensed by the Small Business Administration, and they include Chase Manhattan Capital (owned by the Chase Manhattan Bank) and Small Business Enterprises (owned by the Bank of America). They will accept high-risk loan requests for up to $7.5 million. Basic conditions for acceptance are a good track record over the preceding five years and a convincing growth projection. SBIC loans run for up to twenty years.

Interest rates are substantially higher than prime (the rate banks charge their preferred corporate customers) but can be lowered through an equity-sharing arrangement. That is, a lower-cost loan may be granted if the SBIC is allowed to buy into your corporation on favorable terms. In essence, it becomes part owner of your company.

You can deal with any of about 250 SBICs in the nation. For an SBIC directory, write National Association of SBICs, Washington Building, Washington, DC 20005. Addresses of SBICs are also listed on pages 258 to 284.

4. MINORITY ENTERPRISE SMALL BUSINESS INVESTMENT CORPORATIONS (MESBICS)

Part of the SBIC program, MESBICs differ from their parent organization in several respects. Loans are granted only to firms that are at least 50 percent owned and managed by members of a minority group. Capital for MESBIC loans does not originate solely from the SBA but is supplemented by contributions from organizations and foundations. You can use MESBIC funds to start a business as well as to maintain one. Interest rates are lower than for SBICs, and loans can be repaid in up to twenty years.

For details on MESBIC loans and the address of the MESBIC nearest you, write Minority Business Department, U.S. Department of Commerce, Washington, DC 20230.

5. THE ENVIRONMENTAL PROTECTION AGENCY (EPA)

The EPA makes loans at lower than prevailing rates for periods of up to thirty years to enable small businesses to meet environmental code requirements without straining their financial resources. For details, write Environmental Protection Agency, East Tower, 401 M Street, N.W., Washington, DC 20460.

Keep in mind that commercial banks and government agencies will not loan money to everyone. Come well prepared for your visit to the bank, the SBA or any other source, and you should be better able to persuade the loan officer that you are equipped to make your business idea succeed.

THE BUSINESS PLAN

More than anything else, a "business plan" will help you to get the loan you need. In fact, it can be your most potent piece of ammunition when you set out to obtain serious money. The amount of expertise and sophistication it reflects can literally make or break your chances of getting the money you require to start up and keep going.

In essence, a business plan is a clear blueprint of the business you have in mind. It will show the money people that you have a firm foundation and strong projections for your venture, and that you have the talent and the knowledge to make your business work. Most important, it will clearly show how you plan to reach your profit objectives. A first-rate business plan, you will find, is invaluable not only in getting funding, but also in proving to yourself and your associates that your company is financially viable and has a strong profit potential.

The best business plans are straightforward documents that spell out the "who, what, where, why, and how much" of your existing or proposed company. The plan can be as detailed as you wish (some run over one hundred pages), but an effective and powerful one need not be more than a dozen pages long.

Your business plan, then, is your primary selling tool, a scenario of what you hope for and believe you can accomplish. It should answer the tough questions that a loan officer will probably ask, such as "What have you got to offer that isn't already available from an established firm?" It should clearly demonstrate that you know the field you are about to enter and that you know how to sell what you produce.

In case you've never seen a business plan, I've included one that I put together for a proposed venture called Informex, Inc., for which I sought to raise $250,000 in financing. The Informex business plan was fourteen typed pages long and the table of contents read as follows:

Summary
The Company's Business
Strategy and Product Line
Marketing
Competition
Authors

Production of Proprietary Programs
Financing Requirements
Management
Advisory Board
Expansion Plans
Financial Forecasts
Earning Forecasts
Cash Forecasts
Balance Sheet Forecast
Source and Application of Funds Forecast

I introduced the plan by explaining that Informex was designed to become "a leading producer of
audio cassettes for the fields of business and finance. . . .
The company plans to create, produce, and distribute
informational, educational, and training cassettes, as
well as to market cassettes produced by other companies. The company projects a profitable posture by
the eighth month of operation with achievable sales increases projected for years two and three."

I then explained that the cassette field promised rapid growth, that the sales of cassettes had leaped
from 5 million in 1966 to an expected 200 million by
1975. (It's always effective to cite relevant statistics;
show that you know the field and have done your homework.) I mentioned that in order to minimize the normal, non-income-producing initial time period of the
operation, Informex had begun negotiations with a cas-
sette-producing firm to distribute some of its tapes. This
would allow Informex to realize substantial sales by the
third month of operation. (It is important, obviously, to
indicate to prospective financial backers that your
young, struggling company will have revenue coming in
as quickly as possible.)

I then listed several subjects on which Informex planned to produce tapes. Among them were business and management topics and several series on women's business opportunities and on self-help for career women who wanted to advance in their fields.

As you can see, the business plan is structured to answer the general questions outsiders are going to ask. Few people ever know companies—particularly start-up firms—the way you know your own.

Since I knew that it was essential to prove that my grasp of the current market for my product was firm, and that I knew how to tap it, I then outlined our marketing plan. Informex would use both direct-mail campaigns and space advertising. "For the business tapes, four-part, direct-mail pieces will be sent to small and middle-sized companies, with less emphasis placed on lists such as the _Fortune_ 500" (_Fortune_ magazine's listing of the 500 largest industrial corporations). Plans for other companies to distribute Informex cassette programs were also cited, with the explanation that "these companies will afford the company a highly trained, professional sales force to market its products."

To provide a complete picture of the field I proposed to enter, I listed some of the leading competitors, including such companies as Time-Life and the Success Motivational Institute.

I then reported that Informex was "in final negotiation for material with an author who, we believe, will bring great versatility to Informex. The author was previously director of personnel training for a leading financial institution. . . . Other authors have been tentatively selected for specific topics, but will not be approached until financing for the company has been concluded." Again, this gave the reader of my business plan a chance to see that I was thinking ahead.

A recording studio in the Los Angeles area was named to produce the master tapes. "We do not anticipate doing our own in-house tape duplication until the fourth month, at which time the volume will warrant the purchase of a cassette duplicator." I further explained the rationale behind this decision. "The price difference between in-house duplication and outside duplication is approximately 90 cents per tape, a savings of 15 percent."

Equally interesting to prospective backers, of course, is the precise way in which the financial management of the projected company will be handled. The Informex plan read: "As the 1972 financial forecasts show, Informex requires capital of $250,000 to realize its program. For this equity investment, the company is prepared to issue 40 percent of its common stock to an investment group. The additional financing required to realize the expansion goals will be supplied from profits earned and bank credit which should be available to the company after its first year of operation.

"The earnings forecast projects an efficient operation run with extreme frugality. Capital expenditures will be minimized at the outset in order to preserve the company's capital."

I then projected the first-year earnings which included a gross margin (the difference between sales and cost of sales) of $102,262. This was offset by $125,541 in expenses, including rent, office supplies, travel, postage, insurance, phone and utilities, salaries, and selling expenses. For the first year of operations, I forecast a net loss of $23,279—a realistic and modest loss.

I then included the following chart, explaining a more optimistic outlook for earnings in the second and third years.

My particular prospectus offered a cheerful picture, yes, but not overly optimistic considering the growth industry I was proposing to enter.

I also included a "balance-sheet forecast," and

	Year Two	Year Three
Net sales	$370,000	$585,000
Cost of sales	144,000	222,000
Gross margin	226,000	363,000
Selling and G & A expenses	178,000	282,000
Net profit before taxes	48,000	81,000
Income taxes	18,000	34,000
Net earnings	**$30,000**	**$47,000**

a "source and application of funds forecast" for the first year of operation.

If you need some help assembling this portion of your business plan, you can get such assistance from an accountant, business consultant, or a professional preparer of business plans.

Finally, the plan was professionally typed and bound in a three-ring binder. It projected a serious, businesslike image.

When your plan is complete, review the list of sources described earlier in this chapter and make a decision about who you will approach first.

PRESENTING YOUR PROPOSAL

When you meet with the money people, keep the conversation to the point. They are interested in hard facts. In the initial get-together, they will also be taking your pulse. Your words, your manner, and your dress will all be weighed, in addition to your project. All the rules of negotiating, presented in the next chapter, apply when you are seeking a business loan.

Keep in mind that red tape, papers, and meetings are part of the money-getting game. To minimize snags along the way, insist on dealing with the highest-level officer in the lending institution—usually a vice-president. Top banking officers often have personal signatory capability, meaning that they can approve your loan personally. If you deal with the lower echelons, additional personnel will be required to obtain approval. The fewer people involved in making decisions, the better.

I have always been intrigued by people who possess the entrepreneurial spirit. If you are determined to launch or expand your own business, this chapter should have encouraged you that money _is_ available for those purposes. I believe that with a strong business plan and a powerful sense of what you want to accomplish in your venture, your chances for success are excellent.

CHAPTER 13

NEGOTIATING FOR
MONEY FOR ALL YOUR
NEEDS

A wise business associate once told me, "Whenever money is involved, so is negotiating." It is a point of view that has served me well, both in my business career and in my personal financial activities.

Since America's earliest days, bargaining has been ingrained in our business tradition. Today, whether you're interested in getting a raise, obtaining a loan, or acquiring venture capital, negotiating is the tool that can link you with the money you need. Without a basic knowledge of negotiating techniques, you can easily become a loser in the money-getting field.

Consider the act of securing a loan, whether it's for a car or to pay medical bills. Negotiating is a part of nearly every aspect of the transaction—from the amount, to the length of the loan, to the payment terms. The more money that's involved, the more vital the need for negotiating knowledge and skills. This is an essential fact of financial life for all borrowing professionals.

If you're one of the many people who have never ventured into the world of money negotiating, you might have picked up the notion that there is something repugnant or even demeaning about negotiating. You might think it is a tactic employed only in the souks of Middle Eastern cities or by street vendors in Latin America. But negotiation is actually involved in almost every area of financial life. It is simply a way to make the most of your opportunities. If you are being interviewed for a new job, for example, you may be able to secure as much as $1,000 a year more than you're initially offered, simply by using sound negotiating techniques and holding your ground at the crunch.

Most of us in fact negotiate every day of our lives, even if we're unaware of it. The way you complete a loan application form is a subtle component of the negotiation process. So is the way you dress for meetings with your banker.

In the following pages I'll present a short course in the fine art of negotiation and the tactics that are a part of it. I have personally used each of them in a wide variety of professional situations.

In this chapter you will learn how to prepare for every negotiation involving money; the basic guidelines of every negotiation, coping with fear and anxiety, the importance of "rehearsal" before the meeting, and the eight "don'ts" of negotiating.

As you read this chapter, select only the strategies that are comfortable and appropriate for you and your situation, keeping in mind your own personality, style, and motivations. Also remember that there are some deals that are right—for both parties—from the beginning and that require _no_ negotiation. Don't bargain just for the sake of bargaining. Sign the documents, and be delighted at how easy it was to arrive at an agreement.

No matter how much negotiation is required, however, all of the suggested guidelines in this chapter are designed with one goal in mind: to help you achieve the best money arrangement possible.

PREPARING FOR NEGOTIATIONS

In a recent "60 Minutes" interview with Bobby Knight, the basketball coach of Indiana University, Morley Safer asked, "What do you consider the most essential part of your team's success?" Knight's response was "The courage to prepare."

The most careful preparation is essential for negotiating success. You _must_ do your homework. Draw up a precise blueprint of what you hope to achieve and what you will accept as an absolute minimum. Commit to memory your objectives, needs, alternative offers, fallback positions, as well as what you must gain and what you can concede. Facts and your command of them are vital; the more secure they are in your mind, the greater ease of manner and presentation you'll bring to the table.

Let's take a relatively simple example. You're interested in buying a house. The asking price is $90,000, but the most money you can raise is $82,000. Get out your pencil and pad and set up two columns. Label the left-hand side *What I want,* the other side *What they want.* At the top of each column, write down the price— theirs and yours—then add other appropriate items in each column. On your side, you may want the seller to pay for the title insurance, for example, and any and all repairs you've determined are needed prior to sale. When you look at the situation from the other side, try to analyze what the seller may want—for example, a quick sale or a large down payment.

Now you can evaluate what you may have to give up for an $8,000 compromise. You or someone you know may be a talented carpenter or electrician, in which case you may be able to make the necessary repairs yourself when you can afford to. Or you may want to pick up the escrow costs, which may amount to only a few hundred dollars. A careful itemized breakdown of these costs—a basic part of doing your homework—will enable you to enter into the negotiations with confidence. The more thorough your command of the issues and details, the better your chances of making a good deal.

GUIDELINES FOR
SUCCESSFUL NEGOTIATING

Here are the twelve essential strategies you should keep in mind during any negotiation:

1. Try to hold the negotiating session on your turf—your office or your home—or, second best, on neutral territory such as a restaurant. You'll feel more comfortable in a familiar environment. You won't always have a choice of sites, but when you do, take it.

2. Establish your credibility. Don't be too tough or drive too hard a bargain; no one wants to work with a sharp operator. Impress the other person with your straightforwardness and honesty.

3. Get concessions from the other side as early as possible. For example, if you're negotiating for a lease, ask the lessor for fresh blacktopping on the driveway or new storm sashes—anything, however small, that might induce him or her to make a concession. It will set a precedent for the rest of the meeting. Ease the other person into the habit of saying "yes" by opening with a proposal that is easy to comply with.

4. Early in the discussion, ask questions to which you already know the answers, without being too obvious about your prior knowledge. If the other person corroborates your information, good. If not, you've learned that he or she is either misinformed or is not leveling with you. If that happens, you will need to proceed with caution.

5. Ask for more than you can realistically expect to get. This common negotiating tool leaves you room for maneuvering, for advancing alternatives or counterproposals, and for establishing a fallback position. As a real-estate broker recently told me, "We al-

ways put the house on the 'high side,' knowing that the buyer will want to negotiate."

6. As the bargaining proceeds, make it a give-and-take session. Give the other side some small victories; put up only a token fight on certain minor points. It is best to have a list of issues that are vital to you, as well as a second list of items of virtually no concern. For example, if you're negotiating to buy a house, your primary objectives are getting the house you want, with monthly payments you can afford, at an overall cost within your means. Your "important" list, then, would include these three factors, plus perhaps a new roof, new plumbing, and termite inspection. You have determined that these last points are important because of their cost. But perhaps you're not very concerned about the length of escrow (the arrangement by which the buyer's money is transferred to the seller) and are willing to compromise on this item. And you've determined that you could make your own arrangements for certain necessary repairs. Always leave the other person some room for maneuvering. An inflexible stance can destroy any chance for the compromise that is the essence of any negotiation.

7. Keep the other person's likely psychological motivations in mind. They can often be more important—and decisive—than monetary issues. When someone sells a house, for example, he or she may want more than just attaining top dollar. It may also be important to sell to a sound, reputable family, perhaps because that will make the neighbors happy.

My friend Richard Whittey, a specialist in small businesses, recently told me the story of two partners who were selling their business "for personal reasons." Richard was interested in buying the business and sensed severe tension between the current owners, apparently because of long-term differences over how the business should be run.

After several hours of talks on three different occasions, Richard rather quietly offered $1 million in cash, rather than the $5 million over a three-year period they were asking. Everyone in the room—the lawyers on both sides as well as the two partners—was shocked. But two days later, Richard received a call from one of the partners; they accepted the deal with only a few minor changes.

I asked Richard what prompted him to make such a relatively low offer. His answer was interesting. First, he felt that the partners' asking price was exorbitantly high; second, he knew the cash offer would allow the partners to "cash out" quickly and go their separate ways. Because they had been feuding for months, they decided it was worthwhile to accept the cash right away, even though it was less than they wanted from the longer-term arrangement, and sever their partnership without further delay. Emotional motivations had played an important role in settling the agreement satisfactorily for all involved.

8. Be willing to listen after presenting your viewpoints. Have a list of questions that you need answered, and _listen_ carefully to the responses. Really grasping the other person's point of view can give you the essential key to closing the deal successfully.

Recently, a schoolteacher I know named Michelle Thompson was househunting and, after a thoroughly exhausting three-month search, found _the_ house. In two conversations with the seller, Michelle learned that he was quite eager to close the deal. Consequently, based on what she had learned by doing some careful listening, she decided to propose a smaller down payment, which he eagerly accepted because he was eager to do whatever was necessary to make the deal quickly.

Jackie Lindbergh, a public-relations specialist, underwent quite a different negotiating experience while in the market for a condominium. The owner selling the condo she selected was pleasant, but tough. After two frustrating weeks of telephone calls, Jackie asked, trying to control her exasperation, "Are you honestly interested in selling your condo?" He then claimed that he was and subsequently became a bit more cooperative. Several days—and several more phone calls—later, the deal was finally concluded and the papers were signed, but Jackie was still livid over the way the negotiations had proceeded. She had been in a hurry but the other party hadn't been; she had wanted to buy but he hadn't always seemed sure that he wanted to sell. It had become obvious that he was more interested in the negotiating game than in making the deal.

Watch out for game players. They may take a toll not only on your finances but, more important, on your time and energy. When negotiations drag beyond what seems to you a reasonable time period, step back from the situation, determine as clearly as you can what the other party is aiming for, and take time out to reevaluate your strategy.

9. If possible, always have an associate present during negotiations, particularly if his or her presence is relevant to your business and/or the negotiations themselves. (Obviously, some negotiations are conducted by phone, and others are best conducted one to one.) If your associate cannot make the meeting for any reason, postpone it. Having at least one associate with you can double your negotiating strength and your persuasive power.

This ally can help you in many ways, from observing the "body language" of the opposition to taking notes to simply offering a different viewpoint. Books have been written on the subject of detecting, through physical signs and movement, what someone else is thinking. The crossing of arms or the locking of fingers, a jiggling foot, and scores of other twitches and gestures have their significance for the experienced observer. You and your associate can function as a team, one of you watching while the other concentrates on talking. In fact, you might find it helpful in certain situations to bring along more than one associate. But I suggest that whatever kind of negotiation you're involved in, you officially appoint one person on your side to head the negotiations, perhaps even yourself. It's all too easy to find yourself in the middle of a game with no quarterback; your leader should be charged with the ultimate responsibility of successfully closing the deal.

10. You must clearly understand—and make the most of—*all* your options. If the seller turns down your lower offer because he or she is firm on the price, make sure you leave the door open, concluding your meeting on a pleasant note. "Thanks, we really like the house, but that's really our limit; should your situation change, call us" would be a reasonable exit line; it gives the other person plenty of room to reopen with a counteroffer. Then take the time to analyze where the real problem in the negotiation lay. Was it the monthly payment you wouldn't be able to make? Or is it the down payment? Or are you placing too much emphasis on the overall amount? Always keep in mind that there are plenty of other houses available and there is another one out there that is just right for you. Keeping this in mind will help you to avoid the trap of *forcing* yourself to make a deal, even if it's not advantageous for you.

11. When a basic agreement has been established, put it in writing, even if it's not the ultimate, refined version. Getting *something* in writing effects an immediate commitment. Handwriting is perfectly valid, but both parties should sign immediately. Many an agreement has broken down because of second thoughts while the parties waited for neatly typed copies. Take it upon yourself to pin the deal down—in writing—when *you're* ready.

12. Once an agreement has been reached, stop the meeting, stop selling, and stop talking. You already have what you want. Don't risk fouling things up. As salespeople have learned, to their sorrow, many a deal can sour after it's been made, simply because both parties talked on and on. So when the papers have been signed, don't try to make the other person a lifelong friend, or offer an invitation to lunch or out for drinks.

CONFRONTING AND CONQUERING YOUR FEARS

Some people discover in the course of the negotiation process that their biggest problem is flat-out fear, which can easily overshadow the real issues of the deal.

Harold Schulman, an insurance salesman I know, recently took out a personal loan to finance a car purchase. Almost immediately after signing the loan agreement, he felt himself suffering from "buyer's remorse"—or the "what-have-I-done" syndrome. Knowing that "negotiation anxiety" is normal and to be expected did not immediately cure him of it, but by using a pad and pencil to list his fears, he helped put them in proper perspective. He wrote the following:

My fears about this deal are:
1. Am I paying too much?
2. What if the car turns out to be a lemon?
3. Will I qualify for the loan?
4. Is the interest rate too high?
5. Is the upkeep of this car going to be too expensive?
6. How will I keep up the payments if I lose my job?
7. What if the whole thing is a mistake?

Clearly identifying your fears *before* entering any negotiation can make the difference between devoting your energies effectively to making the deal and unwittingly expending them in breaking up the deal. If you feel confused and uncertain without fully understanding why, you might hold back and disagree at every new turn in the negotiation. You might fundamentally know what you want, but because of emotional and often irrational factors, you could form an invisible but powerful roadblock to your true goals.

First confront your fears, assess whether they're valid, and equip yourself to counter them with strong, positive action. Do some research about the problems that bother you, and try to ease your fears by getting the facts. Don't allow your fears to control you; instead, challenge them and counterbalance them with your own *rational* arguments.

ADAPTING TO CHANGING CONDITIONS

Occasionally I have negotiated with very successful folks who initially held the advantages in the bargaining and then began foot-dragging. In essence, they have said, "If you want it, I'm here." If you perceive that you're facing adversaries with this attitude, you should proceed with caution; you need not necessarily back out altogether.

If you choose to stay in the game, try to even things out when you actually get to executing the contract. You might arrange a face-to-face talk with your adversary at contract time and say, "Look, we can make the deal, but as I see it, this one point is now standing in our way." Delicately persuade the other party to agree to a reasonable midddle ground or solution.

Keep in mind that it's usually foolish to take extreme positions in any negotiation, unless you are adept at the spectacular. Be reasonable, but remember to keep your goals clearly in mind at all times.

REHEARSING THE NEGOTIATION

Some people find it helpful to rehearse the drama of negotiation. You should work up a scenario, starting with your give-and-get list, and anticipate questions and requests that will come up at the meeting.

I use this "anticipate-the-question" approach even when I'm giving a speech. It helps me feel more comfortable and offers me the opportunity to prepare my responses. It also reveals areas where I need to brush up. I find this approach extremely effective—whether I'm negotiating a publishing or television contract or a business deal.

Before the crucial meeting, I make sure to provide for myself some quiet time alone, imagining all the players in the room and their individual motivations (as well as my own, of course). I then imagine what questions both sides are likely to ask during the meeting, and I'll mentally summarize the points I want to make. with this picture of the proceedings in mind, I consult with my negotiating teammates (agent, banker) to develop our mutual strategy.

The scenario that you envision should help you to formulate a game plan that includes introductory gambits, counterproposals, crucial arguments, and a final position. If you don't, you'll be like an actor who hasn't learned his lines—and you'll feel every bit as foolish.

Actual role-playing can be an effective way to prepare for a big meeting. Days before you enter into an actual negotiation you can put yourself through intellectual and emotional conditioning by having an associate play the part of your adversary, in as hard-headed a manner as the real person might at the bargaining table. This can psych you up for the sessions, and it builds confidence to be psychologically honed for the forthcoming big game.

In a sense, negotiating is a form of theater; a certain amount of thespian ability can be a great asset. Maintaining a poker face, for example, can be a very useful technique. If you pretend disinterest in an adversary's proposal while you cite possible alternatives, you may give yourself an advantage. The other person may feel in a position of having to sell you—even if secretly you are quite willing to be sold on the proposition.

One of the most effective bargaining weapons is silence. Nothing unnerves an adversary as much as an impassive, inscrutable, unresponsive exterior. I'm not suggesting, however, that you play _Shōgun_ or behave rudely. But just realize that you don't have to respond to every comment; listening carefully can always help you to assess your adversary's motives and tactics.

You may have to school yourself rigorously. A highly successful agent recently told me about a very poor deal she made early in her career because, in the face of her adversary's stolid silence and because of her own nervousness, she gave away too much. "Through experience," she related, "I've learned that people wouldn't be talking to you at all if they didn't feel *you* had something valuable to offer." So, don't undervalue yourself, no matter whom you are dealing with. It's an easy and self-defeating trap; prepare yourself thoroughly so that you can deal from a position of self-confidence.

A display of controlled anger can also be effective if it is justifiable and used in circumstances with people who might be impressed by it. Let's say that you are truly annoyed because the deal is becoming overly complicated or taking longer to settle than was originally agreed to. In such cases, don't hesitate to let the other party know.

An entrepreneur I know named Steven Dodson once became completely frustrated in the midst of negotiations with a potential investor in his business. The other party was seemingly dragging his feet and made constant use of go-betweens, including two lawyers. After a full month of negotiating, without much forward movement, Steven simply said, "You know, I'm really tired and angry about the time this is taking. Let's either have one meeting with all the parties here at five this afternoon or forget the whole thing." Steven was angry and wasn't afraid to let it be known, politely but firmly. As a result of his controlled straightforwardness, everyone met and pounded out the deal that afternoon. The investment was made in Steven's business, which began to thrive—largely because he was willing to let his exasperation show at a crucial point in the negotiations.

In another incident, my friend Cheryl Serano, a flower-shop owner, was guilty of foot-dragging on a $30,000 bank loan for which she had applied to expand

and remodel her store. She finally realized that her own apprehensions about the deal were prompting her to delay the paperwork that she knew was necessary to get the loan approved. She finally became angry at herself, got the papers completed over the next five hours, and the loan was approved the next morning. Anger can be positively channeled; don't be afraid of it.

THE EIGHT DON'TS OF NEGOTIATING

There are eight vital "don'ts" to keep firmly in mind when you're negotiating.

1. If possible, never enter negotiations unless you're in top shape, physically and mentally. Never negotiate when you're upset, sad, tired, or sick.

2. Don't assume the other party has the same motivations you do. Everyone comes to a negotiation with a different set of objectives and needs. Your job is to assess clearly both your needs and the other side's needs.

3. Although it's fine to have partners on your negotiating team, don't bring a lawyer _until you need one._ Lawyers cost lots of money. I suggest that you meet with your lawyer _beforehand,_ and then not again until a final contract needs to be drafted. Recently, in preparation for a meeting, I had a briefing conference with an attorney to go over what I should do when the deal was ready to wrap up. I spent a solid thirty minutes with him and took extensive notes on his advice. After the conference I felt confident about getting through the meeting, equipped with the information I had gained. (I also made sure I knew where and how to get in touch with him if I needed to during the negotiations.)

The presence of legal counsel tends to make everybody a little nervous. If you bring a lawyer, the other side will quite naturally want to bring one, too. This can often eliminate any of the casual (and necessary) give-and-take. People are prone to become unduly formal, even inflexible, in the company of lawyers.

Note: If your attorney also acts as a deal-maker or an agent, the rules quite clearly are different. In this case the attorney's function is broader, and in certain industries it is quite normal to work hand-in-glove with an attorney who functions more as a facilitator than purely as a legal adviser.

4. If you have an associate with you during the bargaining session, don't be afraid to request a break in the meeting to discuss strategy. It's perfectly all right to say that you want to talk about a few points with your partner outside the conference room. Simply excuse yourself, take a walk in the hallway, or go out for a cup of coffee. This "time-out" is a good way to digest the latest events and jointly decide what action is most appropriate next.

Occasionally you may find that taking a "time-out" ruffles a few feathers on the other side. That risk is worth taking, particularly when the other side is pressing for a decision on an important issue. The rules of negotiating are not cast in concrete; if a meeting with your confederate seems appropriate, do it.

Used wisely, such a maneuver can bemuse the opposition. But you should never use it if you feel indecisive or confused about it. Then you will lose far more than you can hope to gain.

5. Don't agree on any given point—or to the entire package—too quickly, or let yourself be railroaded or hurried unduly. Think the deal through with slow and measured care. Twenty-four hours, if you need it, is a reasonable amount of reflection time.

6. Once you've given your word, stick to it.

There is nothing that will destroy your credibility more thoroughly than a reputation for reneging on a deal. If a deal is wrong for you, the time to say so is *before* you formally agree to it.

7. Don't be afraid to walk out if tempers are becoming too frayed. (It's preferable to getting into a shouting match.) Simply say something like "We're getting a little off the track; why don't we break until tomorrow." Good deals, for both sides, are rarely made when tempers are out of control. Remember: you will have to live with the deal you negotiate today—whether it involves real estate, a raise, a new car, or a million-dollar contract—from that point onward.

8. Never, never assume that the other party isn't as intelligent or as able as you are. More disasters arise from underestimating the capability of one's opponent than from any other single mistake. The shock engendered from a miscalculation of this sort will place you at a disadvantage from which you won't easily recover.

It's just as important, then, to know what you *shouldn't* do in the negotiating process. You can avoid mistakes by adhering to my advice and thus improve your bargaining chances.

SIZING UP THE SITUATION

Negotiating strategies change with each situation and set of players. Negotiating with, for example, a venture-capital group is different from bargaining with a foundation for a grant; you must adhere to the traditions within each industry.

In *all* situations, however, selling yourself is an ongoing process, involving such social graces as being on time and bringing all necessary and helpful printed materials and other required information to the meeting. Effective selling also means being businesslike and meeting deadlines.

After each meeting, it's helpful to review what needs to be done next and who will do it. At the end of a session you can simply say, for instance, "Just to recap what we decided today, I'm going to get the historical papers and send them to your assistant, Mr. Robbins. My associate, Ms. Stevenson, is going to get the current statistics, and I'll expect you to bring the details of your new proposal. We'll all meet back here next Monday at ten A.M."

It's also a good idea to keep a file on the progress of the negotiations, filling it with meeting notes, research materials, and highlights of phone conversations. If your notes are for more than your information, memos are a good idea. I have always discovered that memos are highly appreciated, and they're also a good way to pin down any points you wish to make.

"GIVING" IN ORDER TO WIN

Finally, I have found that giving can be a way of winning in any negotiation, particularly when the bargaining seems stalled. Volunteer to find out a fact or carry some papers to the bank. Actions like these can often facilitate progress, and you won't lose ground.

Throughout the negotiating process, have a list of things you are prepared to offer. This is a winning stance, for whether the other party takes you up on your suggestions or not, you have made the gesture and it will count in your favor.

Being nice, pleasant, and giving doesn't imply weakness or retreat. You can accomplish as much with an amiable attitude as with a harsh one. Wouldn't you rather negotiate in a cheerful environment than in a tense or hostile one?

In my own negotiating experience, I have come to view the process as one of knowledgeable people coming together to see what they can work out. It's an "everybody wins" stance, rather than the "I've-got-to-kill-my-opponent" approach. And it works. The best—and the most satisfying—deals are those in which _everybody_ feels like a winner.

AFTERWORD

Artemus Ward urged us to live within our means—even if we have to borrow to do so; but his advice must be balanced with Shakespeare's warning: "Neither a borrower nor a lender be." We should update that thought with "... unless you have to."

Because obtaining money is essential to modern life, it is wise to be as informed as possible about the system and your options. What I most wanted to give you in this volume is an overview and an understanding of those options and a sense of direction. It is my hope that you will use this information prudently and to your advantage.

The central ingredient to borrowing success—now and in the future—is establishing a consistent record of repayment. Keep your commitment to repay, and don't overdose on borrowed money.

The most important rule of all is to borrow only when it is necessary, and then to be as well informed as you can to obtain the best possible terms.

Here's to your successful money search. Continue that search in the Appendix, which lists additional sources and some of the laws that protect you, the consumer, in various borrowing transactions. Take a few minutes to familiarize yourself with these important laws; knowing your rights is as important as knowing the various sources for the money you need.

—PAULA NELSON
June 1982
Santa Monica, CA

APPENDIX

Appendix Contents

In this book, you've become familiar with the wide array of options that are available to you when you need money, no matter what the purpose. You may have been surprised by the number of alternatives that exist and felt a sense of excitement about taking advantage of one or more of them.

This appendix is designed to give you some supporting information and resources as you enter the money world. I suggest that you read through it now and, in the upcoming months, refer back to specific sections of it whenever they may be relevant to your needs or ventures.

You'll find the appendix divided into several sections. The first part concentrates upon borrower-protection laws with which you should become acquainted. Until relatively recently, the consumer was particularly vulnerable in the lending and credit marketplace, with no strong federal laws to shield him from unscrupulous activities. But fortunately, the number of legal protections has multiplied quickly in the last few years.

Whenever you feel that your rights under these laws have been violated, there are places to turn to that will hear and address your grievances. In this appendix, you'll find a list of agencies to contact in such circumstances.

You'll also become acquainted with some additional material to enhance what you've already learned about credit. Not only will you discover how to obtain and interpret a copy of your own credit report, but you'll also find a list of resources to turn to for information about your credit rights, and the special credit problems and protections unique to women.

In the later sections of this chapter, you'll find lists of resources for obtaining grants, student loans, and business cash. These are names and addresses of specific agencies and corporations that can either provide you with funds directly or point you toward the people who can. There *are* places to obtain money these days, and this appendix will help you find them.

YOUR RIGHTS AS A BORROWER

Over the past fifteen years, a number of laws have been adopted to protect you, the borrower, in all phases of obtaining credit. The first of these was the Consumer Protection Act of 1968, which contained the Truth in Lending Act, requiring lenders to state in plain English the exact cost of credit. A key element in the Truth in Lending Act is the use of a standardized measurement for the cost of credit: the annual percentage rate (APR). The APR provides you with a convenient basis for comparing the actual costs of credit.

In addition to this landmark law affecting the financial specifics of credit, laws have been enacted providing for fairness and equality in reporting of credit information and for your rights to credit regardless of your marital status or sex.

As a consumer and user of credit, you should become particularly familiar with the provisions of three of those laws:

Truth in Lending Act
Fair Credit Reporting Act
Equal Credit Opportunity Act

The highlights of each of those laws are presented here:

Truth in Lending Act:

The Truth in Lending Act is one of the most important and useful consumer-protection laws currently in force. It requires the lender or creditor to specify in writing, and before you sign any agreement, the finance charge and annual percentage rate of the loan or credit. The finance charge is the total dollar amount you pay for the use of the credit, including interest costs and any additional fees, such as service costs, appraisal fees, insurance costs, and points.

The Truth in Lending Act also requires the lender or creditor to state the annual percentage rate of the loan or credit. This is the key to comparing costs, regardless of the amount of the credit or how long you have to repay it. (Note: As mentioned in Chapter 4, check both amounts—the finance charge and the APR—for the actual cost of the loan.)

The law also requires that creditors tell you *when* finance charges will begin on your account, so you'll clearly know how much time you'll have to pay your bills before the finance charges begin accumulating.

Keep in mind that federal law does not set credit charges. But under the Truth in Lending Act, disclosure is required so you can compare credit costs and terms.

Fair Credit Reporting Act

Credit reports—those computerized records of your credit and borrowing history—are a fact of modern life. Their contents often decide the fate of all of your future credit applications.

Too often, there are inaccuracies in these reports, and until recently, the consumer himself had little access to his own report, or recourse to correct any errors in it.

But the Fair Credit Reporting Act has changed that. Primarily it provides you with the following rights:

1. To actually look at your file at any of the credit-reporting agencies that hold information on you.

2. To obtain a free copy of your credit report (from the credit-reporting agency that provides the report) when you have been denied credit within the last thirty days.

3. To know who has received information from your file within the previous six months and, for employment purposes, the past two years.

4. To have the credit-reporting agency reverify any information you consider incomplete or inaccurate.

5. To have information removed which cannot be substantiated or is incorrect.

6. To have the credit agency notify those who have received incorrect information.

7. To provide a one-hundred-word statement to tell your side of the story on your credit report.

8. To have information deleted from your file after seven years, with the exception of bankruptcy, which remains on your credit report for ten years.

9. To receive from creditors a written reason for any turndown of credit.

10. To receive a response within thirty days from creditors whenever you apply for credit.

Equal Credit Opportunity Act

Enacted in 1977, the Equal Credit Opportunity Act prohibits discrimination on the basis of sex, marital status, race, or religion. You are to be judged only on your credit-worthiness.

Since its enactment, this law has been considered an extremely important law for women, because of the long history of credit discrimination that women have experienced. However, the scope of the law is much broader. Here are its most important provisions:

1. You cannot be refused credit solely because you are a woman, or because you are single, married, separated, or widowed.

2. You cannot be refused credit because a creditor won't count income you receive regularly from alimony or child support.

3. You can have credit in your own name if you are creditworthy.

4. If you apply for your own credit and rely on your own income history when you do, you need not submit information about your spouse nor do you need his cosignature.

5. Even if your marital status changes, you can still keep your own accounts and your own credit history.

For more information about women and credit, the following booklets are excellent resources, covering a wide range of details about women's rights and credit:

The Equal Credit Opportunity Act and Women
Publication Services
Division of Support Services
Board of Governors of the Federal Reserve System
Washington, D.C. 20551
(Free of charge)

Borrowing Basics for Women
Public Affairs Department
Citibank
Box 939, Church Street Station
New York, New York 10008
(Free of charge)

How Women Can Get Credit
National Organization for Women
2000 P Street, N.W.
Washington, D.C. 20036
(20¢ per copy)

Some additional booklets containing information about the various laws discussed above are available (free of charge) from the Federal Reserve. They are titled:

What Truth in Lending Means to You
How to File a Consumer Credit Complaint
The Equal Credit Opportunity Act and . . . Age
Fair Credit Billing
Truth in Leasing
Consumer Handbook to Credit Protection Laws

To obtain these booklets, write to:
Publication Services
Division of Support Services
Board of Governors of the Federal Reserve System
Washington, D.C. 20551

HOW TO OBTAIN A COPY OF YOUR CREDIT REPORT

If you would like a copy of your credit report, it is your right to obtain it, typically at a minimal fee of $4 to $10. There is no charge if you have been denied credit (based on the facts in the report) within the previous thirty days.

If your credit application has been turned down, the source of any credit information that may have influenced that decision must be supplied on a letter from this creditor. Contact the credit-reporting agency listed on the letter.

In other cases, to locate the credit-reporting agency nearest you, contact:

Associated Credit Bureaus
16211 Park Place
Houston, Texas 77218
(713) 492-9155

The accompanying form is a sample credit report from TRW Credit Data, the largest credit bureau in the nation. To give you an idea of how to read such a form, here is what the information in the first entry means.

- The account of SPNB is a "current account"—that is, it is in good standing.
- The account was opened in June 1977 and reported on in July 1980.
- It is an individual (1), revolving (REV) credit-card account (CRC), with a $1,000 credit limit. The present balance is $242, and there is no money past due.
- The account has had a current (C) payment history during the past twelve months—that is, the bills have been paid on time for the past year.

The back of the actual credit report contains full explanations of all symbols and abbreviations used on the form.

TRW CREDIT DATA   UPDATED CREDIT PROFILE   CONFIDENTIAL

TCR2   INQUIRY INFORMATION

DFD2 9999999ABC CONSUMER JANE Q.., 1825 H 90027, P-2234 W 92667,
S-548926847, M-1825 HILL STREET?LOS ANGELES CA 90027

PAGE 1	DATE 09-11-80	TIME 15:19:14	PORT AL11	H/V A14	CONSUMER				02-999999/99

JANE Q CONSUMER
1825 HILL STREET
LOS ANGELES, CA 90027

2-80 A & B SALES
1350 4TH STREET
LOS ANGELES, CA 90067
3388338

SS# 548926847

YOB-1952

ACCOUNT PROFILE POS NON NEG	SUBSCRIBER NAME/COURT NAME — STATUS COMMENT	DATE REPORTED INQUIRY	DATE OPENED	SUBSCRIBER COURT CODE — TYPE	ASSN CODE — TERMS	AMOUNT	BALANCE	ACCOUNT NUMBER/DOCKET — BALANCE DATE	AMOUNT PAST DUE	PAYMENT PROFILE NUMBER OF MONTHS PRIOR TO BALANCE DATE 1 2 3 4 5 6 7 8 9 10 11 12
A	SPNB CURR ACCT	7-80	6-77	3900900 CRC	1 REV	$1000	$242	40245566789 7-15-80		CCCCCCCCCCCC
A	CITIBANK PAID SATIS	1-80	1-77	3900900 AUT	36	$5000		892939495969		CCCCC
A	SEARS CURR ACCT	7-80	3-75	3647586 CHG	2 REV	$500	$0	8384858687777 7-28-80		CCCCCCCCCCCC
A	JC PENNEY CURR ACCT	7-80	2-79	3494959 CHG	1 REV	$200	$149	59697989493922 7-21-80		CCCCCCCCCCCC
A	MAY CO CURR ACCT	6-80	2-80	3388338 CHG	2 REV	$200	$0	77000412233333 6-28-80		CCCCCCCCCCCC
M	MAY CO INQUIRY	2-09-80		3388338						
M	B OF A INQUIRY	9-21-80		3892212 CHG	REV					

©TRW INC. 1971, 1978

WHEN YOU FEEL YOUR RIGHTS HAVE BEEN VIOLATED

If your application for credit has been denied, and you feel that the reason for denial involves a violation of law, first bring the matter up directly with the credit grantor (bank, finance company, department store, etc.). If that action fails to bring satisfactory results you can file a formal complaint.

When you feel that a bank has violated any federal credit laws, or if a bank has handled your application or credit procedures unfairly or deceptively, submit a complaint (in writing) to the Federal Reserve System—either to the national office in Washington, D.C., or to the district office nearest you. Describe your complaint in detail, and the Federal Reserve will respond within fifteen days, helping you enforce the law if a violation has occurred.

Here are the addresses of the nation's Federal Reserve offices:

Board of Governors of the Federal Reserve System
20th and Constitution Avenue, N.W.
Washington, D.C. 20551
(202) 452-3000

Atlanta, Georgia
104 Marietta Street, N.W.
30303
(404) 586-8500

Boston, Massachusetts
600 Atlantic Avenue
02106
(617) 973-3000

Chicago, Illinois
230 South LaSalle Street
P.O. Box 834
60690
(312) 322-5322

Cleveland, Ohio
1455 East Sixth Street
P.O. Box 6387
44101
(216) 241-2800

Dallas, Texas
400 South Akard Street
Station K 75222
(214) 651-6111

Kansas City, Missouri
925 Grand Avenue
64198
(816) 881-2000

Minneapolis, Minnesota
250 Marquette Avenue
55480
(612) 340-2345

New York, New York
33 Liberty Street
Federal Reserve P.O. Station
10045
(212) 791-5000

Philadelphia, Pennsylvania
100 North Sixth Street
P.O. Box 66
19105
(215) 574-6000

Richmond, Virginia
701 East Byrd Street
P.O. Box 27622
23219
(804) 643-1250

St. Louis, Missouri
411 Locust Street
P.O. Box 442
63166
(314) 444-8444

San Francisco, California
400 Sansome Street
P.O. Box 7702
94120
(415) 544-2000

If your complaint is with a business other than a bank, you should contact the appropriate regulatory agency listed below:

Federal Credit Unions
Regional Office of the National Credit Union Administration serving the area in which the Federal Credit Union is located.

Creditors Subject to Civil Aeronautics Board
Director, Bureau of Enforcement
Civil Aeronautics Board
1825 Connecticut Avenue, N.W.
Washington, D.C. 20428

Creditors Subject to Interstate Commerce Commission
Office of Proceedings
Interstate Commerce Commission
Washington, D.C. 20523

Creditors Subject to Packers and Stockyards Act
Nearest Packers and Stockyards Administration area supervisor.

Small Business Investment Companies
U.S. Small Business Administration
1441 L Street, N.W.
Washington, D.C. 20416

Brokers and Dealers
Securities and Exchange Commission
Washington, D.C. 20549

STUDENT LOANS AND STUDENT AID

As you learned in Chapter 10, your primary source of information about student financial aid is the financial-aid officer at the college you (or your child) are attending.

However, information can be obtained from other sources as well. The offices listed below should be helpful. Find those nearest the college you or your child will be attending and contact them directly. They can provide you with information ranging from special funding to a list of the leading lenders active in the student loan program:

ALABAMA
ALABAMA COMMISSION ON
HIGHER EDUCATION
1 Court Square, Suite 221
Montgomery, Alabama 36197
GSL and State Aid:
(205) 832-3790

ALASKA
ALASKA COMMISSION ON
POSTSECONDARY EDUCA-
TION
400 Willoughby Avenue
Pouch FP
Juneau, Alaska 99801
GSL and State Aid:
(907) 465-2962

ARIZONA
GSL: ARIZONA EDUCATIONAL
LOAN PROGRAM
301 East Virginia Avenue
Phoenix, Arizona 85004
(602) 252-5793

State Aid: ARIZONA COMMIS-
SION FOR POSTSECONDARY
EDUCATION
1937 West Jefferson
Phoenix, Arizona 85009
(602) 255-3109

ARKANSAS
GSL: STUDENT LOAN GUAR-
ANTEE FOUNDATIONS OF AR-
KANSAS
1515 West 7th Street—Suite 515

Little Rock, Arkansas 72202
(501) 371-2634

State Aid: DEPARTMENT OF
HIGHER EDUCATION
1301 West Seventh Street
Little Rock, Arkansas 72201
(501) 371-1441, Ext. 56

CALIFORNIA
CALIFORNIA STUDENT AID
COMMISSION
1410 Fifth Street
Sacramento, California 95814
GSL: (916) 322-0435
State Aid: (916) 445-0880

COLORADO
GSL: COLORADO GUARAN-
TEED STUDENT LOAN PRO-
GRAM
7000 N. Broadway, Suite 100
Denver, Colorado 80221
(303) 427-0259

State Aid: COLORADO COM-
MISSION ON HIGHER EDUCA-
TION
1550 Lincoln Street, Room 210
Denver, Colorado 80203
(303) 866-2748

CONNECTICUT
GSL: CONNECTICUT STU-
DENT LOAN FOUNDATION
25 Pratt Street
Hartford, Connecticut 06103
(203) 547-1510

State Aid: CONNECTICUT
BOARD OF HIGHER EDUCA-
TION
61 Woodland Street
Hartford, Connecticut 06105
(203) 566-6218

DELAWARE
GSL: DELAWARE HIGHER
EDUCATION LOAN PROGRAM
c/o Brandywine College
Post Office Box 7139
Wilmington, Delaware 19803
(302) 478-3000 Ext. 201

State Aid: DELAWARE POST-
SECONDARY EDUCATION
COMMISSION
Carvel State Office Building
220 French Street
Wilmington, Delaware 19801
(302) 571-3240

DISTRICT OF COLUMBIA
GSL: HIGHER EDUCATION AS-
SISTANCE FOUNDATION
HIGHER EDUCATION LOAN
PROGRAM (HELP) OF D.C.,
INC.
1001 Connecticut Avenue, N.W.
Suite 825
Washington, D.C. 20036
(202) 861-0701

State Aid: OFFICE OF STATE
EDUCATION AFFAIRS
614 H Street, N.W.
8th Floor, Room 817
Washington, D.C. 20001
(202) 727-3688

FLORIDA
FLORIDA STUDENT FINAN-
CIAL ASSISTANCE COMMIS-
SION
Knott Building
Tallahassee, Florida 32301
GSL and State Aid:
(904) 487-1800

GEORGIA
GEORGIA HIGHER
EDUCATION
ASSISTANCE CORPORATION
9 LaVista Perimeter Park
2187 Northlake Parkway
Suite 110
Tucker, Georgia 30084
GSL: (404) 393-7241
State Aid: (404) 393-7253

HAWAII
GSL: HAWAII EDUCATION
LOAN PROGRAM
1314 South King Street, Suite 603
Honolulu, Hawaii 96814
(808) 536-3731

State Aid: STATE POSTSEC-
ONDARY EDUCATION COM-
MISSION
124F Bachman Hall, University of
Hawaii
2444 Dole Street
Honolulu, Hawaii 96822
(808) 938-6862

IDAHO
GSL: STUDENT LOAN FUND
OF IDAHO, INC.
Processing Center
Route 2, North Whitley Drive
Fruitland, Idaho 83619
(208) 452-4058

State Aid: OFFICE OF STATE
BOARD OF EDUCATION
650 West State Street, Room 307
Boise, Idaho 83720
(208) 334-2270

ILLINOIS
GSL: ILLINOIS GUARANTEED
LOAN PROGRAM
102 Wilmot Road
Deerfield, Illinois 60015
(312) 945-7040

State Aid: ILLINOIS STATE
SCHOLARSHIP COMMISSION
102 Wilmot Road
Deerfield, Illinois 60015
(312) 948-8550

INDIANA
STATE STUDENT ASSIS-
TANCE COMMISSION OF INDI-
ANA
219 North Senate Avenue, 1st
Floor
Indianapolis, Indiana 46202
GSL: (317) 232-2366
State Aid: (317) 232-2351

IOWA
IOWA COLLEGE AID COMMIS-
SION
201 Jewett Building
9th and Grand
Des Moines, Iowa 50309
GSL: (515) 281-8537
State Aid: (515) 281-3501

KANSAS
GSL: HIGHER EDUCATION AS-
SISTANCE FOUNDATION
34 Corporate Woods
10950 Grand View Drive
Overland Park, Kansas 66210
(913) 648-4255

State Aid: BOARD OF RE-
GENTS—STATE OF KANSAS
1416 Merchants National Bank
Topeka, Kansas 66612
(913) 296-3421

KENTUCKY
KENTUCKY HIGHER EDUCA-
TION ASSISTANCE AU-
THORITY
1050 U.S. 127 South
West Frankfort Office Complex
Frankfort, Kentucky 40601
GSL and State Aid:
(502) 564-7990

LOUISIANA
GOVERNOR'S SPECIAL COM-
MISSION ON EDUCATION
SERVICES
4637 Jamestown Street
Post Office Box 44127
Baton Rouge, Louisiana 70804
GSL and State Aid:
(504) 925-3630

MAINE
STATE DEPARTMENT OF
EDUCATIONAL AND CUL-
TURAL SERVICES
Division of Higher Education Ser-
vices
State House Station 23
Augusta, Maine 04333
GSL and State Aid:
(207) 289-2183

MARYLAND
GSL: MARYLAND HIGHER
EDUCATION LOAN CORPORA-
TION
2100 Guilford Avenue
Baltimore, Maryland 21218
(301) 659-6555

State Aid: MARYLAND STATE
SCHOLARSHIP BOARD
2100 Guilford Avenue
Baltimore, Maryland 21218
(301) 659-6420

MASSACHUSETTS
GSL: MASSACHUSETTS
HIGHER EDUCATION ASSIS-
TANCE CORPORATION
330 Stuart Street
Boston, Massachusetts 02116
(617) 426-9796

State Aid: MASSACHUSETTS
BOARD OF REGENTS OF
HIGHER EDUCATION
Scholarship Office
330 Stuart Street
Boston, Massachusetts 02116
(617) 727-9420

MICHIGAN
GSL: MICHIGAN DEPART-
MENT OF EDUCATION
Guaranteed Student Loan Pro-
gram
Box 30047
Lansing, Michigan 48909
(517) 373-0760

State Aid: MICHIGAN DEPART-
MENT OF EDUCATION
Post Office Box 30008
Lansing, Michigan 48909
(517) 373-3394

MINNESOTA
GSL: HIGHER EDUCATION AS-
SISTANCE FOUNDATION
900 American National Bank
Building
Fifth and Minnesota Streets
St. Paul, Minnesota 55101
(612) 227-7661

State Aid: MINNESOTA
HIGHER EDUCATION COOR-
DINATING BOARD
400 Capitol Square
550 Cedar Street
St. Paul, Minnesota 55101
(612) 296-3974

MISSISSIPPI
GSL: STUDENT FINANCIAL
ASSISTANCE U.S. DEPART-
MENT OF EDUCATION
101 Marietta Tower—Suite 423
Atlanta, Georgia 30323
(404) 221-5658

State Aid: MISSISSIPPI POST-
SECONDARY EDUCATION FI-
NANCIAL ASSISTANCE
BOARD
Post Office Box 2336
Jackson, Mississippi 39205
(601) 982-6168

MISSOURI
GSL: MISSOURI DEPART-
MENT OF HIGHER EDUCA-
TION
Post Office Box 1438
Jefferson City, Missouri 65102
(314) 751-3940

State Aid: MISSOURI DEPART-
MENT OF HIGHER EDUCA-
TION
Post Office Box 1437
Jefferson City, Missouri 65102
(314) 751-3940

MONTANA
GSL and State Aid: MONTANA
UNIVERSITY SYSTEM
33 South Last Chance Gulch
Helena, Montana 59601
(406) 449-3024

NEBRASKA
Cornhusker Bank Building
11th and Cornhusker Highway
Suite 304
Lincoln, Nebraska 68521
(402) 476-9129

State Aid: NEBRASKA COOR-
DINATING COMMISSION FOR
POSTSECONDARY EDUCA-
TION
301 Centennial Mall South
Post Office Box 95005
Lincoln, Nebraska 68509
(402) 471-2847

NEVADA
GSL: NEVADA STATE DE-
PARTMENT OF EDUCATION
400 West King Street
Carson City, Nevada 89710
(702) 885-3107

State Aid: UNIVERSITY OF NE-
VADA SYSTEM
405 Marsh Avenue
Reno, Nevada 89509
(702) 784-4666

NEW HAMPSHIRE
GSL: NEW HAMPSHIRE
HIGHER EDUCATION ASSIS-
TANCE FOUNDATION
143 North Main Street
Post Office Box 877
Concord, New Hampshire 03301
(603) 225-6612

State Aid: NEW HAMPSHIRE
POSTSECONDARY EDUCA-
TION COMMISSION
61 South Spring Street
Concord, New Hampshire 03301
(603) 271-2555

NEW JERSEY
GSL: NEW JERSEY HIGHER
EDUCATION ASSISTANCE AU-
THORITY
C. N. 00538
Trenton, New Jersey 08638
(609) 292-3906

State Aid: DEPARTMENT OF
HIGHER EDUCATION
Office of Student Assistance
Number 4 Quakerbridge Plaza
C. N. 540
Trenton, New Jersey 08625
(609) 292-4646

NEW MEXICO
GSL: NEW MEXICO EDUCA-
TIONAL ASSISTANCE FOUN-
DATION
2301 Yale S.E., Building F
Albuquerque, New Mexico 87106
(505) 277-6304

State Aid: BOARD OF EDUCA-
TION FINANCE
1068 Cerrillos Road
Santa Fe, New Mexico 87503
(505) 827-5017

NEW YORK
NEW YORK STATE HIGHER
EDUCATION SERVICES COR-
PORATION
99 Washington Ave.
Albany, New York 12255
GSL: (518) 473-1574
State Aid: (518) 474-5642

NORTH CAROLINA
NORTH CAROLINA STATE
EDUCATION ASSISTANCE AU-
THORITY
Post Office Box 2688
Chapel Hill, North Carolina 27514
GSL and State Aid:
(919) 473-1688

NORTH DAKOTA
GSL: STUDENT FINANCIAL
ASSISTANCE DEPARTMENT
OF EDUCATION
11037 Federal Office Building
19th and Stout Streets
Denver, Colorado 80294
(303) 837-3676

State Aid: NORTH DAKOTA
STUDENT FINANCIAL ASSIS-
TANCE PROGRAM
10th Floor, State Capitol
Bismarck, North Dakota 58505
(701) 224-4114

OHIO
GSL: OHIO STUDENT LOAN
COMMISSION
P.O. Box 16610
Columbus, Ohio 43216
(614) 466-3091

State Aid: OHIO BOARD OF RE-
GENTS
3600 State Office Tower
30 East Broad Street
Columbus, Ohio 43215
(614) 466-7420

OKLAHOMA
OKLAHOMA STATE REGENTS
FOR HIGHER EDUCATION
500 Education Building
State Capitol Complex
Oklahoma City, Oklahoma 73105
GSL and State Aid:
(405) 521-8262

OREGON
OREGON STATE SCHOLAR-
SHIP COMMISSION
1445 Willamette Street
Eugene, Oregon 97401
GSL: (800) 452-8807 (within OR),
(503) 686-3200
State Aid: (503) 686-4166

PENNSYLVANIA
PENNSYLVANIA HIGHER
EDUCATION ASSISTANCE
AGENCY
660 Boas Street
Harrisburg, Pennsylvania 17102
GSL: (800) 692-7392 (within PA),
(717) 787-1932
State Aid: (800) 692-7435 (within
PA), (717) 787-1937

RHODE ISLAND
RHODE ISLAND HIGHER
EDUCATION ASSISTANCE AU-
THORITY
274 Weybosset Street
Providence, Rhode Island 02903
GSL and State Aid: (401) 277-2050

SOUTH CAROLINA
GSL: SOUTH CAROLINA STU-
DENT LOAN CORPORATION
Interstate Center, Suite 210
Post Office Box 21337
Columbia, South Carolina 29221
(803) 798-0916

State Aid: HIGHER EDUCA-
TION TUITION GRANTS
AGENCY
411 Keenan Building, Box 11638
Columbia, South Carolina 29211
(803) 758-7070

SOUTH DAKOTA
GSL: SOUTH DAKOTA EDUCA-
TION ASSISTANCE CORPORA-
TION
105 First Ave. SW
Aberdeen, South Dakota 57401
(605) 225-6423

State Aid: DEPARTMENT OF
EDUCATION AND CULTURAL
AFFAIRS
Richard F. Kneip Building
Pierre, South Dakota 57501
(605) 773-3134

TENNESSEE
TENNESSEE STUDENT AS-
SISTANCE CORPORATION
B-3 Capitol Towers—Suite 9
Nashville, Tennessee 37219
GSL and State Aid:
(800) 342-1663
(within TN)
(615) 741-1346

TEXAS
GSL: TEXAS GUARANTEED
STUDENT LOAN CORPORA-
TION
Champion Tower, Suite 510
Austin, Texas 78752
(512) 835-1900

State Aid: COORDINATING
BOARD TEXAS COLLEGE AND
UNIVERSITY SYSTEM
Post Office Box 12788, Capitol Sta-
tion
Austin, Texas 78711
(512) 475-8169

UTAH
GSL: UTAH EDUCATION LOAN
SERVICE
1800 South West Temple
Suite 101
Salt Lake City, Utah 84108
(801) 486-5921

State Aid: UTAH STATE
BOARD OF REGENTS
807 East South Temple
Suite 204
Salt Lake City, Utah 84102
(801) 533-5617

VERMONT
VERMONT STUDENT ASSIST-
ANCE CORPORATION
5 Burlington Square
Burlington, Vermont 05401
GSL and State Aid:
(800) 642-3177 (within VT),
(802) 758-4530

VIRGINIA
GSL: VIRGINIA STATE EDU-
CATION ASSISTANCE AU-
THORITY
6 North Sixth Street
Suite 400
Richmond, Virginia 23219
(804) 786-2035

State Aid: STATE COUNCIL OF
HIGHER EDUCATION FOR
VIRGINIA
James Monroe Building
101 N. 14th Street
Richmond, Virginia 23219
(804) 225-2141

WASHINGTON
GSL: WASHINGTON STUDENT
LOAN GUARANTY ASSOCIA-
TION
100 South King Street, Suite 560
Westland Building
Seattle, Washington 98104
(206) 625-1030

State Aid: COUNCIL FOR POST-
SECONDARY EDUCATION
908 East Fifth Avenue
Olympia, Washington 98504
(206) 753-3571

WEST VIRGINIA
GSL: HIGHER EDUCATION AS-
SISTANCE FOUNDATION
HIGHER EDUCATION LOAN
PROGRAM OF WEST VIR-
GINIA, INC.
Post Office Box 591
Union Building, Suite 900
723 Kanawha Boulevard East
Charleston, West Virginia 25322
(304) 345-7211

State Aid: WEST VIRGINIA
BOARD OF REGENTS
950 Kanawha Boulevard East
Charleston, West Virginia 25301
(304) 348-0112

WISCONSIN
GSL: WISCONSIN HIGHER
EDUCATION CORPORA-
TION
137 East Wilson Street
Madison, Wisconsin 53702
(608) 266-1653

State Aid: WISCONSIN HIGHER
EDUCATIONAL AIDS BOARD
Post Office Box 7858
Madison, Wisconsin 53707
(608) 266-2897

WYOMING
GSL: HIGHER EDUCATION AS-
SISTANCE FOUNDATION
American National Bank Building
20 Street at Capitol, Suite 320
Cheyenne, Wyoming 82001
(307) 635-3259

State Aid: WYOMING COMMU-
NITY COLLEGE COMMISSION
1720 Carey Avenue
Boyd Building, Fifth Floor
Cheyenne, Wyoming 82002
(307) 777-7763

AMERICAN SAMOA
GSL: STUDENT FINANCIAL
ASSISTANCE U.S. DEPART-
MENT OF EDUCATION
50 United Nations Plaza, Rm. 250
San Francisco, California
(415) 556-0137

State Aid: DEPARTMENT OF
EDUCATION GOVERNMENT
OF AMERICAN SAMOA
Pago Pago, American Samoa 96799
(Overseas) 633-4256

**COMMONWEALTH OF THE
NORTHERN MARIANA IS-
LANDS**
GSL: See American Samoa

State Aid: DEPARTMENT OF
EDUCATION COMMON-
WEALTH OF THE NORTHERN
MARIANA ISLANDS
Saipan, Mariana Islands 96950
(Saipan) 98 12/9311

GUAM
GSL: See American Samoa

State Aid: UNIVERSITY OF
GUAM
Post Office Box EK
Agana, Guam 96910
(734) 2177

PUERTO RICO
GSL: STUDENT FINANCIAL
ASSISTANCE DEPARTMENT
OF EDUCATION
26 Federal Plaza
New York, New York 10007
(212) 264-4022

State Aid: COUNCIL ON
HIGHER EDUCATION
Box F-UPR Station
Rio Piedras, Puerto Rico 00931
(809) 751-5082/1136

**TRUST TERRITORY OF THE
PACIFIC ISLANDS AND
WAKE ISLAND**
GSL: See American Samoa

State Aid: OFFICE OF THE
HIGH COMMISSIONER TRUST
TERRITORY OF THE PACIFIC
ISLANDS
Saipan, Mariana Islands 96950
(Saipan) 9870

VIRGIN ISLANDS
BOARD OF EDUCATION
Post Office Box 9128
St. Thomas, Virgin Islands 00801
GSL and State Aid:
(809) 774-4546

USAF, INC.
(800) 227-3037 (West Coast)
(800) 382-4506 (Indiana only)
(800) 428-9250 (All other states)
UNITED STUDENT AID
FUNDS PROCESSING CENTER
Post Office Box 50827
Indianapolis, Indiana 46250

GRANTS AND FOUNDATIONS

As a supplement to the information presented
in Chapter 11, the following organizations, books, and
booklets should be particularly helpful as you make your

way through the process of applying for grant funding.
Two excellent sources of general information
and guidance are:

1. The Grantsmanship Center
   1031 South Grand Avenue
   Los Angeles, California 90015

This nonprofit organization provides a wide
range of services directed at nonprofit organizations, including:

- A monthly magazine aimed at grantee groups,
  human service agencies, and community-based
  organizations. It provides articles and how-to information
  on fund-raising, program management,
  and grantsmanship.
- A seminar series on subjects like grant writing,
  fund-raising, finding funding, corporate funding,
  federal block grants, direct mail fund-raising, special
  events fund-raising and business ventures for
  nonprofit organizations.

A complete listing of services is available
through *The Source,* a publication provided free of
charge from the Grantsmanship Center.

2. The Foundation Center
   888 Seventh Avenue
   New York, New York 10019

The Foundation Center is the central national
organization chartered to help you and/or your organization
match your grant requirements with the 22,000
active U.S. foundations. They offer a number of services,
including computer printouts and directories. The com-

puter service, called COMSEARCH, offers printouts by category and geography, listing the active foundations in each area. Categories include: Communications, Education, Health, Humanities, Population Groups, Physical and Life Sciences, Social Sciences, and Welfare.

The price per subject for a printout is $12. (Contact the Foundation Center for ordering details.)

A printout by geographic location can be obtained for any of the following geographic areas: California, Illinois, Massachusetts, Michigan, Minnesota, New Jersey, New York State, Ohio, Pennsylvania, Texas, Washington, D.C., and New York City.

The price is $25 each for New York City and California, and $15 for all the others.

Useful publications offered by the Foundation Center are:

About Foundations: How to Find the Facts You Need to Get a Grant. This is a simple step-by-step guide to the research process for finding a grantor.

Foundation Grants to Individuals. If you decide to go it alone, this is your bible. It's a specialized directory of about 1,000 foundations that have awarded as much as $96 million to over 40,000 individuals. (Price: $15.)

The Foundation Center National Data Book, Volumes One and Two, contains material on thousands of smaller foundations not listed in _The Foundation Directory._ (Price: $40.)

Other publications that may be useful in the grant-getting process include:

The Foundation Directory contains 2,818 entries on those foundations that contribute about 80 percent of all private grants in the United States. (Order from Columbia University Press, 136 South Broadway, Irvington, N.Y. 10533. Price: $36.)

The Corporate Foundation Directory lists corporate foundations and officials and is indexed by state, field of interest, and types of grants offered. (Order from Taft Corporation, 1000 Vermont Avenue, N.W., Washington, D.C. 20005.)

Catalog of Federal Domestic Assistance is a must for seekers of federal funds—a comprehensive guide to whom to contact, and how to go about getting U.S. grants. (Get price information and order from Superintendent of Documents, U.S. Government Printing Office, Washington, D.C. 20402.)

Researching Foundations: How to Identify Those That May Support Your Organization, Parts I and II. (Order from The Grantsmanship Center, 1031 South Grand Avenue, Los Angeles, California 90015. Price: $1.55 per part.)

BUSINESS CASH

When you need money to launch or sustain your small business, you can use one or more of the following lists to help you make contact with money sources.

Government loan sources are a good place to start, since when federal money can be obtained, it is often under excellent loan terms. Check the list on pages 252 through 255 for the Small Business Administration office nearest you.

Then, beginning on page 257, you'll find a list of venture-capital sources, members of the National Association of Small Business Investment Companies. These are financial institutions created to make equity capital and long-term credit available to small independent businessmen.

Finally, a list of investment bankers is included on pages 283 through 290. These are firms that specialize in providing capital to businessmen and range from well-known companies (like the E. F. Hutton Group and Dean Witter Reynolds) to smaller firms.

SMALL BUSINESS ADMINISTRATION OFFICES

Midwest

IDAHO
216 N. 8th Street
Boise, ID 83702

ILLINOIS
Federal Office Building
219 S. Dearborn Street
Chicago, IL 60604

502 Monroe Street
Springfield, IL 63701

INDIANA
26 S. Pennsylvania Street
Indianapolis, IN 46204

IOWA
New Federal Building
210 Walnut Street
Des Moines, IA 50309

KANSAS
120 S. Market Street
Wichita, KS 67202

MICHIGAN
1249 Washington Boulevard
Detroit, MI 48226

502 W. Kaye Avenue
Marquette, MI 49885

MINNESOTA
816-2nd Avenue S.
Minneapolis, MN 55402

MISSOURI
Federal Building
210 N. 12th Street
St. Louis, MO 63102

NEBRASKA
Federal Building
215 N. 17th Street
Omaha, NE 68102

NORTH DAKOTA
653-2nd Avenue N.
Fargo, ND 58102

OHIO
5026 Federal Building
550 Main Street
Cincinnati, OH 45202

1240 E. 9th Street
Cleveland, OH 44199

50 W. Gay Street
Columbus, OH 43215

OKLAHOMA
30 N. Hudson Street
Oklahoma City, OK 73102

SOUTH DAKOTA
National Bank Building
8th and Main Avenue
Sioux Falls, SD 57102

WISCONSIN
510 S. Barstow Street
Eau Claire, WI 54701

25 W. Main Street
Madison, WI 53703

238 W. Wisconsin Avenue
Milwaukee, WI 53202

Northeast

CONNECTICUT
Federal Office Building
450 Maine Street
Hartford, CT 06103

DELAWARE
6th and King Streets
Wilmington, DE 19801

DISTRICT OF COLUMBIA
1405 "I" Street N.W.
Washington, DC 20417

MAINE
Federal Building
U.S. Post Office
40 Western Avenue
Augusta, ME 04330

MARYLAND
113 Federal Building
Hopkins Plaza
Baltimore, MD 21202

MASSACHUSETTS
John Fitzgerald Federal Building
Boston, MA 02203

326 Appleton Street
Holyoke, MA 01040

NEW HAMPSHIRE
55 Pleasant Street
Concord, NH 03301

NEW JERSEY
970 Broad Street, Room 1636
Newark, NJ 07102

NEW YORK
91 State Street
Albany, NY 12297

Federal Building, Room 9
121 Ellicott Street
Buffalo, NY 14203

26 Federal Plaza, Room 3930
New York, NY 10007

Hunter Plaza
Fayette and Salina Streets
Syracuse, NY 13202

PENNSYLVANIA
1 Decker Square
Bala Cynwyd
Philadelphia, PA 19004

Federal Building
1000 Liberty Avenue
Pittsburgh, PA 15222

RHODE ISLAND
702 Smith Building
57 Eddy Street
Providence, RI 02903

VERMONT
Federal Building, 2nd Floor
87 State Street
Montpelier, VT 05601

Northwest

MONTANA
Power Block Building
Main and 6th Avenue
Helena, MT 59601

OREGON
921 S.W. Washington Street
Portland, OR 97205

WASHINGTON
506 Second Street
Seattle, WA 98104

Courthouse Building, Room 651
Spokane, WA 99210

WYOMING
300 N. Center Street
Casper, WY 82601

Southeast

ALABAMA
908 S. 20th Street
Birmingham, AL 35205

ARKANSAS
377 Post Office and Courthouse
    Bldg.
600 W. Capitol Avenue
Little Rock, AR 72203

FLORIDA
Federal Office Building
400 W. Bay Street
Jacksonville, FL 32202

Federal Building
51 S.W. 1st Avenue
Miami, FL 33130

Federal Building
500 Zack Street
Tampa, FL 33602

GEORGIA
1401 Peachtree Street N.E.
Atlanta, GA 30309

KENTUCKY
Federal Office Building
600 Federal Place
Louisville, KY 40202

LOUISIANA
124 Camp Street
New Orleans, LA 70130

MISSISSIPPI
2500-14th Street
Gulfport, MS 39501

245 E. Capitol Street
Jackson, MS 39205

NORTH CAROLINA
Addison Building
222 S. Church Street
Charlotte, NC 28202

PUERTO RICO
255 Ponce de Leon Avenue
Hato Rey, PR 00919

SOUTH CAROLINA
1801 Assembly Street
Columbia, SC 29201

TENNESSEE
502 S. Gay Street
Knoxville, TN 37902

Federal Building
167 N. Main Street
Memphis, TN 38103

500 Union Street
Nashville, TN 37219

VIRGINIA
Federal Building
400 N. 8th Street
Richmond, VA 23240

WEST VIRGINIA
3410 Courthouse and Federal Bldg.
500 Quarrier Street
Charleston, WV 25301

Lowndes Bank Building
119 N. 3rd Street
Clarksburg, WV 26301

Southwest

ARIZONA
122 N. Central Avenue
Phoenix, AZ 85004

Federal Building
155 E. Alamenda Street
Tucson, AZ 85701

CALIFORNIA
Federal Building
1130 "O" Street
Fresno, CA 93721

849 S. Broadway
Los Angeles, CA 90014

532 N. Mountain Avenue
San Bernardino, CA 92401

COLORADO
721-19th Street
Denver, CO 80202

NEVADA
300 Las Vegas Boulevard S.
Las Vegas, NV 98101

NEW MEXICO
Federal Building
550 Gold Avenue S.W.
Albuquerque, NM 87101

1015 El Paso Road
Los Cruces, NM 88001

TEXAS
Post Office and Custom House
 Bldg.
Corpus Christi, TX

1309 Main Street
Dallas, TX 75202

109 N. Oregon Street
El Paso, TX 79901

219 E. Jackson Street
Harlingen, TX 78550

Federal Office Building
1616-19th Street
Lubbock, TX 79408

505 E. Travis Street
Marshall, TX 75670

302 Broadway
San Antonio, TX 78205

UTAH
2237 Federal Building
125 S. State Street
Salt Lake City, UT 84111

West Pacific

ALASKA
1016 W. Sixth Street
Anchorage, AK 99501

510 Third Avenue
Fairbanks, Ak 99701

Federal Building
Juneau, AK 99801

GUAM
Ada Plaza Center Building
Agana, GU 96910

HAWAII
1149 Bethel Street
Honolulu, HI 96813

VENTURE-CAPITAL SOURCES

The following list of venture-capital sources has been provided courtesy of the National Association of Small Business Investment Companies. Each of the firms listed has been approved and licensed by the Small Business Administration to provide equity capital and long-term credit to small independent companies.

Following each entry is a code which will help

you locate the most promising firm for your industry or location. The key to the code appears at the bottom of this page. If you would like more information on NASBIC, you can write to them at:

National Association of Small Business Investment
  Companies
618 Washington Building
Washington, D.C. 20005
(202) 638-3411

EXPLANATION OF CODES

Preferred Limit for Loans or Investments

A — up to $100,000
B — up to $250,000
C — up to $500,000
D — up to $1-million
E — Above $1-million

Investment Policy

* — Will consider either loans or investments
** — Prefers to make long-term loans
*** — Prefers financings with right to acquire stock interest

Industry Preferences

1. Communications and Movies
2. Construction and Development
3. Natural Resources
4. Hotels, Motels, and Restaurants
5. Manufacturing and Processing
6. Medical and Other Health Services
7. Recreation and Amusements
8. Research and Technology
9. Retailing, Wholesaling, and Distribution
10. Service Trades
11. Transportation
12. Diversified

MESBIC—an SBIC which concentrates in placing its loans and investments with a small businessperson who is socially or economically disadvantaged

ALABAMA

Coastal Capital Co.
Mr. David C. De Laney, Inv. Mgr.
3201 Dauphin St., Ste. B
Mobile, AL 36606
(205) 476-0700
C * 12

First SBIC of Alabama
Mr. David C. De Laney, Pres.
3201 Dauphin St., Ste. B
Mobile, AL 36606
(205) 476-0700
C * 12

Western Financial Capital Corp.
Dr. Frederic M. Rosemore, Pres.
306 Temple Ave. No.
Fayette, AL 35555
(205) 932-3528
B * 6,12

ARIZONA

American Business Capital Corp.
Mr. Leonard A. Frankel, Pres.
3550 N. Central, Ste. 1305
Phoenix, AZ 85012
(602) 277-6259
A ** 12

ARKANSAS

First SBIC of Arkansas, Inc.
Mr. Fred C. Burns, Pres.
702 Worthen Bank Bldg.
Little Rock, AR 72201
(501) 378-1876
A *** 12

Kar-Mal Venture Capital, Inc.
Mr. Tommy Karam, Pres.
610 Plaza West
Little Rock, AR 72205
(501) 661-0010
MESBIC B *** 9

Small Business Investment Capital, Inc.
Mr. C. E. Toland, Pres.
10003 New Benton Hwy.
Little Rock, AR 72203
(501) 455-2234
A ** 9

CALIFORNIA

Bay Area Western Venture Capital Group, Inc.
Mr. Jack Wong, Sec./Treas.
383 Diablo Rd., Ste. 100
Danville, CA 94526
(415) 820-8079
MESBIC *** 2,8

Brantman Capital Corp.
Mr. W. T. Brantman, Pres.
P.O. Box 877
Tiburon, CA 94920
(415) 435-4747
A *** 4,5,6,7,8,9,10,11,12

Brentwood Capital Corp.
Mr. Timothy M. Pennington, Gen. Ptnr.
Mr. Frederick J. Warren, Gen. Ptnr.
11661 San Vicente Blvd.
Los Angeles, CA 90049
(213) 826-6581
D *** 1,3,5,6,8,10,12

Builders Capital Corp.
Mr. Victor Indiek, Pres.
2716 Ocean Park Blvd.
Santa Monica, CA 90406
(213) 450-0779
C * 2

Business Equity & Dev. Corp.
Mr. Ricardo J. Olivarez, Pres.
1411 W. Olympic Blvd., Ste. 200
Los Angeles, CA 90015
(213) 385-0351
MESBIC B * 5,12

California Northwest Fund, Inc.
Mr. Kirk L. Knight, Managing Dir.
Mr. Ken E. Joy, Managing Dir.
Mr. H. DuBose Montgomery, Managing Dir.
3000 Sand Hill Rd.
Menlo Park, CA 94025
(415) 854-2940
D * 12
(Branch Office: NY)

California Partners
Mr. William H. Draper, III, Pres.
Two Palo Alto Square

Palo Alto, CA 94304
(415) 493-5600
A *** 8

Crocker Ventures, Inc.
Mr. John M. Boyle, VP
#10 Montgomery St.
San Francisco, CA 94104
(415) 983-7024
B *** 1,5,8,11

Crosspoint Investment Corp.
Mr. Max S. Simpson, Pres.
1015 Corporation Way
P.O. Box 10101
Palo Alto, CA 94303
(415) 964-3545
B *** 1,5,8

Developers Equity Capital Corp.
Mr. Larry Sade, Pres.
9201 Wilshire Blvd., Ste. 204
Beverly Hills, CA 90210
(213) 278-3611
B * 2,4,6,11

Equitable Capital Corp.
Mr. John C. Lee, Pres.
855 Sansome St., Ste. 200
San Francisco, CA 94111
(415) 434-4114
MESBIC B * 12

Florists' Capital Corp.
Mr. Christopher M. Conroy, Pres.
10514 West Pico Blvd.
Los Angeles, CA 90064
(213) 204-6956
D *** 9,12

Grocers Capital Co.
Mr. William Christy, Pres.
2601 S. Eastern Ave.
Los Angeles, CA 90040
(213) 728-3322
B ** 9

HUB Enterprises, Ltd.
Mr. Richard Magary, Gen Mgr.
5874 Doyle St.
Emeryville, CA 94608
(415) 653-5707
MESBIC A * 2,5,6,8,10,12

Krasne Fund for Small Business, Inc.

Mr. Clyde A. Krasne, Pres.
P.O. Box 5257
Beverly Hills, CA 90210
(213) 274-7007
A ** 2,12

Lasung Investment & Finance Co., Inc.
Mr. Jung S. Lee, Pres.
3121 W. Olympic Blvd., #201
Los Angeles, CA 90006
(213) 384-7548
MESBIC A * 4

Lucky Star Investment Co.
Mr. Sinclair Louie, Pres.
665 Grant Ave.
San Francisco, CA 94108
(415) 982-5729
C * 2,4,5,6,9,10

Marwit Capital Corp.
Mr. Martin W. Witte, Pres.
The Marwit Bldg.
180 Newport Center Dr., Ste. 200
Newport Beach, CA 92660
(714) 640-6234
D *** 1,2,4,5,6,8,10,12

MCA New Ventures, Inc.
Mr. Robert B. Braswell, Chmn. & Pres.
100 Universal City Plaza
Universal City, CA 91608
(213) 508-2937
MESBIC B * 1,5,7,12

Merrill, Pickard Capital Co.
Mr. Steven L. Merrill
Mr. Jeff Pickard
650 California St., 31st Fl.
San Francisco, CA 94108
(415) 397-8800
E *** 1,5,6

Branch Office:
Nelson Capital Corp.
Mr. Norman Tulchin, Chmn.
1901 Ave. of the Stars, Ste. 584
Los Angeles, CA 90067
(213) 556-1944
D ** 12
(Main Office: NY)

Novus Capital Corp.
Mr. Errol M. Gerson, Pres.
5670 Wilshire Blvd.
Los Angeles, CA 90036
(213) 932-4051/4077
C * 2

Oceanic Capital Corp.
Mr. Robert C. Weeks, Pres.
350 California St., Ste. 2090
San Francisco, CA 94104
(415) 398-7677
C * 1,5,8

Opportunity Capital Corp.
Mr. J. Peter Thompson, Pres.
100 California St., Ste. 714
San Francisco, CA 94111
(415) 421-5935
MESBIC B *** 1,3,5,6,9,12

Oxford Capital Corp.
Mr. Richard R. Lorenz, Pres.
3700 Wilshire Blvd.
Los Angeles, CA 90010
(213) 381-8743
B *** 12

Pan American Investment Co.
Mr. Spencer W. Hoopes, Pres.
350 California St., #2090
San Francisco, CA 94104
(415) 398-7677
D *** 1,5,6,8

PBC Venture Capital, Inc.
Mr. Richard Robins, VP & Inv.
   Mgr.
1408 18th St., P.O. Box 6008
Bakersfield, CA 93386
(805) 395-3555
B *** 1,5,8,12

San Joaquin Capital Corp.
Mr. Chester W. Troudy, Exec. VP
P.O. Box 2538
Bakersfield, CA 93303
(805) 323-7581
D *** 2,5

San Jose Capital Corp.
Mr. H. Bruce Furchtenicht, Pres.
130 Park Center Plaza, Ste. 132
San Jose, CA 95113
(408) 293-8052
B *** 1,5,6,8

Solid Capital Corp.
Mr. Lusing Ty, Chief Financial
   Officer
652 Kearny St., Stes. 1 & 2
San Francisco, CA 94108
(415) 434-3371
MESBIC A * 2,4,9,12

Space Ventures, Inc.
Mr. Leslie R. Brewer, Gen. Mgr.
3901 MacArthur Blvd., Ste. 101
Newport Beach, CA 92660
(714) 851-0855
MESBIC B *** 1,2,4,5,7,8,9,10,11,12

TELACU Investment Co.
Mr. Gilberto Padilla, Pres.
1330 So. Atlantic Blvd.
Los Angeles, CA 90022
(213) 268-6745
MESBIC B * 5,9,10,12

Union Venture Corp.
Mr. Brent T. Rider, Pres.
445 S. Figueroa St.
Los Angeles, CA 90071
(213) 687-6959
E *** 1,3,5,6,8,12

Unity Capital Corp.
Mr. Frank W. Owen, Pres.
362 30th St. "B"
San Diego, CA 92104
(714) 295-6768
MESBIC C *** 2,4,5,9,12

Branch Office:
Washington Capital Corp.
601 University Ave.
Campus Commons
Sacramento, CA 95825
D * 12
(Main Office: WA)

WESTAMCO Investment Co.
Mr. Leonard G. Muskin, Pres.
8929 Wilshire Blvd., Ste. 400
Beverly Hills, CA 90211
(213) 652-8288
B * 2,3,5,8,9,12

West Coast Venture Capital
Mr. Gary W. Kalbach, Gen. Ptnr.
10440 So. DeAnza Blvd., Ste. D-2
Cupertino, CA 95014
(408) 996-2702
C *** 1,5,8

Western Bancorp Venture Capital Co.
(Effective June 1, 1981:
First Interstate Capital, Inc.)
Mr. David B. Jones, Pres.
707 Wilshire Blvd., Ste. 1850
Los Angeles, CA 90017
(213) 614-5903
D *** 12

COLORADO

Branch Office:
Central Investment Corp. of Denver
Mr. Blaine E. D'Arcey, Gen. Mgr.
7625 W. Fifth Ave., Ste. 202N
Lakewood, CO 80226
(303) 232-3018
D *** 12
(Main Office: Northwest Growth Fund, Inc., MN)

Colorado Growth Capital, Inc.
Mr. Nicholas H. C. Davis, Pres.
950 17th St., #1630
Denver, CO 80202
(303) 629-0205
B * 1,3,7,8,9

Enervest, Inc.
Mr. Mark Kimmel, Pres.
7000 E. Belleview Ave. #310
Englewood, CO 80111
(303) 771-9650
C *** 1,3,5,6,7,8,12

CONNECTICUT

Activest Capital Corp.
Mr. William N. Vitalis, Pres.
P.O. Box 76
Cornwall Bridge, CT 06754
(203) 672-6651
A * 2,4

Asset Capital & Mgmt. Corp.
Mr. Ralph Smith, Pres.
608 Ferry Blvd.
Stratford, CT 06497
(203) 375-0299
A * 1,2,6,9

Capital Resource Company of Connecticut
Mr. I. Martin Fierberg, Pres.
345 N. Main St., Ste. 304
West Hartford, CT 06117
(203) 232-1769
A * 12

The First Connecticut SBIC
Mr. James Breiner, Chmn.
Mr. David Engelson, Pres.
177 State St.
Bridgeport, CT 06604
(203) 366-4726
D * 1,2,5,6,9,12
(Branch Office: NY)

Foster Management Co.
Mr. John H. Foster, Pres.
1010 Summer St.
Stamford, CT 06905
(203) 348-4385
C *** 1,3,5,6,8,11

Manufacturers SBIC, Inc.
Mr. Louis W. Mingione, Exec. Dir.
310 Main St.
East Haven, CT 06512
(203) 469-7901
A * 12

Marcon Capital Corp.
Mr. Martin Cohen, Pres.
49 Riverside Ave.
Westport, CT 06880
(203) 226-7751
C ** 1,12

Regional Financial Enterprises, Inc.
Mr. Robert M. Williams, Chmn.
1111 Summer St.
Stamford, CT 06905
(203) 356-1730
D * 1,3,5,6,8,12

Small Business Investment Co. of Connecticut
Mr. Kenneth F. Zarrilli, Pres.
c/o E&F Construction Co.
505 Sylvan Ave.
Bridgeport, CT 06604
(203) 367-3282
A ** 12

DISTRICT OF COLUMBIA

Allied Capital Corp.
Mr. George C. Williams, Pres.
Mr. David Gladstone, Exec. VP
1625 I St., NW
Washington, DC 20006
(202) 331-1112
C * 1,2,4,5,6,8,9,11,12
(Branch Office: FL)

Branch Office:
Broad Arrow Investment Corp.
Mr. C. N. Bellm, Pres.
1701 Pennsylvania Ave., NW
Washington, DC 20006
(202) 452-6680
MESBIC A * 5,9,12
(Main Office: NJ)

Capital Investment Company of
Washington
Mr. Jayrel Goldberg, Pres.
1010 Wisconsin Ave., NW, #900
Washington, DC 20007
(202) 298-3214
A * 6,12

Columbia Ventures, Inc.
Mr. Richard Whitney, Pres.
1828 L St., NW
Washington, DC 20036
(202) 659-0033
Fully Invested
(Branch Office: MS)

Continental Investors, Inc.
Mr. Lac Thantrong, Pres.
2020 K St., NW, Ste. 350
Washington, DC 20006
(202) 466-3709
MESBIC A * 12

Fulcrum Venture Capital Corp.
Mr. Steven L. Lilly, Pres.
2021 K St., NW, Ste. 714
Washington, DC 20006
(202) 833-9590
MESBIC C *** 1,5,8,9,11

Greater Washington Investors, Inc.
Mr. Don A. Christensen, Pres. &
Treas.
1015 - 18th St., NW
Washington, DC 20036
(202) 466-2210
B *** 1,5,8,12

FLORIDA

Branch Office:
Allied Capital Corp.
Mr. George C. Williams, Pres.
Mr. Warren Miller, Reg. VP
1614 One Financial Plaza
Ft. Lauderdale, FL 33394
(305) 763-8484
C * 1,2,4,5,6,8,9,11,12
(Main Office: DC)

CUBICO, Ltd.
Mr. Anthony G. Marina, Pres.
7425 NW 79th St.
Miami, FL 33166
(305) 885-8881
MESBIC B * 12

The First American Lending Corp.
Mr. G. M. Caughlin, Pres.
1200 N. Dixie Hwy., P.O. Box 1449
Lake Worth, FL 33460
(305) 582-3322
MESBIC A * 12

First Miami SBIC
Mr. Irve L. Libby, Pres.
1195 NE 125th St.
North Miami, FL 33161
(305) 891-2534
B * 2,6,7,12

Branch Office:
First Miami SBIC
Mr. Irve L. Libby, Pres.
Suite 18-D
250 S. Ocean Blvd.
Boca Raton, FL 33432
(305) 392-4424
B * 2,6,7,12

Gulf Coast Capital Corp.
Mr. Oscar M. Tharp, Pres.
70 N. Baylen St.
P.O. Box 12790
Pensacola, FL 32575
(904) 434-1361
A *** 2,10

J & D Capital Corp.
Mr. Jack Carmel, Pres.
12747 Biscayne Blvd.
North Miami, FL 33181
(305) 893-0303
C * 10,12

Market Capital Corp.
Mr. E. E. Eads, Pres.
P.O. Box 22667
Tampa, FL 33622
(813) 248-5781
A *** 9,11

Branch Office:
Massachusetts Capital Corp.
Mr. David Harkins, Pres.
Mr. Warren Miller, Reg. VP
1614 One Financial Plaza
Ft. Lauderdale, FL 33394
(305) 763-8484
B *** 1,3,5,6,10,11,12
(Main Office: MA)

The Quiet SBIC
Mr. Edward Gray, III, VP
105 E. Garden St.
Pensacola, FL 32501
(904) 434-5090
A * 12

Servico Business Investment Corp.
Mr. Gary O. Marino, Pres.
2000 Palm Beach Lakes Blvd.
Ste. 1000
West Palm Beach, FL 33409
(305) 689-5031
A * 12

Small Business Assistance Corp.
Mr. Charles S. Smith, Pres.
2612 W. 15th St.
Panama City, FL 32401
(904) 785-9577
B * 4

Southeast SBIC, Inc.
Mr. C. L. Hofmann, Pres.
100 S. Biscayne Blvd.
Miami, FL 33131
(305) 577-4680
C *** 1,5,6,8,12

Universal Financial Services, Inc.
Mr. Norman N. Zipkin, CEO
Ste. B, 225 NE 35th St.
Miami, FL 33137
(305) 573-6326
MESBIC A * 12

Venture Capital Corp. of America
Mr. Richard A. Osias, Pres.
4875 N. Federal Hwy.

Ft. Lauderdale, FL 33308
(305) 772-1800
B *** 12

Verde Capital Corp.
Mr. Jose Dearing, Pres.
6701 Sunset Dr., Ste. 104
Miami, FL 33143
(305) 666-8789
MESBIC B * 1,2,5,11,12

GEORGIA

Affiliated Investment Fund, Ltd.
Mr. Samuel Weissman, Pres.
2225 Shurfine Dr.
College Park, GA 30337
(404) 766-0221
A ** 9

CSRA Capital Corp.
Mr. Allen F. Caldwell, Jr., Pres.
P.O. Box 11045
1058 Claussen Rd., Ste. 102
Augusta, GA 30907
(404) 736-2236
B *** 2

Fidelity Capital Corp.
Mr. Alfred F. Skiba, Pres.
180 Interstate No. Pkwy., Ste. 400
Atlanta, GA 30339
(404) 955-4313
C * 1,2,5,11

Investor's Equity, Inc.
Mr. Ronald W. White
Managing Dir.
3517 First Nat'l Bank Tower
Atlanta, GA 30383
(404) 523-3999
B *** 1,2,3,4,5,6,8

Peachtree Capital Corp.
Mr. David W. Howe, Pres.
1611 Gas Light Tower
Peachtree Center
Atlanta, GA 30303
(404) 522-9000
A *** 12

Southeastern Capital SBIC
Mr. J. Ray Efird, Pres.
100 Northcreek, Ste. 600

3715 Northside Pkwy., NW
Atlanta, GA 30327
(404) 237-1567
B *** 12

Sunbelt Funding Corp.
Mr. Charles H. Jones, Pres.
P.O. Box 7006
Macon, GA 31298
(912) 742-0177
MESBIC A * 12

HAWAII

Pacific Venture Capital, Ltd.
Mr. Dexter J. Taniguchi, Pres.
1505 Dillingham Blvd.
Honolulu, HI 96817
(808) 847-6502
MESBIC A * 12

Small Business Investment Co. of
   Hawaii, Inc.
Mr. James W. Y. Wong, Chmn.
1575 S. Beretania St.
Honolulu, HI 96826
(808) 946-1171
A *** 2,12

IDAHO

First Idaho Venture Capital Co.
Mr. Jack J. Winderl, Pres.
P.O. Box 1739
Boise, ID 83701
(208) 345-3460
B ** 12

ILLINOIS

Abbott Capital Corp.
Mr. Richard E. Lassar, Pres.
120 S. LaSalle St., Ste. 1100
Chicago, IL 60603
(312) 726-3803
C *** 5,6,8,10

Amoco Venture Capital Co.
Mr. L. E. Schaffer, Pres.
200 E. Randolph
Chicago, IL 60601
(312) 856-6523
MESBIC B * 12

CEDCO Capital Corp.
Mr. Frank B. Brooks, Pres.
Mr. Joseph W. Miller, VP
180 N. Michigan Ave., Ste. 333
Chicago, IL 60601
(312) 984-5971
MESBIC A *** 12

Chicago Community Ventures, Inc.
Ms. Phyllis George, Pres.
108 N. State St., Ste. 902
Chicago, IL 60602
(312) 726-6084
MESBIC B *** 12

Chicago Equity Corp.
Mr. Morris Weiser, Pres.
One IBM Plaza, Ste. 2424
Chicago, IL 60611
(312) 321-9662
A *** 12

Claremont/LaSalle Corp.
Mr. Steven B. Randall, Pres.
29 S. LaSalle St.
Chicago, IL 60603
(312) 236-5888
D *** 1,3,5,6,7,8,12

Combined Opportunities, Inc.
Mr. E. Patric Jones, Asst. VP
300 N. State St.
Chicago, IL 60610
(312) 266-3091
MESBIC B * 1,5,12

Continental Illinois Venture Corp.
Mr. John L. Hines, Pres.
231 S. LaSalle St., Ste. 1617
Chicago, IL 60693
(312) 828-8021
E *** 1,3,5,6,8,9,11,12

First Capital Corp. of Chicago
Mr. John A. Canning, Jr., Pres.
One 1st Nat'l Plaza, Ste. 2628
Chicago, IL 60670
(312) 732-5400
E *** 12

Frontenac Capital Corp.
Mr. David A. R. Dullum, Pres.
208 S. LaSalle St.
Chicago, IL 60604
(312) 368-0047
C *** 1,5,6,8,12

Heizer Corporation
Mr. E. F. Heizer, Jr., Chmn.
20 N. Wacker Dr.
Chicago, IL 60606
(312) 641-2200
E *** 1,3,5,6,7,8,11,12

Branch Office:
Nelson Capital Corp.
Mr. Irwin B. Nelson, Pres.
8550 W. Bryn Mawr Ave., Ste. 515
Chicago, IL 60631
(312) 693-5990
D ** 12
(Main Office: NY)

Tower Ventures, Inc.
Mr. R. A. Comey, Pres.
Sears Tower, BSC 9-29
Chicago, IL 60684
(312) 875-0583
MESBIC B * 12

United Capital Corp. of Illinois
Mr. Jack K. Ahrens, VP
United Center
State & Wyman Sts.
Rockford, IL 61101
(815) 987-2179
C *** 1,5,6,8

The Urban Fund of IL, Inc.
Mr. E. Patric Jones, Pres.
300 N. State St.
Chicago, IL 60610
(312) 266-3050
MESBIC B * 12

Woodland Capital Co.
Mr. James W. Erickson, Pres.
1401 N. Western Ave.
Lake Forest, IL 60045
(312) 295-6300
C *** 12

IOWA

R. W. Allsop Capital Corp.
Mr. Robert W. Allsop, Pres.
1241 Park Place NE
Cedar Rapids, IA 52402
(319) 393-6911
D *** 1,5,6,12
(Branch Offices: KS, WI, MO)

MorAmerica Capital Corp.
Mr. Jerry M. Burrows, Pres.
300 American Bldg.
Cedar Rapids, IA 52401
(319) 363-8249
D *** 12
(Branch Offices: MO, WI)

KANSAS

Branch Office:
R. W. Allsop Capital Corp.
Mr. Larry C. Maddox
35 Corporate Woods, Ste. 229
9101 W. 10th St.
Overland Park, KS 66210
(913) 642-4719
D *** 1,5,6,12
(Main Office: IA)

Kansas Venture Capital, Inc.
Mr. George L. Doak, Pres.
First Nat'l Bank Towers
One Townsite Plaza, Ste. 1030
Topeka, KS 66603
(913) 233-1368
A *** 5

KENTUCKY

Equal Opportunity Finance, Inc.
Mr. Frank P. Justice, Jr., Pres.
9502 Williamsburg Plaza
Louisville, KY 40222
(502) 423-1943
MESBIC A * 12

Financial Opportunities, Inc.
Mr. Gary J. Miller, Gen. Mgr.
981 S. Third St.
Louisville, KY 40203
(502) 584-1281
A * 9

Mountain Ventures, Inc.
Mr. Frederick J. Beste, III, Pres.
911 N. Main St., Box 628
London, KY 40741
(606) 878-6635
D *** 12

LOUISIANA

Business Capital Corp.
Mr. David R. Burrus, Pres.
1732 Canal St.
New Orleans, LA 70112
(504) 581-4002
MESBIC D * 12

CADDO Capital Corp.
Mr. Thomas L. Young, Jr., Pres.
820 Jordan St., Ste. 504
Shreveport, LA 71101
(318) 424-0505
D *** 3,5,12

Capital for Terrebonne, Inc.
Mr. Hartwell A. Lewis, Pres.
1613 Barrow St., P.O. Box 1868
Houma, LA 70361
(504) 868-3933
A ** 12

Commercial Capital, Inc.
Mr. F. W. Pierce, Pres.
200 Belle Terre Blvd.
Covington, LA 70433
(504) 892-4921 Ext. 261
A * 1,2,4,6,7,9,10,12

Branch Offices:
Commercial Capital, Inc.
c/o Northlake Insurance, Inc.
Bogue Falaya Plaza Shopping Center
Covington, LA 70433

Commercial Capital, Inc.
c/o Central Progressive Bank
1809 W. Thomas
Hammond, La 70401

Dixie Business Investment Co.
Mr. Steve K. Cheek, Pres.
P.O. Box 588
Lake Providence, LA 71254
(318) 559-1558
A ** 12

EDICT Investment Corp.
Mr. Gregory B. Johnson, Exec. VP
2908 S. Carrollton Ave.
New Orleans, LA 70118
(504) 861-2364
MESBIC A ** 12

First SBIC of Louisiana
Mrs. Alma O. Galle, Pres.
2852 Carey St., P.O. Box 1336
Slidell, LA 70459
(504) 561-0017/641-2404
A * 12

First Southern Capital Corp.
Mr. John H. Crabtree, Chmn. & Pres.
P.O. Box 14205
Baton Rouge, LA 70898
(504) 769-3004
D *** 1,5,12

Louisiana Equity Capital Corp.
Mr. Charles A. Beard, Exec. VP
c/o Louisiana Nat'l Bank
P.O. Box 1511
Baton Rouge, LA 70821
(504) 389-4421
C ** 5,9

Royal Street Investment Corp.
Mr. William D. Humphries, Pres.
618 Baronne St.
New Orleans, LA 70113
(504) 588-9271
B *** 12

Savings Venture Capital Corp.
Mr. David R. Dixon, Exec. VP
6001 Financial Plaza
Shreveport, LA 71130
(318) 686-9200
B ** 12

Venturtech Capital, Inc.
Mr. E. M. Charlet, Pres.
Ste. 602, Republic Tower
5700 Florida Blvd.
Baton Rouge, LA 70806
(504) 926-5482
B *** 1,6,8

MAINE

Maine Capital Corp.
Mr. Lloyd D. Brace, Jr.
VP & Dir. of Finance
One Memorial Circle
Augusta, ME 04330
(207) 623-1686
B * 1,2,3,5,8,11,12

MARYLAND
Albright Venture Capital, Inc.
Mr. William A. Albright, Pres.
8005 Rappahannock Ave.
Jessup, MD 20794
(301) 799-7935
MESBIC A * 2,4,9,10,11,12

MASSACHUSETTS
Advent Capital Corp.
Mr. David D. Croll, Chmn. & CEO
111 Devonshire St.
Boston, MA 02109
(617) 725-2301
E * 1,3,5,6,8,12

Alta Capital Corp.
Mr. William P. Egan, Pres.
175 Federal St.
Boston, MA 02110
(617) 482-8020
D * 1,6,9,12

Atlas Capital Corp.
Mr. Herbert Carver, Pres.
55 Court St., Ste. 200
Boston, MA 02108
(617) 482-1218
B ** 12

Boston Hambro Corp.
Mr. Edwin A. Goodman, Pres.
One Boston Place
Boston, MA 02106
(617) 722-7055
D * 1,2,3,5,6,8,12
(Branch Office: NY)

Chestnut Capital Corp.
Mr. David D. Croll, Chmn. & CEO
111 Devonshire St.
Boston, MA 02109
(617) 725-2302
E * 1,3,5,6,8,12

Cohasset Capital Corp.
Mr. Grant Wilson, Pres.
4 Tupelo Rd.
Cohasset, MA 02025
(617) 383-0758
A *** 1,12

Devonshire Capital Corp.
Mr. David D. Croll, Chmn. & CEO

111 Devonshire St.
Boston, MA 02109
(617) 725-2300
E * 1,3,5,6,8,12

First Capital Corp. of Boston
Mr. George Rooks, Pres.
100 Federal St.
Boston, MA 02110
(617) 434-2442
D *** 1,3,5,6,8,9

Massachusetts Capital Corp.
Mr. David Harkins, Pres.
Mr. Christopher Lynch, VP
75 Federal St.
Boston, MA 01945
(617) 426-2488
B *** 1,3,5,6,10,11,12
(Branch Office: FL)

Massachusetts Venture Capital
   Corp.
Mr. Charles Grigsby, Pres.
59 Temple Place
Boston, MA 02111
(617) 426-0208
MESBIC B *** 12

New England Enterprise Capital
   Corp.
Mr. Z. David Patterson, VP
28 State St.
Boston, MA 02106
(617) 742-0285
C *** 1,5,6,8,10,12

Schooner Capital Corp.
Mr. Vincent J. Ryan, Jr., Pres.
77 Franklin St.
Boston, MA 02110
(617) 357-9031
B *** 1,3

Transatlantic Capital Corp.
Mr. Bayard Henry, Pres.
60 Batterymarch St., Room 728
Boston, MA 02110
(617) 482-0015
C *** 1,5,6,8,10

UST Capital Corp.
Mr. Stephen R. Lewinstein, Pres.
40 Court St.

Boston, MA 02108
(617) 726-7260
A * 1,2,3,5,6,8,11

W.C.C.I. Capital Corp.
Ms. Deborah G. Nurse, VP
791 Main St.
Worcester, MA 01610
(617) 791-0941
MESBIC A *** 12

Worcester Capital Corp.
Mr. W. Kenneth Kidd, VP
446 Main St.
Worcester, MA 01608
(617) 853-7508
A *** 5,8

MICHIGAN

DBT Capital Corp.
Mr. John D. Berkaw, Pres.
211 W. Fort St.
Detroit, MI 48231
(313) 222-3907
C *** 5,6,8,12

Doan Resources Corp.
Mr. Ian R. N. Bund, VP
110 East Grove
Midland, MI 48640
(517) 631-2471
C *** 1,5,6,8

Federated Capital Corp.
Mr. Louis P. Ferris, Jr., Pres.
20000 W. Twelve Mile Rd.
Southfield, MI 48076
(313) 559-0554
A ** 12

Independence Capital Formation,
Inc.
Mr. Walter M. McMurtry, Jr.,
Pres.
1505 Woodward Ave., Pierson
Bldg.
Ste. 700
Detroit, MI 48226
(313) 961-2470
MESBIC B * 1,5,8,9,11

Metro-Detroit Investment Co.
Mr. William J. Fowler, Pres.
18481 W. Ten Mile Rd.

Southfield, MI 48075
(313) 557-3818/19
MESBIC A ** 9

Michigan Capital & Service, Inc.
Mr. Joseph F. Conway, Pres.
740 City Center Bldg.
Ann Arbor, MI 48104
(313) 663-0702
C *** 1,3,5,6,8,12

Motor Enterprises, Inc.
Mr. James Kobus, Mgr.
General Motors Bldg.
Rm. 6-248
3044 W. Grand Blvd.
Detroit, MI 48202
(313) 556-4273
MESBIC B ** 5

Mutual Investment Co., Inc.
Mr. Timothy J. Taylor, Treas.
17348 W. Twelve Mile Rd.
Ste. 104
Southfield, MI 48076
(313) 552-8515
MESBIC A * 9

PRIME, Inc.
Mr. Jimmy N. Hill, Pres.
1845 David Whitney Bldg.
Detroit, MI 48226
(313) 964-3380
MESBIC B * 12

Tyler Refrigeration Capital Corp.
Mr. Gary J. Slock, Chmn.
1329 Lake
Niles, MI 49120
(616) 683-1610
A * 2

MINNESOTA

Consumer Growth Capital, Inc.
Mr. John T. Gerlach, Pres.
430 Oak Grove
Minneapolis, MN 55403
(612) 874-0694
C *** 1,4,5,10,12

Control Data Capital Corp.
Mr. John F. Tracy, Pres.
8100 34th Ave. S.

Minneapolis, MN 55440
(612) 853-6537
B * 1,5,6,8,12

Eagle Ventures, Inc.
Mr. Thomas M. Neitge, VP
700 Soo Line Bldg.
Minneapolis, MN 55422
(612) 339-9694
C *** 1,5,6,7,8

First Midwest Capital Corp.
Mr. Alan K. Ruvelson, Pres.
Ste. 700 Chamber of Commerce
    Bldg.
15 S. Fifth St.
Minneapolis, MN 55402
(612) 339-9391
B *** 1,5,6,8,9,10,12

Northland Capital Corp.
Mr. George G. Barnum, Jr., Pres.
613 Missabe Bldg.
Duluth, MN 55802
(218) 722-0545
B *** 12

North Star Ventures, Inc.
Mr. Terrence W. Glarner, Exec.
    VP & Gen. Mgr.
Ste. 1258, NFC Bldg.
7900 Xerxes Ave., S.
Minneapolis, MN 55431
(612) 830-4550
C *** 1,5,6,7,8,12

Northwest Growth Fund, Inc.
Mr. Robert F. Zicarelli, Chmn.
1730 Midwest Plaza Bldg.
801 Nicollet Mall
Minneapolis, MN 55402
(612) 372-8770
D *** 12
(Branch Offices: OR, CO)

Pathfinder Venture Capital Fund
Mr. A. J. Greenshields, Ptnr.
7300 Metro Blvd., Ste. 585
Minneapolis, MN 55435
(612) 835-1121
E *** 1,5,6,8

P. R. Peterson Venture Capital
    Corp.
Mr. P. R. Peterson, Pres.
7301 Washington Ave., S.

Edina, MN 55435
(612) 941-8171
A *** 6,8

Retailers Growth Fund, Inc.
Mr. Cornell L. Moore
Chmn. & Pres.
5100 Gamble Dr., Ste. 380
Minneapolis, MN 55416
(612) 546-8989
A * 9

Shared Ventures, Inc.
Mr. Howard Weiner, Pres.
4601 Excelsior Blvd., Ste. 411
Minneapolis, MN 55416
(612) 925-3411
A * 12

MISSISSIPPI

Branch Office:
Columbia Ventures, Inc.
809 State St.
Jackson, MS 39201
FULLY INVESTED
(Main Office: DC)

DeSoto Capital Corp.
Mr. William B. Rudner, Pres.
8885 E. Goodman
Olive Branch, MS 38654
(601) 895-4145
A *** 12

Invesat Corporation
Mr. J. Thomas Noojin, Pres.
162 E. Amite St., Ste. 204
Jackson, MS 39207
(601) 969-3242
C * 12

Sun Delta Capital Access Center,
    Inc.
Mr. Charles Bannerman, Pres.
819 Main St., Box 588
Greenville, MS 38701
(601) 335-5291
MESBIC B * 12

Vicksburg Small Business Invest-
    ment Co.
Mr. David L. May, Pres.
First Nat'l Bank Bldg.
P.O. Box 852

Vicksburg, MS 39180
(601) 636-4762
A * 5,9,12

MISSOURI
Branch Office:
R. W. Alisop Capital Corp.
Mr. Robert L. Kuk
111 W. Port Plaza, Ste. 600
St. Louis, MO 63141
(314) 434-1688
D *** 1,5,6,12
(Main Office: IA)

Bankers Capital Corp.
Mr. Raymond E. Glasnapp, Pres.
4049 Pennsylvania, Ste. 304
Kansas City, MO 64111
(816) 531-1600
A * 12

Intercapco West, Inc.
Mr. Thomas E. Phelps, Pres.
7800 Bonhomme
Clayton, MO 63105
(314) 863-0600
A *** 1,2,3,5,6,8,9,11,12

Branch Office:
MorAmerica Capital Corp.
Mr. Rex E. Wiggins, Reg. VP
Ste. 2724A - Commerce Tower
911 Main St.
Kansas City, MO 64105
(816) 842-0114
D *** 12
(Main Office: IA)

NEBRASKA
Community Equity Corp. of Ne-
braska
Mr. William C. Moore, Pres.
5620 Ames Ave., Ste. 109
Omaha, NE 68104
(402) 455-7722
MESBIC A ** 12

NEVADA
Westland Capital Corp.
Mr. Morton B. Phillips, Chmn.

100 W. Grove St., Ste. 550
Reno, NV 89509
(702) 826-6307
B * 12

NEW HAMPSHIRE
Hampshire Capital Corp.
Mr. Philip G. Baker, Pres.
48 Congress St.
P.O. Box 468
Portsmouth, NH 03801
(603) 431-1415
A *** 5,9,12

NEW JERSEY
Broad Arrow Investment Corp.
Mr. C. N. Bellm, Pres.
P.O. Box 2231-R
Morristown, NJ 07960
(201) 766-2835
MESBIC A * 5,9,12
(Branch Office: DC)

Engle Investment Co.
Mr. Murray Hendel, Pres.
35 Essex St.
Hackensack, NJ 07601
(201) 489-3583
A * 12
(Branch Office: NY)

Eslo Capital Corp.
Mr. Leo Katz, Pres.
485 Morris Ave.
Springfield, NJ 07081
(201) 467-2545
A ** 12

Lloyd Capital Corp.
Mr. Solomon T. Scharf, Pres.
77 State Highway #5
Edgewater, NJ 07020
(201) 947-6000
C * 2,4,6,9,12

Main Capital Investment Corp.
Mr. Sam Klotz, Pres.
818 Main St.
Hackensack, NJ 07601
(201) 489-2080
A *** 1,2,3,4,7,10,12

Monmouth Capital Corp.
Mr. Eugene W. Landy, Pres.
125 Wyckoff Rd.
P.O. Box 335
Eatontown, NJ 07724
(201) 542-4927
B * 12

Quidnet Capital Corp.
Mr. Stephen W. Fillo, Pres.
909 State Rd.
Princeton, NJ 08540
(609) 924-7665
C *** 12

Rutgers Minority Investment Co.
Mr. Louis T. German, Pres.
92 New St.
Newark, NJ 07102
(201) 648-5287
MESBIC A * 5,9

NEW MEXICO

Albuquerque SBIC
Mr. Albert T. Ussery, Pres.
P.O. Box 487
Albuquerque, NM 87103
(505) 247-4089
A *** 12

Associated Southwest Investors,
    Inc.
Mr. John R. Rice, Pres.
2425 Alamo SE
Albuquerque, NM 87106
(505) 842-5955
MESBIC B * 1,5,6,8,12

First Capital Corp. of New Mexico
Ms. Shirley A. Williams, Pres.
8425 Osuna Rd., NE
Albuquerque, NM 87112
(505) 292-2300
A * 12

Fluid Capital Corp.
Mr. George T. Slaughter, Pres.
200 Lomas, NW, Ste. 527
Albuquerque, NM 87102
(505) 243-2279
B * 2,12

Branch Office:
The Franklin Corp.

Mr. Herman E. Goodman, Pres.
4209 San Mateo NE
Albuquerque, NM 87110
(505) 243-9680
D *** 1,5,6,7,8,11,12
(Main Office: NY)

New Mexico Capital Corp.
Mr. S. P. Hidalgo, II, Exec. VP
2900 Louisiana Blvd., NE, Ste. 201
Albuquerque, NM 87110
(505) 884-3600
C * 12

Southwest Capital Investments,
    Inc.
Mr. Martin J. Roe, Pres.
8000 Pennsylvania Circle, NE
Albuquerque, NM 87110
(505) 265-9564
A * 5,10,12

Venture Capital Corp. of New
    Mexico
Mr. Ben Bronstein, Chmn.
5301 Central Ave., NE
Ste. 1600
Albuquerque, NM 87108
(505) 266-0066
B *** 12

NEW YORK

AMEV Capital Corp.
Mr. Martin S. Orland, Pres.
Two World Trade Center, #9766
New York, NY 10048
(212) 775-1912
D *** 1,4,5,6,7,9,10,12

Amistad DOT Venture Capital,
    Inc.
Mr. Percy E. Sutton, Chmn. &
    Pres.
801 Second Ave., Ste. 303
New York, NY 10017
(212) 573-6600
MESBIC C * 5,8,11

BanCap Corporation
Mr. William L. Whitely, Pres.
155 E. 42nd St.
New York, NY 10017
(212) 784-6470
MESBIC B *** 1,3,5,12

Beneficial Capital Corp.
Mr. John J. Hoey, Pres.
645 Fifth Ave.
New York, NY 10022
(212) 752-1291
A * 3,12

Bohlen Capital Corp.
Mr. Harvey Wertheim, Pres.
230 Park Ave.
New York, NY 10169
(212) 867-9535
D *** 1,3,5,6,8

Branch Office:
Boston Hambro Corp.
Mr. Edwin A. Goodman, Pres.
17 E. 71st St.
New York, NY 10021
(212) 288-7778
D * 1,2,3,5,6,8,12
(Main Office: MA)

BT Capital Corp.
Mr. James G. Hellmuth, Pres.
280 Park Ave.
New York, NY 10017
(212) 692-4840
D * 12

Branch Office:
California Northwest Fund, Inc.
Dr. Yung Wong, Managing Dir.
230 Park Ave., Third Floor
New York, NY 10017
(212) 935-0997
D * 12
(Main Office: CA)

Central New York SBIC, Inc.
Mr. Robert E. Romig, Pres.
351 S. Warren St.
Syracuse, NY 13202
(315) 478-5026
FULLY INVESTED

Citicorp Venture Capital, Ltd.
Mr. William T. Comfort, Chmn.
399 Park Ave., 20th Floor
New York, NY 10043
(212) 559-1127
C *** 12

Clinton Capital Corp.
Mr. Mark Scharfman, Pres.

35 Middagh St.
Brooklyn, NY 11201
(212) 858-0920
C *** 12

CMNY Capital Co., Inc.
Mr. Robert Davidoff, VP
77 Water St.
New York, NY 10005
(212) 437-7078
B *** 1,5,6,7,8,9,10,12

College Venture Equity Corp.
Mr. Francis M. Williams, Pres.
Mr. William J. MacDougall, VP
1222 Main St., P.O. Box 791
Niagara Falls, NY 14301
(716) 285-8455
A * 12

Cornell Capital Corp.
Mr. Barry M. Bloom, Pres.
8-B Main St.
East Hampton, NY 11937
(516) 324-0408
D * 4,12

EAB Venture Corp.
Mr. Richard C. Burcaw, Pres.
Mr. Mark R. Littell, VP & Treas.
90 Park Ave.
New York, NY 10016
(212) 437-4182
C * 1,3,5,6,8,10,12

Edwards Capital Corp.
Mr. Edward H. Teitelbaum, Pres.
215 Lexington Ave.
New York, NY 10016
(212) 686-2568
B * 12

Branch Office:
Engle Investment Co.
Mr. Murray Hendel, Pres.
135 W. 50th St.
New York, NY 10020
(212) 757-9580
A * 12
(Main Office: NJ)

Equico Capital Corp.
Mr. Carlos R. Evering, Exec. VP
1211 Ave. of the Americas, Ste.
    2905

New York, NY 10020
(212) 921-2290
MESBIC C *** 12

Equitable SBIC
Mr. David Goldberg, Pres.
350 Fifth Ave., Ste. 5805
New York, NY 10118
(212) 564-5420
A * 6

ESIC Capital, Inc.
Mr. George H. Bookbinder, Pres.
110 E. 59th St.
New York, NY 10022
(212) 421-1605
C ** 12

European Development Capital
    Corp.
Mr. Harvey Wertheim, Pres.
230 Park Ave.
New York, NY 10169
(212) 867-9535
D *** 1,3,5,6,8

Exim Capital Corp.
Mr. Victor Chun, Pres.
290 Madison Ave.
New York, NY 10017
(212) 683-3200
MESBIC A *** 5

Fairfield Equity Corp.
Mr. Matthew A. Berdon, Pres.
200 E. 42nd St.
New York, NY 10017
(212) 867-0150
B *** 1,5,7,9,10,12

Fifty-Third Street Ventures, Inc.
Mr. Alan J. Patricof, Chmn.
1 E. 53rd St.
New York, NY 10023
(212) 753-6300
D *** 1,3,5,6,8,12

Branch Office:
The First Connecticut SBIC
Mr. James Breiner, Chmn.
Mr. David Engelson, Pres.
680 Fifth Ave.
New York, NY 10019
(Main Office: CT)

First Wall Street SBIC, Inc.
Mr. John W. Chappell, Pres.

767 Fifth Ave., Ste. 4403
New York, NY 10153
(212) 355-6540
A *** 3

The Franklin Corp.
Mr. Herman E. Goodman, Pres.
1 Rockefeller Plaza
New York, NY 10020
(212) 581-4900
D *** 1,5,6,7,8,11,12
(Branch Office: NM)

Fundex Capital Corp.
Mr. Howard Sommer, Pres.
525 Northern Blvd.
Great Neck, NY 11021
(516) 466-8550
(212) 895-7361
C ** 12

Hanover Capital Corp.
Mr. Daniel J. Sullivan, Pres.
233 E. 62nd St.
New York, NY 10021
(212) 752-5173
B * 12

Heller Capital Services, Inc.
Mr. Jack A. Prizzi, Exec. VP
200 Park Ave.
New York, NY 10166
(212) 880-7198
E * 1,3,5,6,7,8,9,11,12

Ibero-American Investors Corp.
Mr. Emilio Serrano, Gen. Mgr.
954 Clifford Ave.
Rochester, NY 14621
(716) 544-7420
MESBIC A *** 5,9,12

Intercoastal Capital Corp.
Mr. Herbert Krasnow, Pres.
380 Madison Ave.
New York, NY 10017
(212) 986-0482
D * 1,2,4,6,7,10,11,12

Intergroup Venture Capital Corp.
Mr. Ben Hauben, Pres.
230 Park Ave.
New York, NY 10169
(212) 661-5428
A * 12

International Film Investors, Inc.
Mr. Neil Braun, VP-Finance
595 Madison Ave.
New York, NY 10022
(212) 310-1500
E *** 7

Irving Capital Corp.
Mr. J. Andrew McWethy, Exec.
VP
1290 Ave. of the Americas
Third Floor
New York, NY 10019
(212) 922-8790
E *** 1,3,5,8,9

Japanese American Capital Corp.
Mr. Stephen Huang, Pres.
120 Broadway
New York, NY 10271
(212) 964-4077
MESBIC B * 2,4,12

Korean Capital Corp.
Ms. Min-ja Oh, Pres.
222-48 Birmington Pkwy.
Bayside, NY 11364
(212) 224-5891
MESBIC C * 12

Lincoln Capital Corp.
Mr. Martin Lifton, Pres.
41 E. 42nd St., Ste. 1510
New York, NY 10017
(212) 697-0610
C * 2,12

Medallion Funding Corp.
Mr. Alvin Murstein, Pres.
86 Glen Cove Rd.
East Hills, NY 11576
(212) 682-3300
MESBIC A * 11

Branch Office:
Medallion Funding Corp.
Mr. Alvin Murstein, Pres.
205 E. 42nd St., Rm. 2020
New York, NY 10017
(212) 682-3300
MESBIC A * 11
(Main Office: NY)

Midland Capital Corp.
Mr. Michael R. Stanfield, Managing Dir.

Mr. Robert B. Machinist, Managing Dir.
110 William St.
New York, NY 10038
(212) 577-0750
E * 1,3,12

Minority Equity Capital Co., Inc.
(MECCO)
Mr. Patrick Owen Burns, Pres.
275 Madison Ave., Ste. 1901
New York, NY 10016
(212) 686-9710
MESBIC C *** 1,5,6,9,12

M & T Capital Corp.
Mr. Harold M. Small, Pres.
One M & T Plaza
Buffalo, NY 14240
(716) 842-4881
C *** 12

Multi-Purpose Capital Corp.
Mr. Eli B. Fine, Pres.
31 S. Broadway
Yonkers, NY 10701
(914) 963-2733
A * 1,2,3,4,5,6,7,8,9,10,11,12

Nelson Capital Corp.
Mr. Irwin B. Nelson, Pres.
591 Stewart Ave.
Garden City, NY 11530
(516) 222-2555
D ** 12
(Branch Offices: CA, IL)

New Oasis Capital Corp.
Mr. James J. H. Huang, Pres.
114 Liberty St., Ste. 404
New York, NY 10006
(212) 394-2804/5
MESBIC B * 12

Noro Capital Corp.
Mr. Harvey Wertheim, Pres.
230 Park Ave.
New York, NY 10169
(212) 867-9535
D *** 1,3,5,6,8

North Street Capital Corp.
Mr. Ralph L. McNeal, Sr., Pres.
250 North St., TA-2
White Plains, NY 10625

(914) 683-6306
MESBIC A *** 1,5,11,12

NYBDC Capital Corp.
Mr. Marshall R. Lustig, Pres.
41 State St.
Albany, NY 12209
(518) 463-2268
A *** 5

Pioneer Investors
Mr. James G. Niven, Pres.
113 E. 55th St.
New York, NY 10022
(212) 980-9090
C *** 1,3,5,6,8

Rand SBIC, Inc.
Mr. Donald A. Ross, Pres. & CEO
2600 Rand Bldg.
Buffalo, NY 14203
(716) 853-0802
A * 12

Realty Growth Capital Corp.
Mr. Lawrence A. Benenson, Pres.
575 Lexington Ave.
New York, NY 10022
(212) 755-9044
A ** 11

Royal Business Funds Corp.
Mr. I. S. Goodman, Exec. VP
60 E. 42nd St., Ste. 2530
New York, NY 10165
(212) 986-8463
E * 2,7

R & R Financial Corp.
Mr. Imre J. Rosenthal, Pres.
1451 Broadway
New York, NY 10036
(212) 790-1400
A * 12

Peter J. Schmitt Co., Inc.
Mr. Denis G. Riley, Mgr.
678 Bailey Ave.
Buffalo, NY 14206
(716) 825-1111
A *** 5,8,9

Sherwood Business Capital Corp.
Mr. Lewis R. Eisner, Pres.
770 King St.
Port Chester, NY 10573

(914) 937-6000
B ** 12

Branch Office:
Sherwood Business Capital Corp.
Mr. Lewis R. Eisner, Pres.
230 Park Ave.
New York, NY 10169
(212) 661-2424
B ** 12

Small Business Electronics Investment Corp.
Mr. Stanley Meisels, Pres.
60 Broad St.
New York, NY 10004
(212) 952-7531
A ** 12

Southern Tier Capital Corp.
Mr. Irving Brizel, Pres.
55 S. Main St.
Liberty, NY 12754
(914) 292-3030
A * 2,4,9,12

Sprout Capital Corp.
Mr. L. Robert Johnson, Pres.
140 Broadway
New York, NY 10005
(212) 943-0300
D *** 1,3,5,6,8,9

Tappan Zee Capital Corp.
Mr. Jack Birnberg, Exec. VP
120 North Main St.
New City, NY 10956
(914) 634-8890
C ** 12

Taroco Capital Corp.
Mr. David Chang, Pres.
120 Broadway
New York, NY 10271
(212) 964-4210
MESBIC B * 2,4,5,6,7,8,9,10

Telesciences Capital Corp.
Mr. George E. Carmody, Pres.
135 E. 54th St.
New York, NY 10022
(212) 935-2550
B *** 1,8

TLC Funding Corp.
Mr. Phillip G. Kass, Pres.
200 E. 42nd St.

New York, NY 10017
(212) 682-0790
B ** 1,4,5,7,9,10,11

Transportation SBIC, Inc.
Mr. Melvin L. Hirsch, Pres.
122 E. 42nd St., 46th Fl.
New York, NY 10168
(212) 986-6050
MESBIC A ** 11

Van Rietschoten Capital Corp.
Mr. Harvey Wertheim, Pres.
230 Park Ave.
New York, NY 10169
(212) 867-9535
D *** 1,3,5,6,8

Vega Capital Corp.
Mr. Victor Harz, Pres.
10 E. 40th St.
New York, NY 10016
(212) 685-8222
C * 12

Watchung Capital Corp.
Mr. Thomas S. T. Jeng, Pres.
111 Broadway, Rm. 2002
New York, NY 10006
(212) 227-4597
MESBIC A * 2,4

Winfield Capital Corp.
Mr. Stan Pechman, Pres.
237 Mamaroneck Ave.
White Plains, NY 10605
(914) 949-2600
C * 12

Wood River Capital Corp.
Mr. Richard M. Drysdale, Pres.
767 Fifth Ave., 27th Fl.
New York, NY 10053
(212) 750-9420
D *** 1,5,6,8,12

NORTH CAROLINA

Delta Capital, Inc.
Mr. Alex Wilkins, Pres.
202 Latta Arcade
320 S. Tryon St.
Charlotte, NC 28202
(704) 372-1410
C *** 12

Heritage Capital Corp.
Mr. J. Randolph Gregory, Pres.
2290 First Union Plaza
Charlotte, NC 28282
(704) 334-2867
C *** 12

Kitty Hawk Capital, Ltd.
Mr. Walter Wilkinson, Pres.
2195 First Union Plaza
Charlotte, NC 28282
(704) 333-3777
B *** 1,5,6,9,12

Vanguard Investment Co., Inc.
Mr. James F. Hansley, Pres.
309 Pepper Bldg.
Winston-Salem, NC 27101
(919) 724-3676
MESBIC B * 1,5,6,11,12

NORTH DAKOTA

First Dakota Capital Corp.
Mr. David L. Johnson, VP
52 Broadway
Fargo, ND 58102
(701) 237-0450
A *** 12

OHIO

Clarion Capital Corp.
Mr. Peter Van Oosterhout, Pres.
The Chesterfield
1801 E. 12th St., Rm. 201
Cleveland, OH 44114
(216) 687-1096
D *** 2,3,5,12

Dycap, Inc.
Mr. A. Gordon Imhoff, Pres.
Ste. 1980, 88 E. Broad St.
Columbus, OH 43215
(614) 228-6641
A * 1,3,6,12

Glenco Enterprises, Inc.
Dr. Lewis F. Wright, Jr., VP
1464 E. 105th St.
Cleveland, OH 44106
(216) 721-1200
MESBIC A *** 12

Greater Miami Investment Service, Inc.
Mr. Emmett B. Lewis, Pres.
3131 S. Dixie Dr., Ste. 505
Dayton, OH 45439
(513) 294-6124
A *** 5,8

Gries Investment Co.
Mr. Robert D. Gries, Pres.
2310 Terminal Tower Bldg.
Cleveland, OH 44113
(216) 861-1146
B *** 12

Intercapco, Inc.
Mr. Robert B. Haas, Exec. VP
One Erieview Plaza
Cleveland, OH 44114
(216) 241-7170
C *** 12

National City Capital Corp.
Mr. Michael Sherwin, Pres.
National City Center
1900 E. Ninth St.
Cleveland, OH 44114
(216) 575-2491
C *** 12

Tamco Investors SBIC, Inc.
Mr. Nathan H. Monus, Pres.
375 Victoria Rd.
P.O. Box 1588
Youngstown, OH 44501
(216) 792-3811
A * 9

Tomlinson Capital Corp.
Mr. Donald R. Calkins, VP
3055 E. 63rd St.
Cleveland, OH 44127
(216) 271-2103
A *** 12

OKLAHOMA

Alliance Business Investment Co.
Mr. Barry M. Davis, Pres.
500 McFarlin Bldg., 11 E. 5th St.
Tulsa, OK 74103
(918) 584-3581
C *** 3,5,11,12
(Branch office in TX)

Bartlesville Investment Corp.
Mr. J. L. Diamond, Pres.
P.O. Box 548
Bartlesville, OK 74003
(918) 333-3022
A *** 2,3,12

First Oklahoma Investment Capital Corp.
Mr. Gary Bunch, Sr., VP
P.O. Box 25189
Oklahoma City, OK 73125
(405) 272-4338
B *** 12

Investment Capital, Inc.
Mr. James J. Wasson, Pres.
300 N. Harrison
P.O. Box 1071
Cushing, OK 74023
(918) 225-5850
B * 12

Oklahoma Capital Corp.
Mr. William T. Daniel, Chmn.
2200 Classen Blvd., Ste. 540
Oklahoma City, OK 73106
(405) 525-5544
A * 6

Southwest Venture Capital, Inc.
Mr. D. J. Rubottom, Pres.
1920 First Place
Tulsa, OK 74103
(918) 583-4663
A * 8,11,12

Utica Investment Corp.
Mr. David D. Nunneley, Pres.
1924 S. Utica
Tulsa, OK 74104
(918) 749-9976
A *** 12

OREGON

Branch Office:
Cascade Capital Corp.
Mr. Wayne B. Kingsley, VP
3018 First Nat'l Tower
1300 S. W. 5th Ave.
Portland, OR 97201
(503) 223-6622
D *** 12

(Main Office: Northwest Growth
   Fund, Inc., MN)

Northern Pacific Capital Corp.
Mr. John J. Tennant, Jr., Pres.
P.O. Box 1530
Portland, OR 97207
(503) 245-3147
B *** 5,11

Branch Office:
Washington Capital Corp.
1335 S.W. Fifth Ave.
Portland, OR 97201
(503) 243-1850
D * 12
(Main Office: WA)

PENNSYLVANIA
Alliance Enterprise Corp.
Mr. Richard H. Cummings, Jr.,
   Pres.
2000 Market St., 2nd Fl.
Philadelphia, PA 19103
(215) 972-4230
MESBIC B *** 1,5

American Venture Capital Co.
Mr. Knute C. Albrecht, Pres.
Ste. 122, Blue Bell W.
Blue Bell, PA 19422
(215) 278-8905
B *** 12

Central Capital Corp.
Mr. Robert A. Rupel, VP
1097 Commercial Ave.
P.O. Box 3959
Lancaster, PA 17604
(717) 569-9650
B * 12

Greater Philadelphia Venture Capital Corp., Inc.
Mr. Wilson E. DeWald, VP
225 S. 15th St., Ste. 920
Philadelphia, PA 19102
(215) 732-3415
MESBIC B *** 12

Osher Capital Corp.
Mr. L. Cantor, Pres.
Wyncote House

Township Line Rd. & Washington
   Lane
Wyncote, PA 19095
(215) 624-4800
C *** 5,6,8,9,10,12

TDH Capital Corp.
Mr. J. Mahlon Buck, Jr., Pres.
P.O. Box 234
Two Radnor Corporate Ctr.
Radnor, PA 19087
(215) 297-9787
C *** 12

PUERTO RICO
CREDI-I-F.A.C., Inc.
Mr. Manuel L. Prats, Inv. Adv.
Banco Cooperativo Plaza, Ste.
   1001
Ave. Ponce de Leon #623
Hato Rey, PR 00917
(809) 765-0070
MESBIC A * 12

First Puerto Rico Capital, Inc.
Mr. Eliseo E. Font, Pres.
52 McKinley St., Box 816
Mayaguez, PR 00708
(809) 832-9171
MESBIC B ** 12

North America Investment Corp.
Mr. Santiago Ruiz Betancourt,
   Pres.
P.O. Box 1831
Hato Rey, PR 00918
(809) 754-6177
MESBIC B * 1,5,9,12

Venture Capital Puerto Rico, Inc.
Mr. Manuel L. Prats, Pres.
Banco Cooperativo Plaza, Ste. 602
Hato Rey, PR 00917
(809) 751-8040/8138
MESBIC A * 12

RHODE ISLAND
Industrial Capital Corp.
Mr. A. A. T. Wickersham, Pres.
111 Westminster St.
Providence, RI 02903
(401) 278-6770
C *** 12

Narragansett Capital Corp.
Mr. Arthur D. Little, Chmn.
40 Westminster St.
Providence, RI 02903
(401) 751-1000
E *** 1,5,6,12

SOUTH CAROLINA
Carolina Venture Capital Corp.
Mr. Thomas H. Harvey, III, Pres.
P.O. Box 3110
Hilton Head Island, SC 29928
(803) 842-3101
B * 1,2,4,7,8,12

Charleston Capital Corp.
Mr. I. J. Futeral, VP
P.O. Box 30895
Charleston, SC 29407
(803) 723-6464
A *** 2,9,10

Reedy River Ventures
Mr. John M. Sterling, Pres.
P.O. Box 8931
Greenville, SC 29604
(803) 233-2374
B *** 12

TENNESSEE
C & C Capital Corp.
Mr. T. Wendell Holliday, Pres.
531 S. Gay St., 14th Fl.
Knoxville, TN 37901
(615) 637-0521
A *** 12

Chickasaw Capital Corp.
Mr. Wayne J. Haskins, Pres.
P.O. Box 387, 67 Madison
Memphis, TN 38147
(901) 523-6404
MESBIC A ** 12

Financial Resources, Inc.
Mr. Milton C. Picard, Chmn.
Ste. 2800, Sterick Bldg.
Memphis, TN 38103
(901) 527-9411
A * 12

Tennessee Equity Capital Corp.
Mr. Richard Kantor, Pres.
4515 Poplar Ave., Ste. 222
Memphis, TN 38117
(901) 761-3410
MESBIC E *** 12

TEXAS
Branch Office:
Alliance Business Investment Co.
Mr. Leon Davis, Chmn.
2660 South Tower, Pennzoil Place
Houston, TX 77002
(713) 224-8224
C *** 3,5,11,12
(Main Office in OK)

Allied Bancshares Capital Corp.
Mr. D. Kent Anderson, Pres.
808 Travis
Houston, TX 77002
(713) 224-6611
C * 3,5,10,12

Bow Lane Capital Corp.
Mr. Stuart Schube, Pres.
2411 Fountainview, Ste. 250
Houston, TX 77079
(713) 977-8882
D *** 12

Brittany Capital Corp.
Mr. Robert E. Clements, Pres.
2424 LTV Tower
Dallas, TX 75201
(214) 742-5810
A *** 1,3,6,8

Capital Marketing Corp.
Mr. Nathaniel Gibbs, Chmn.
9004 Ambassador Row
P.O. Box 225293
Dallas, TX 75222
(214) 638-1913
D ** 9

CSC Capital Corp.
Mr. William R. Thomas, Pres.
12900 Preston Rd., Ste. 700
Dallas, TX 75230
(214) 233-8242
C *** 1,3,5,6,7,8,9,11,12

Diman Financial Corp.
Mr. David S. Willis, Pres.
13601 Preston Road, 717E
Dallas, TX 75240
(214) 233-7610
A * 2,3,5,8

Energy Assets, Inc.
Mr. L. E. Simmons, VP
1800 S. Tower Pennzoil Place
Houston, TX 77002
(713) 236-9999
A * 3

Energy Capital Corp.
Mr. Herbert F. Poyner, Jr., Pres.
953 Esperson Bldg.
Houston, TX 77002
(713) 236-0006
E *** 3

First City Capital Corp.
Mr. William E. Ladin, Pres.
One West Loop S., Ste. 809
Houston, TX 77027
(713) 623-6151
A *** 12

First Dallas Capital Corp.
Mr. Eric C. Neuman, Pres.
P.O. Box 83385
Dallas, TX 75283
(214) 744-8050
D *** 1,3,5,11

Great American Capital Investors
Mr. Albert Dillard, Pres.
1006 Holliday
Wichita Falls, TX 76301
(817) 322-5554
A *** 12

The Grocers SBIC
Mr. Milton Levit, Pres.
3131 E. Holcombe Blvd.
Houston, TX 77021
(713) 747-7913
A ** 9

Livingston Capital, Ltd.
Mr. J. Livingston Kosberg, Pres.
5701 Woodway
Houston, TX 77057
(713) 977-4040
D *** 12

Mapleleaf Capital Corp.
Mr. Edward B. Scott, Pres.
7500 San Felipe, Ste. 100
Houston, TX 77063
(713) 975-8060
D ** 3,8

Mercantile Dallas Corp.
Mr. J. Wayne Gaylord, Sr. VP
P.O. Box 222090
Dallas, TX 75222
(214) 741-1469
E * 3,5,12

MESBIC Financial Corp. of Dallas
Mr. Walter W. Durham, Pres.
7701 N. Stemmons Freeway, Ste.
  850
Dallas, TX 75247
(214) 637-0445
MESBIC C *** 12

MESBIC Financial Corp. of Houston
Mr. Richard Rothfeld, Pres.
717 Travis, Ste. 600
Houston, TX 77061
(713) 228-8321
MESBIC B * 12

MESBIC of San Antonio, Inc.
Mr. William A. Fagan, Jr.
2300 W. Commerce
San Antonio, TX 78207
(512) 225-4241
MESBIC A *** 1,4,5,11

Permian Basin Capital Corp.
Mr. Douglas B. Henson, Pres.
303 W. Wall
P.O. Box 1599
Midland, TX 79702
(915) 685-2000
A *** 5,12

Rainbow Capital Corp.
Mr. W. A. Anderson, Jr., Pres.
1470 One Allen Ctr.
Houston, TX 77002
(713) 757-0461
A * 2,3,5,11

Red River Ventures, Inc.
Mr. Thomas H. Schnitzius, Pres.
2050 Houston Natural Gas Bldg.

Houston, TX 77002
(713) 658-9806
B *** 1,3,5,6

Republic Venture Group, Inc.
Mr. Robert H. Wellborn, VP
P.O. Box 225961
Dallas, TX 75265
(214) 653-5078
D *** 12

Retail Capital Corp.
Mr. William J. Boschma, Pres.
13403 Northwest Freeway, Ste. 160
Houston, TX 77040
(713) 462-8517
A ** 9

Rust Capital, Ltd.
Mr. Jeffrey C. Garvey, Exec. VP
605 Brazos, Ste. 300
Austin, TX 78701
(512) 479-0055
C * 1,5,12

Rice Country Capital, Inc.
Mr. William H. Harrison, Jr., Pres.
100 Commerce, P.O. Box 215
Eagle Lake, TX 77434
(713) 234-2506
A * 12

San Antonio Venture Group, Inc.
Mr. William A. Fagan, Jr., Pres.
2300 W. Commerce
San Antonio, TX 78207
(512) 223-3633
A *** 1,3,4,5,6,11

Southwestern Venture Capital of
   Texas, Inc.
Mr. J. A. Bettersworth, Pres.
113 S. River St.
Ste. 108, La Plaza Bldg.
Seguin, TX 78155
(512) 379-2258
B * 2,3,5,12

Texas Capital Corp.
Mr. W. Grogan Lord, Chmn.
2424 Houston Natural Gas Bldg.
Houston, TX 77002
(713) 658-9961
C *** 12

Trammell Crow Investment Company
Mr. Henry Billingsley, Pres.
2001 Bryan Tower, #3900
Dallas, TX 75201
(214) 747-0643
A ** 2

TSM Corp.
Mr. Joe Justice
444 Executive Center Blvd.
Ste. 237
El Paso, TX 79902
(915) 533-6375
A * 12

West Central Capital Corp.
Mr. Howard W. Jacob, Pres.
440 Northlake Ctr., Ste. 206
Dallas, TX 75238
(214) 348-3969
A *** 2,4,5,6,12

Zenith Capital Corp.
Mr. Andrew L. Johnston, Sec.-
   Treas.
5150 N. Shepherd, Ste. 218
Houston, TX 77018
(713) 692-6121
A * 12

VERMONT

Mansfield Capital Corp.
Mr. Stephen H. Farrington, Pres.
Box 986, Mountain Rd.
Stowe, VT 05672
(802) 253-9400
A * 2,9,11,12

Vermont Investment Capital, Inc.
Mr. Harold Jacobs, Pres.
Route 14, Box 84
South Royalton, VT 05068
(802) 763-8878
A * 12

VIRGINIA

East West United Investment Co.
Mr. Doug Bui, Pres.
6723 Whittier Ave., Ste. 206-B
McLean, VA 22101

(703) 821-6616
MESBIC A ** 4,12
Inverness Capital Corp.
Mr. Harry Flemming, Pres.
424 N. Washington St.
Alexandria, VA 22314
(703) 549-5730
C *** 12
Metropolitan Capital Corp.
Mr. Fred Scoville, Pres.
2550 Huntington Ave.
Alexandria, VA 22193
(703) 960-4698
A *** 12

Norfolk Investment Co., Inc.
Mr. Kirk W. Saunders, Pres.
201 Granby Mall Bldg., Ste. 515
Norfolk, VA 23510
(804) 623-1042
MESBIC B * 5,9,12

Tidewater Small Business Investment Corp.
Mr. Robert H. Schmidt, Chmn.
1106 Maritime Tower
234 Monticello Ave.
Norfolk, VA 23510
(804) 627-2315
B ** 5

Virginia Capital Corp.
Mr. Robert H. Pratt, Pres.
P.O. Box 1493
Richmond, VA 23212
(804) 644-5496
B *** 12

WASHINGTON

Capital Resource Corp.
Mr. Theodore M. Wight, Gen. Mgr.
1001 Logan Bldg.
Seattle, WA 98101
(201) 623-6550
D *** 1,5,6,7,8,12

Northwest Capital Investment Corp.
Mr. Dale H. Zeigler, Pres.
1940 116th Ave., NE
P.O. Box 3500

Bellevue, WA 98009
(206) 455-3049
D *** 12

Seafirst Capital Corp.
Mr. Steven G. Blanchard, VP & Gen. Mgr.
Fourth & Blanchard Bldg.
Seattle, WA 98121
(206) 583-3278
C * 5,9

Washington Capital Corp.
Mr. James F. Aylward, Pres.
David A. Kohls, VP
1417 Fourth Ave.
Seattle, WA 98101
(206) 682-5400
D * 12
(Branch Offices: OR, CA, WA)

Branch Office:
Washington Capital Corp.
North 920 Washington
Spokane, WA 99201
(509) 326-6940
D * 12
(Main Office: Seattle, WA)

Washington Trust Equity Corp.
Mr. Alan Bradley, Pres.
Washington Trust Financial Ctr.
Spokane, WA 99210
(509) 455-4106
C * 12

WISCONSIN

Branch Office:
R. W. Allsop Capital Corp.
Mr. Gregory B. Bultman
815 E. Mason St., Ste. 1501
P.O. Box 1368
Milwaukee, WI 53201
(414) 271-6510
D *** 1,5,6,12
(Main Office: IA)

Bando-McGlocklin Investment Co., Inc.
Mr. Salvatore L. Bando, Pres.
13555 Bishops Crt., Ste. 225
Brookfield, WI 53005
(414) 784-9010
B ** 5,9

CERTO Capital Corp.
Mr. Howard E. Hill, Pres.
6150 McKee Rd.
Madison, WI 53711
(608) 271-4500
A ** 9

Branch Office:
MorAmerica Capital Corp.
Mr. H. Wayne Foreman, Reg. VP
Ste. 333, 710 N. Plankinton Ave.
Milwaukee, WI 53203
(414) 276-3839
D *** 12
(Main Office: IA)

SC Opportunities, Inc.
Mr. Robert L. Ableman, VP & Sec.
1112 7th Ave.
Monroe, WI 53566
(608) 325-3134
MESBIC A *** 9

77 Capital Corporation
Mr. Sheldon B. Lubar, Pres.
3060 First Wisconsin Ctr.
777 E. Wisconsin Ave.
Milwaukee, WI 53202
(414) 291-9000
C * 3,5,8,12

Super Market Investors, Inc.
Mr. John W. Andorfer, Pres.
P.O. Box 473
Milwaukee, WI 53201
(414) 453-8200
A ** 9

WYOMING

Capital Corp. of Wyoming, Inc.
Mr. Larry McDonald, Exec. VP
P.O. Box 612
145 S. Durbin, Ste. 201
Casper, WY 82602
(307) 234-5438
A * 12

NON-SBIC MEMBERS

Adler & Company
Mr. James R. Swartz, Ptnr.
280 Park Ave.

New York, NY 10017
(212) 986-3010
*** 1,2,3,4,5,6,7,8,9,10,11,12

A. G. Capital Corp.
Mr. Robert Metge, Pres.
701 SE Shurfine Dr.
Ankeny, IA 50021
(515) 964-7300
A * 9

A. J. Armstrong Co., Inc.
Mr. Robert Spitalnic, VP
850 Third Ave.
New York, NY 10022
(212) 826-3172

Alaska Renewable Resources Corp.
Mr. Wayne C. Littleton, Pres. &
  CEO
P.O. Box 828
Anchorage, AK 99510
(907) 279-5602
E * 3

Atlantic American Capital Corp.
Mr. J. Patrick Michaels, Jr., Pres.
Lincoln Center, Ste. 851
5401 W. Kennedy Blvd.
Tampa, FL 33609
(813) 877-8844
B *** 1

Beacon Partners
Mr. Leonard Vignola, Jr., Manag-
  ing Ptnr.
111 Hubbard Ave.
Stamford, CT 06905
(203) 348-8858
D * 1,4,5,6,9,11,12
(Branch Office: NY)

Branch Office:
Beacon Partners
Mr. Leonard Vignola, Jr., Manag-
  ing Ptnr.
733 Third Ave., Ste. 901
New York, NY 10017
(212) 265-0177
D * 1,4,5,6,9,11,12
(Main Office: CT)

Broventure Co., Inc.
Mr. William Gust, Pres.
Two Hopkins Plaza

Baltimore, MD 21201
(301) 727-4520
D *** 1,5,6,8,11

Malcolm Bund & Associates
Mr. Malcolm Bund, Pres.
Ste. 301, 1111 19th St., NW
Washington, DC 20036
(202) 293-2910
E * 1,5,7,12

The Business Development Corp.
  of Georgia, Inc.
Mr. Mike Johnson, Exec. VP
558 South Omni Internat'l
Atlanta, GA 30303
(404) 577-5715
D ** 5,6,8,9,10

The Business Development Corp.
  of North Carolina
Mr. Gary M. Underhill, Pres.
P.O. Box 10665
505 Oberlin Rd.
Raleigh, NC 27605

INVESTMENT BANKERS

Midwest

ILLINOIS

Bacon, Whipple & Co.
135 South Street
Chicago, IL 60603
(312) 782-3100

William Blair & Co.
135 S. LaSalle Street
Chicago, IL 60603
(312) 236-1600

**Burton J. Vincent, Chesley &
  Co.**
105 W. Adams
Chicago, IL 60603
(312) 641-7800

INDIANA

K. J. Brown & Co. Inc.
122 E. Main Street
Muncie, IN 47305
(317) 284-9791

(919) 828-2331
D ** 5

Cap-Form, Inc.
Mr. John H. Rubel, Pres.
327 S. LaSalle St.
Chicago, IL 60604
(312) 939-6070

Capital Designs, Ltd.
Mr. Dale H. Zeigler, Pres.
1940 116th Ave., NE
P.O. Box 3500
Bellevue, WA 98009
(206) 455-3037

Capital Publishing Corp.
Mr. Stanley E. Pratt, Pres.
P.O. Box 348, 2 Laurel Ave.
Wellesley Hills, MA 02181
(617) 235-5405

Capital Resources Corp.
Mr. W. Denis O'Connell, Pres.
1624 Letitia St.
Baton Rouge, LA 70808
(504) 387-0806

City Securities Corp.
400 Circle Tower
Indianapolis, IN 46204
(317) 634-4400

**Raffensperger, Hughes & Co.
  Inc.**
20 N. Meridian Street
Indianapolis, IN 46204
(317) 635-4551

IOWA

R. G. Dickinson & Co.
910 Grand Avenue
Des Moines, IA 50309
(515) 247-8100

Equity Dynamics Inc.
2116 Financial Center
Des Moines, IA 50309
(515) 244-5746

Iowa Capital Corp.
1110 Financial Center
Des Moines, IA 50309
(515) 280-8363

KANSAS

Beecroft, Cole & Co.
First National Bank Building
Sixth and Kansas Avenue
Topeka, KS 66603
(913) 234-5671

MICHIGAN

EVR Management & Development Inc.
P.O. Box 7299
Ann Arbor, MI
(313) 529-2318

William C. Roney & Co.
2 Buhl Building
Detroit, MI 48226
(313) 963-6700

MINNESOTA

Dain, Kalman & Quail, Inc.
100 Dain Tower
Minneapolis, MN 55402
(612) 371-2711

Piper Jaffray & Hopwood, Inc.
800 Multifoods Building
733 Marquette Avenue
Minneapolis, MN 55435
(612) 371-8378

MISSOURI

George K. Baum & Co. Inc.
1016 Baltimore Avenue
Kansas City, MO 64105
(816) 474-1100

B. C. Christopher & Co.
4800 Main Street
Kansas City, MO 64112
(816) 932-7000

A. G. Edwards & Sons Inc.
One N. Jefferson
St. Louis, MO 63103
(314) 289-3000

Reinholdt & Gardner
506 Olive Street
St. Louis, MO 63101
(314) 444-5080

NEBRASKA

Chiles, Heider & Co. Inc.
1300 Woodmen Tower
Omaha, NE 68102
(402) 346-6677

Kirkpatrick, Pettis, Smith & Polian Inc.
1623 Farnam Street, Suite 700
Omaha, NE 68102
(402) 449-1400

OHIO

The Ohio Co.
155 E. Broad Street
Columbus, OH 43215
(614) 464-6811

Prescott, Ball & Turben
900 National City Bank Building
Cleveland, OH 44114
(216) 687-4000

WISCONSIN

Robert W. Baird & Co. Inc.
777 E. Wisconsin Avenue
Milwaukee, WI 53201
(414) 765-3750

Northeast

CONNECTICUT

Advest Inc.
Six Central Row
Hartford, CT 06103
(203) 525-1421

B. L. McTeague & Co.
1 Constitution Plaza
Hartford, CT 06103
(203) 246-8897

DISTRICT OF COLUMBIA

Berg & Co. Inc.
1250 Connecticut Avenue
Washington, DC
(202) 659-9091

First Washington Securities Corp.
1735 "I" Street N.W., Suite 605
Washington, DC 20006
(202) 296-2394

Legg Mason Wood Walker Inc.
1747 Pennsylvania Avenue
Washington, DC 20006
(301) 539-3400

MARYLAND

Alex, Brown & Sons
135 E. Baltimore Street
Baltimore, MD 21202
(301) 727-1700

Legg Mason Wood Walker Inc.
7 E. Redwood Street
Baltimore, MD 21203
(301) 539-3400

MASSACHUSETTS

Berg & Co. Inc.
21 Merchants Row
Boston, MA 02109
(617) 723-2710

Burgess & Leith Inc.
60 State Street
Boston, MA 02109
(617) 742-5900

Foster Dykema Cabot & Co. Inc.
One Boston Place
Boston, MA 02108
(617) 723-4433

Peter A. Ulin
75 Federal Street
Boston, MA 02110
(617) 482-8912

NEW JERSEY

Amswiss International Corp.
One Exchange Place
Jersey City, NJ 07302
(201) 451-3576

NEW YORK

Adventura Corp.
85 Livingston Street, Suite 15M
Brooklyn, NY 11201
(212) 834-1818

ABD Securities Corp.
One Battery Park Plaza
New York, NY 10004
(212) 952-7700

A. E. Ames & Co. Inc.
Two Wall Street
New York, NY 10005
(212) 766-9350

Allen & Co. [Inc.]
711 Fifth Avenue
New York, NY 10022
(212) 832-8000

Altgelt & Co. Inc.
45 Wall Street
New York, NY 10005
(212) 425-6240

Asiel & Co.
20 Broad Street
New York, NY 10005
(212) 747-1000

Atlantic Capital Corp.
40 Wall Street
New York, NY 10005
(212) 363-5600

Bache Halsey Stuart Shields Inc.
100 Gold Street
New York, NY 10038
(212) 791-1000

Bear, Stearns & Co.
55 Water Street
New York, NY 10041
(212) 952-5000

Blyth Eastman Dillon & Co. Inc.
1221 Avenue of the Americas
New York, NY 10020
(212) 730-8500

A. T. Brod & Co.
110 Wall Street
New York, NY 10005
(212) 422-5900

Burns Fry & Timmins Inc.
100 Wall Street
New York, NY 10005
(212) 269-6950

Daiwa Securities America Inc.
One Liberty Plaza
New York, NY 10006
(212) 732-6600

Dean Witter Reynolds Inc.
130 Liberty Street
New York, NY 10006
(212) 437-3000

Dillon, Read & Co. Inc.
46 William Street
New York, NY 10005
(212) 285-5656

Dominick & Dominick Inc.
55 Water Street
New York, NY 10041
(212) 952-6000

Dominion Securities Inc.
100 Wall Street
New York, NY 10005
(212) 344-8160

Donaldson, Lufkin & Jenrette Inc.
140 Broadway
New York, NY 10005
(212) 943-0300

Drexel Burnham Lambert Group Inc.
60 Broad Street
New York, NY 10004
(212) 480-6000

F. Eberstadt & Co. Inc.
61 Broadway
New York, NY 10006
(212) 480-0800

Europartners Securities Corp.
One World Trade Center, Suite 3411
New York, NY 10048
(212) 466-6100

Evans & Co.
300 Park Avenue
New York, NY 10022
(212) 832-3300

First Boston Inc.
20 Exchange Place
New York, NY 10005
(212) 825-2000

First Jersey Securities Inc.
80 Broad Street
New York, NY 10004
(212) 269-5500

Goldman, Sachs & Co.
55 Broad Street
New York, NY 10004
(212) 676-8000

E. F. Hutton Group
1 Battery Park Plaza
New York, NY 10004
(212) 742-5000

Keefe Bruyette & Woods Inc.
1 Liberty Plaza
New York, NY 10006
(212) 349-4321

Kidder, Peabody & Co. Inc.
10 Hanover Square
New York, NY 10005
(212) 747-2000

Laidlaw-Adams & Peck Inc.
20 Broad Street
New York, NY 10005
(212) 363-3200

Lazard Freres & Co.
1 Rockefeller Plaza
New York, NY 10020
(212) 489-6600

Lehman Brothers Kuhn Loeb Inc.
1 William Street
New York, NY 10004
(212) 558-1500

Loeb Rhoades, Hornblower & Co.
14 Wall Street
New York, NY 10005
(212) 742-7000

Carl Marks & Co. Inc.
77 Water Street
New York, NY 10005
(212) 437-7078

Merrill Lynch White Weld Capital Markets Group
1 Liberty Plaza
New York, NY 10006
(212) 285-2000

Moore & Schley, Cameron & Co.
2 Broadway
New York, NY 10004
(212) 483-1800

Morgan Stanley & Co. Inc.
1251 Avenue of the Americas
New York, NY 10020
(212) 974-4000

Moseley, Hallgarten & Estabrook Inc.
1 New York Plaza
New York, NY 10004
(212) 363-3500

Nesbitt Thomson Securities Inc.
1 Battery Park Plaza
New York, NY 10004
(212) 248-3200

New Japan Securities International Inc.
80 Pine Street
New York, NY 10005
(212) 747-1810

Nikko Securities Co. International Inc.
Subsidiary of Nikko Securities Co. Ltd.
140 Broadway
New York, NY 10005
(212) 747-9800

Nomura Securities International Inc.
100 Wall Street
New York, NY 10005
(212) 483-9700

Paine, Webber, Jackson & Curtis Inc.
140 Broadway
New York, NY 10005
(212) 437-2837

Patricof, Tessler & Co.
1 E. 53rd Street
New York, NY 10022
(212) 753-6796

Pitfield, Mackay & Co. Inc.
30 Broad Street

New York, NY 10004
(212) 422-9247

Richardson Securities Inc.
Subsidiary of Richardson Securities of Canada Ltd.
40 Wall Street
New York, NY 10005
(212) 483-0750

L. F. Rothschild, Unterberg, Towbin
55 Water Street
New York, NY 10041
(212) 425-3300

Salomon Brothers
1 New York Plaza
New York, NY 10004
(212) 747-7000

J. Henry Schroder Corp.
1 State Street
New York, NY 10004
(212) 269-6500

Shearson Hayden Stone Inc.
767 Fifth Avenue
New York, NY 10022
(212) 350-0500

Shelby Cullom Davis & Co.
70 Pine Street
New York, NY 10005
(212) 425-3212

Smith Barney, Harris Upham & Co. Inc.
1345 Avenue of the Americas
New York, NY 10019
(212) 399-6000

SoGen-Swiss International Corp.
245 Park Avenue
New York, NY 10017
(212) 578-0100

Thomson McKinnon Securities Inc.
1 New York Plaza
New York, NY 10004
(212) 482-7000

Warburg Paribas Becker Inc.
55 Water Street
New York, NY 10041
(212) 747-4400

Wertheim & Co.
200 Park Avenue
New York, NY 10017
(212) 578-0200

Winthrop Ventures
74 Trinity Place
New York, NY 10006
(212) 422-0100

Wood Gundy Inc.
100 Wall Street
New York, NY 10005
(212) 344-0633

PENNSYLVANIA

Arthurs, Lestrange & Short
2 Gateway Center
Pittsburgh, PA 15222
(412) 566-6800

Babbitt, Meyers & Co.
155 Union Trust Building
Pittsburgh, PA 15219
(412) 391-6500

Butcher & Singer Inc.
1500 Walnut Street
Philadelphia, PA 19102
(215) 985-5000

Cunningham, Schmertz & Co. Inc.
1900 Union Bank Building
Pittsburgh, PA 15222
(412) 434-8750

Elkins, Stroud, Suplee & Co.
1500 Walnut Street
Philadelphia, PA 19102
(215) 568-1975

Parker/Hunter Inc.
4000 United States Steel Building
Pittsburgh, PA 15219
(412) 562-8000

E. W. Smith Co.
1513 Walnut Street
Philadelphia, PA 19102
(215) 241-6500

Northwest

MONTANA

D. A. Davidson & Co. Inc.
P.O. Box 5015
Great Falls, MT 59403
(406) 727-4200

WASHINGTON

Foster & Marshall Inc.
205 Columbia Street
Seattle, WA 98104
(206) 344-2465

Interpacific Investors Services Inc.
1111 Norton Building
Seattle, WA 98104
(206) 623-2784

Southeast

FLORIDA

Raymond, James & Assoc. Inc.
6090 Central Avenue
St. Petersburg, FL 33707
(813) 381-3800

GEORGIA

Robinson-Humphrey Co. Inc.
2 Peachtree Street
Atlanta, GA 30303
(404) 581-7111

KENTUCKY

Almstedt Brothers Inc.
425 W. Market Street
Louisville, KY 40202
(502) 589-7660

J. J. B. Hilliard, W. L. Lyons Inc.
545 S. Third Street
Louisville, KY 40202
(502) 583-6651

LOUISIANA

Howard, Weil, Labouisse, Friedrichs Inc.
211 Carondelet Street
New Orleans, LA 70130
(504) 588-2941

TENNESSEE

J. C. Bradford & Co.
170 Fourth Avenue N.
Nashville, TN 37219
(615) 748-9310

Equitable Securities Corp.
First American Center
Nashville, TN 37238
(615) 244-9420

Morgan, Keegan & Co. Inc.
2800 One Commerce Square
Memphis, TN 38103
(901) 523-1501

VIRGINIA

DeRand Corp. of America
2201 Wilshire Boulevard, Suite 300
Arlington, VA 22201
(703) 527-3827

Wheat, First Securities Inc.
707 E. Main Street
Richmond, VA 23219
(804) 649-2311

Southwest

ARIZONA

Continental American Securities Inc.
3201 N. 1st Place
Phoenix, AZ 85012
(602) 263-0020

CALIFORNIA

Ashfield & Co. Inc.
303 Sacramento Street, Suite 400
San Francisco, CA 94111
(415) 391-4747

Bangert, Dawes, Reade, Davis & Thom Inc.
650 California Street
San Francisco, CA 94108
(415) 421-0846

Bateman Eichler, Hill Richards Inc.
700 S. Flower Street
Los Angeles, CA 90017
(213) 625-3545

Crowell, Weedon & Co.
One Wilshre Boulevard
Los Angeles, CA 90017
(213) 620-1850

Davis, Skaggs & Co. Inc.
160 Sansome Street
San Francisco, CA 94104
(415) 392-7700

Hambrecht & Quist
235 Montgomery Street
San Francisco, CA 94104
(415) 433-1720

Montgomery Securities
235 Montgomery Street
San Francisco, CA 94104
(415) 989-2050

J. A. Overton & Co.
1110 Orange Avenue, Box 326
Coronado, CA 92118
(714) 435-6241

Robertson, Colman, Siebel & Weisel
235 Montgomery Street, Suite 2100
San Francisco, CA 94104
(415) 989-2050

Stone & Youngberg
One California Street, Suite 2800
San Francisco, CA 94111
(415) 981-1314

Sutro & Co. Inc.
460 Montgomery Street

San Francisco, CA 94104
(415) 445-8500

Wallace and Schilling
235 Montgomery Street
San Francisco, CA 94104
(415) 421-9762

Wedbush, Noble, Cooke Inc.
615 S. Flower Street, 3rd Floor
Los Angeles, CA 90017
(213) 485-1931

COLORADO

Boettcher & Co.
828-317th Street
Denver, CO 80202
(303) 629-2020

Bosworth Sullivan
Division of Dain, Kalman & Quail
950-17th Street
Denver, CO 80202
(303) 534-1177

Hanifen, Imhoff & Samford Inc.
624-17th Street
Denver, CO 80202
(303) 534-0221

TEXAS

Eppler, Guerin & Turner Inc.
2300 Bryan Tower
P.O. Box 508
Dallas, TX 75221
(214) 744-0511

Rauscher Pierce Refsnes Inc.
900 Mercantile Dallas Building
Dallas, TX 75201
(214) 748-0111

Rotan Mosle Inc.
1500 South Tower
Pennzoil Place
Houston, TX 77002
(713) 236-3000

Underwood, Neuhaus & Co. Inc.
724 Travis Street at Rusk Avenue
Houston, TX 77002
(713) 224-1224

INDEX